ARE YOU READ

The world hurtles like a runaway train to-ward an abyss known as Armageddon—the final world war. Meanwhile, its passengers, ignoring their true plight, hold a party and pretend that the journey is peaceful and safe. They shut their eyes to all evidence of impending destruction. They close their ears to the hard voices of history tell-ing them that such times as these are precursors of disaster.

The Western world watches in smug compla-cency as the Soviet empire, the most powerful military force in history, begins its tortuous col-lapse into anarchy and civil war. Naive commen-tators craft grandiose plans of an immediate millennium of peace in our time, refusing to rec-ognize that the earth is teetering on the brink of World War III.

Is there any hope for the world? Or will the century end in the worst disaster in human his-tory?

Find the answers in
MESSIAH

QUANTITY SALES

Most Bantam books are available at special quantity discounts when purchased in bulk by corporations, organizations or groups. Special imprints, messages and excerpts can be produced to meet your needs. For more information, write to:

Bantam Books
666 Fifth Avenue
New York, NY 10103
Attention: Director, Diversified Sales

Please specify how you intend to use the books (i.e., promotion, resale, etc.).

INDIVIDUAL SALES

Are there any Bantam books you want but cannot find in your local stores? If so, you can order them directly from us. You can get any Bantam book currently in print. For a complete, up-to-date listing of our books, and information on how to order, write to:

Bantam Books
666 Fifth Avenue
New York, NY 10103
Attn: Customer Service

MESSIAH

WAR
IN THE
MIDDLE EAST
&
THE ROAD TO
ARMAGEDDON

Grant R. Jeffrey

BANTAM BOOKS
NEW YORK · TORONTO · LONDON · SYDNEY · AUCKLAND

MESSIAH

*A Bantam Nonfiction Book/published by arrangement
with Frontier Research Publications*

PUBLISHING HISTORY
Frontier Research Publications edition published 1991
Bantam revised edition / November 1992

ISBN 0-553-29958-1

Published simultaneously in the United States and Canada

*Bantam Books are published by Bantam Books, a division of
Bantam Doubleday Dell Publishing Group, Inc. Its trademark,
consisting of the words "Bantam Books" and the portrayal of
a rooster, is Registered in U.S. Patent and Trademark Office
and in other countries. Marca Registrada. Bantam Books, 666
Fifth Avenue, New York, New York 10103.*

PRINTED IN THE UNITED STATES OF AMERICA

OPM   0 9 8 7 6 5 4 3 2 1

TABLE OF CONTENTS

ACKNOWLEDGEMENT

MESSIAH represents a lifetime of research and Bible study concerning the role of Jesus as the coming Messiah. This study has transformed my life and my outlook on the coming Kingdom of God. I am grateful to the hundreds of men and women who have written the great books which have guided my own explorations. Many of these books are listed in the select bibliography. However, the inspired Word of God has been the major source and primary guide in all my studies. Most of all I am thankful to Jesus Christ who has opened my eyes to see Him in an entirely new light — as the coming Messiah, the Lord of Hosts and King of Kings.

I would like to thank my wife Kaye for her selfless dedication to the publication of this book. Her loving concern is demonstrated in every aspect of our publications, television programs and speaking ministry. A special thanks to my parents Lyle and Florence Jeffrey who have inspired me with a great love for the Bible and a longing for our coming Messiah.

My hope is that this book will encourage you to study the Scriptures and find your own personal relationship with Jesus the Messiah.

INTRODUCTION

Keys to Understanding Prophecy

The world hurtles like a runaway train towards an abyss known as Armageddon—the final world war. Meanwhile, its passengers, ignoring their true plight, hold a party and pretend that the journey is peaceful and safe. They shut their eyes to all evidence of impending destruction. They close their ears to the hard voices of history telling them that such times as these are precursors of disaster.

The Western world watches in smug complacency as the Soviet Empire, the most powerful military force in history, begins its tortuous collapse into anarchy and civil war. Naive commentators craft grandiose plans of an immediate millennium of "peace in our time," refusing to recognize that the Earth is teetering on the brink of World War III. Those who take the time to contemplate the condition of the world observe with growing concern the awesome armaments build-up in all nations. The potential of a cataclysmic war can quickly develop out of the unbridled ambition of dictators such as Saddam Hussein. This "butcher of Baghdad" swallowed up the country of Kuwait, and defied the whole world to stop him. His boasts and threats not only focused on the United Nations alliance, but also on his hated enemy, Israel. The devastation unleashed by Iraq's war in the Persian Gulf led to wholesale death, bombing, and ecological disaster with enormous oil spills and oil wells set afire. Yet, if Hussein were to read the Bible's prophecies he would know that his aggressive defiance of the world is leading the Middle East to Armageddon.

Is there any hope for the world? Or will the century end in the worst disaster in human history? The prophecies in the Bible outline very clearly a series of events that will signal the final conflict of history. These incredible events will lead to the culmination of God's great plan, the hope of the coming Messiah and the establishing of His kingdom on the Earth.

Among those prophesied events, the most prominent was the rebirth of the nation of Israel. This notable event began in the 1880's. A wave of spiritual excitement began to course through the veins of Jews exiled into the many countries of the Diaspora. Young men and women packed their belongings and commenced the arduous journey back to their Promised Land. Wave after wave of immigrants endured the perils of enemy territory, persecution, extortion, and government opposition as they battled their way to their ancestral home. The small trickle of Jews became a stream and then a rushing river of returning humanity.

God promised that when the Jews began to return to their desolate country, the land would respond to the sounds of their feet and begin once more to yield its bounty to become the "land flowing with milk and honey." Just as the prophet declared, as the people filled the land the heavens opened with ever-increasing amounts of rainfall year after year. This century has seen the fulfillment of the prophecy, "Ask the Lord for rain in the time of the latter rain. The Lord will make flashing clouds; He will give them showers of rain, grass in the field for everyone" (Zechariah 10:1).

Abundant rainfall, new fertilizers, and the blood, sweat and tears of generations of Jewish settlers combined with the blessings of the Almighty to produce the most astonishing agricultural transformation in the history of the world. Two thousand years of neglect by the Romans, Arabs, and the Turkish Empire had left Palestine a veritable wasteland. In the devastating Roman-Jewish wars from A.D. 66 to A.D. 70, and continuing into centuries of land erosion under Turkish rule, Israel's wonderful forests were systematically destroyed until she became a land of deserts.

Samuel Clemens, better known as Mark Twain, traveled through the barren desertland of Palestine in 1863. He

8

claimed in his book *Innocence Abroad* that in his journey from Jerusalem to Galilee he saw only one Arab. Aside from Jerusalem and Jaffa, most of Palestine was very sparsely settled, primarily because no one could live in the barren land. However, one hundred and thirty years later, the land is truly blossoming as a rose. Israel now provides 90 percent of all citrus fruit consumed in Europe. Fifteen years ago no one had tried to grow cotton in Israel, and today the land provides a tremendous amount of cotton for export. Since the great migration of 1948 the Jews have planted more than two hundred million trees. Not only has this reforestation beautified the land, it has also contributed in great measure to the transformation of the precipitation cycle which governs the weather system of Palestine; this generation has truly become the "time of the latter rain" which the prophet foretold.

Over one-fourth of the Bible focuses on prophecy. According to an analysis by J. Barton Payne, "Out of the Old Testament's 23,210 verses, 6,641 contain predictive material, or 28 1/2 percent. Out of the New Testament, 7,914 verses, 1,711 contain predictive material, or 21 1/2 percent. So, for the entire Bible's 31,124 verses, 8,352 contain predictive material, or 27 percent of the whole Bible." If the Holy Spirit directed the writers to include this much prophetic matter throughout the Bible we must conclude that God wanted to convey some very important messages to everyone, Jew, Gentile, believer and non-believer.

The words translated "prophet" or "prophecy" occur more than four hundred times throughout the Scriptures. They convey two different meanings, depending on the context. In one, the word focuses on the predictive element of the message: foretelling; in the other the meaning conveyed is the exhortation by the prophet of the message of God to His people: forth-telling. In the original Hebrew, the word portrays the image of an overflowing fountain, bubbling forth as the prophets speak—not from themselves, but rather as the Spirit of God "gave them utterance" (Acts 2:4).

When we study the prophetic portions of Scripture we discover that the Holy Spirit, as the Spirit of truth (see John 14:17; 15:26; 16:13; 1 John 4:6), led the prophets to full

9

understanding of God's unfolding purpose in history. Since the Holy Spirit initially inspired Bible writers, He will also awaken spiritual understanding of these prophetic truths within us.

There are several reasons why we should study the prophecies in the Bible: they are (1) important, (2) unique, and (3) practical.

The Importance of Bible Prophecy

While some suggest that those who focus on prophecy become so heavenly minded they are no earthly good, the problem in our carnally minded, materialistic, Laodicean Church today is quite the reverse. We have become so earthly minded that we are in serious danger of becoming no heavenly good to our Father. Historically, Christians who are interested in prophecy and the soon return of Christ have been at the forefront of the great movements of evangelism, missions, third-world relief efforts, and the active fulfillment of Jesus' command to "occupy till I come" (Luke 19:13 KJV). Our interest in prophecy must increase concern for our sin-sick world and motivate us to actively go and "make disciples of all the nations, baptizing them in the name of the Father and of the Son and of the Holy Spirit, teaching them to observe all things that I have commanded you; and lo, I am with you always, even to the end of the age" (Matthew 28:19-20).

John the Elder, in the Revelation of Jesus Christ, revealed the centrality of prophecy to Christians: "The testimony of Jesus is the spirit of prophecy" (Revelation 19:10). Jesus Christ, as the Living Word, is the supreme revealer of the Word to us just as He was to two of His disciples that day on the road to Emmaus when, "Beginning at Moses and all the Prophets, He expounded on them in all the Scriptures the things concerning Himself" (Luke 24:27). What a joy it must have been to listen to Jesus open the hidden treasures of Scripture. Some day in heaven, all those who love Him will have the glorious experience of listening to the greatest teacher of all as He opens all the truth concerning Himself.

Facts about life, death, resurrection and the second coming of Jesus make up the major focus of Bible prophecy. Old Testament prophets declared that the Messiah and the Kingdom of God are the ultimate goals toward which all history is leading. If we want to understand God's ultimate redemptive purpose for us we must examine the Scriptures for His progressive revelation of the role of the Messiah.

While Jesus Christ is the subject of thousands of Old and New Testament prophecies, He is also the supreme Prophet who declares God's purpose in history. Through Scripture He reveals the place and role of the nations and allows us to judge the "times and seasons" of our lives. Rather than forbid humankind to look into these things, the Son of God severely criticized the religious people of His day for ignoring the clear Old Testament prophecies about the coming of the Messiah. He scolded them for understanding the signs of the seasons but neglecting to comprehend the signs of the Son of Man. It is very important that we study God's Word and try to understand the prophecies within it. No other written word can reveal the destiny of our world or of our souls.

The Uniqueness of Bible Prophecy

The Bible is the only religious book in existence that dared to detail thousands of prophecies concerning the rise and fall of empires, most of which, historically, have already been fulfilled. In no other religious literature will you find hundreds of detailed predictions that have been fulfilled precisely as they were predicted. In my earlier book, Armageddon – Appointment With Destiny, I present a mathematical analysis which shows that it is impossible for any human—not inspired by Almighty God—to predict accurately a series of sequential events, events that can be historically verified. No human has ever presented such detailed predictions of future events. Those who point to the occasional lucky "guess" of Nostradamus or Mother Shipton ignore the hundreds of totally incorrect predictions they also made.

Justin Martyr, a great writer in the early Church, pinpointed the importance of prophecy with these words:

11

"To declare a thing shall come to pass long before it is in being, and to bring it to pass; this or nothing is the work of God." God claims that the ability to predict and fulfill prophecy is a unique attribute of His nature as the Lord of Hosts: "For I am God, and there is no other; I am God and there is none like Me, declaring the end from the beginning, and from ancient times things that are not yet done, saying, 'My counsel shall stand, and I will do all My pleasure'" (Isaiah 46:9-10). In this passage, the prophet Isaiah declares that not only does God foreknow future events, He also declares them and then brings them to pass.

The Lord Jesus told His listeners that all of God's prophecy as recorded in His Word would ultimately be fulfilled: "For assuredly, I say to you, till heaven and earth pass away, one jot or one tittle will by no means pass from the law till all is fulfilled" (Matthew 5:18).

In this book we will examine the great number of prophecies about the Messiah which have not yet been fulfilled. In Christ's first advent two thousand years ago, all of the Old Testament prophecies concerning His birth, ministry, suffering, crucifixion, death, and resurrection were fulfilled to the precise letter by Jesus of Nazareth; therefore, we can confidently believe that the remaining messianic prophecies will also be fulfilled precisely. As a matter of fact, many of the Old Testament prophecies give details about the Messiah in both His first and second advents in the same sentence. For example, the prophet Isaiah declares that the Messiah will "proclaim liberty to the captives, and the opening of the prison to those who are bound; to proclaim the acceptable year of the Lord, and the day of vengeance of our God" (Isaiah 61:1-2). In His first advent, Jesus the Messiah proclaimed liberty to the captives in prison and the acceptable year of the Lord when He redeemed all repentant sinners through His atoning work on the cross. Yet, the last phrase in this prophecy concerning Armageddon—to proclaim "the day of vengeance of our God"—will not be fulfilled until Christ's second coming. When Jesus chose this passage to preach about in the synagogue at Nazareth, He read the first part of the prophecy, then "closed the book, and gave it back to the attendant and sat down." He continued by saying, "Today this Scripture is

12

fulfilled in your hearing," but He did not read the second part which He knew would be fulfilled two thousand years later. The prophecies in the Bible are unique in that they *always* come to pass exactly as they were prophesied.

The Practical Value of Prophecy

Christians should prayerfully study biblical prophecies, because in understanding them we can begin to see God's unfolding plan of redemption. As we become more familiar with prophecy we will see how we fit in a practical way into Christ's redemptive purpose for our world. This practical value of prophecy is illustrated many times in the lives of historical figures during periods of extreme danger and crisis.

For example, King Hezekiah of Judah found his city of Jerusalem surrounded by a vastly superior force of Assyrian soldiers led by King Sennacherib. To his human mind the situation was hopeless. The city was under siege, the people were starving, and the enemy king was taunting them by telling them that their God was not big enough to deliver them from his hand. But Hezekiah trusted God. He "went into the house of the Lord. Then he sent Eliakim...to Isaiah the prophet." Isaiah sent back word that Hezekiah was not to be afraid, because God would "cause him to fall by the sword in his own land." (See 2 Kings 18 and 19). Isaiah records the exact words of the prophecy: "'He shall not come into this city, nor shoot an arrow there, or come before it with shield, nor build a siege mound against it. By the way that he came, by the same shall he return, and he shall not come into this city,' says the Lord. 'For I will defend this city, to save it for My own sake and for My servant David's sake'" (Isaiah 37:33-35).

In short, God promised to deliver the city of Jerusalem from her enemies for the sanctity of His own name and also because He loved Hezekiah's ancestor, King David, "a man after His own heart" (1 Samuel 13:14; Acts 13:22). Soon after this prophecy, "on a certain night," the Angel of the Lord (which is a title for Jesus Christ in His pre-incarnate form) "went out, and killed in the camp of the Assyrians one hundred and eighty-five thousand; and when people arose early in the morning, there were the corpses—all dead" (2 Kings 19:35). Thus, God's prophecy and command to King Hezekiah to refuse to surrender to the enemy was precisely fulfilled. The Lord Himself personally killed thousands of Assyrian soldiers who were intent on blaspheming God's name and destroying the chosen people. A brief review of the Bible's historical passages, together with the prophetic accounts of Christ's future destruction of the evil armies of the Antichrist, reveals that there is no contradiction between God's justice and a just defense of one's homeland.

Another example of the practical value of prophecy is when King Zedekiah of Judah asked the prophet of God what to do when still another army was besieging Jerusalem. Surprisingly, God gave a command that was opposite to the earlier one. He told the prophet Jeremiah that the king should not resist the enemy but rather he should "surrender to the king of Babylon's princes" so that "this city shall not be burned with fire, and you and your house shall live" (Jeremiah 38:17). God's purpose was to deliver Jerusalem and all of the countries of the known world into the hand of the rising Babylonian Empire. Due to centuries of accumulated sin and contempt of His Holy name, God decided to permit Judah to endure seventy years of captivity in Babylon, to purge their rebellious spirit and pagan idolatry.

This news of impending judgment was not exactly welcomed by King Zedekiah and his nobles, so they refused to accept the words of the prophet. They reacted by throwing Jeremiah into a dungeon made from a household cistern. Rather than heed what God was telling them, the king and the nobles chose to trust the words of false prophets who looked to the natural defenses of high walls, enormous water cisterns filled to the brim, and huge grain supplies. The tragic result was a siege of two years. Finally, when the king, his family, and his army fled through the mile-and-a-half long tunnel north of the Temple Mount, just ahead of the conquering Babylonians, they were captured outside the city walls, just as Jeremiah had promised. His children were killed, his eyes blinded, and he was taken to Babylon in chains as the Temple burned to the ground. What a tragic result of not heeding the prophetic command of the Lord.

In almost identical circumstances, two kings of Judah were given opposite prophetic advice from God. King Hezekiah listened and obeyed the prophecy and saw a miraculous deliverance of his city. King Zedekiah refused to submit to the prophecy, resisted Babylon in his own strength, and lost the nation.

The Babylonian captivity of Judah in 606 B.C. was the beginning of the times of the Gentiles. World sovereignty which God had planned for Israel was now passed to "those who were not My people," the Gentiles (see Hosea 2:23; Romans 9:25). After they returned from captivity, the people of Israel were never again tempted with idolatry.

When nearly seventy years had past, the length of time God had said His people would be in bondage, the prophet Daniel, a contemporary of Jeremiah, began to pray for their return to Jerusalem. Daniel wrote: "In the first year of Darius the son of Ahasuerus . . .I, Daniel, understood by the books the number of years specified by the word of the Lord, given through Jeremiah the prophet, that He would accomplish seventy years in the desolations of Jerusalem. Then I set my face toward the Lord God to make request by prayer and supplications, with fasting, sackcloth, and ashes. And I prayed to the Lord my God, and made confession and said,... "O Lord, hear! O Lord, forgive! O Lord, listen and act! Do not delay for Your own sake, my God, for Your city and Your people are called by Your name" (Daniel 9:2-3,19). This prophecy was fulfilled within two years when the Media-Persian ruler Cyrus, who then ruled the Babylonian empire, decreed that the Jews could return to Jerusalem (536 B.C.).

Daniel's prayer was that God would deliver Israel "for Your own sake" because "Your city and Your people are called by Your name." Throughout Bible history and into the future of prophecies yet to be fulfilled, God delivers His people Israel, and also His Church, so that His name and purpose will be honored.

Still another incidence of the practical value of prophecy is seen in the experience of the Christian Church in Jerusalem during the years A.D. 66 to 70, the time of the tragic Jewish-Roman wars. Jerusalem was once again a massive citadel with huge stone walls, grain reserves to last for seventeen years, unlimited water supply, and excellent well-motivated soldiers. The Roman General Flavius Titus captured the city of Jerusalem. He declared that he was victorious because the God of Israel had delivered up the city to Rome due to the unparalleled wickedness of its inhabitants. Various factions, after rebelling against Rome, showed their contempt for God and broke into civil war within Jerusalem. They burned grain supplies and forced a famine that ultimately killed more than a million and a quarter of its citizens.

Amazingly, contemporary documents claim that when the city and the Temple finally were destroyed on the ninth day of Av (August) in A.D. 70, no Christians were captured or killed. Emperor Nero had ordered General Vespasian and his son, General Titus, to conquer Galilee first, and then to destroy Jerusalem. As Galilee fell to Rome, many of the Jews, believing that its defenses were strong enough to withstand a siege, fled to Jerusalem for safety.

Christians in Palestine did just the opposite. They fled Jerusalem to Syria, Petra and Egypt. At one point in the siege, Roman legions withdrew several miles from Jerusalem, preparing to return to Rome to back up General Vespasian's claim to succeed the emperor. During the lull in battle, the last remaining Christians left the city and escaped the final destruction of Jerusalem. When Vespasian won, his son, General Titus, resumed the siege.

Thirty-eight years earlier, Jesus Christ told His disciples, as they sat on the Mount of Olives where Titus ultimately headquartered his Tenth Legion, that the enemy would come and surround Jerusalem, besiege her and destroy the city so that "not one stone shall be left upon another that shall not be thrown down." But then Jesus went on to say, "When you see Jerusalem surrounded by armies, then know that its desolation is near. Then let those in Judea flee to the mountains, let those who are in the midst of her depart, and let not those who are in the country enter her. For these are the days of vengeance, that all things which are written may be fulfilled" (Luke 24:6,20-22). While the first part of this prophecy was fulfilled a few years later, the last part had to do with the last days. We still await the fulfillment of the second part of the two-fold prophecy.

Therefore, since we are living in the last days, it is vital that we study the Bible so that we will know what it has to say about our future. There are many prophecies that must still be fulfilled, and "Blessed is he who reads and those who hear the words of this prophecy, and keep those things which are written in it; for the time is near" (Revelation 1:3).

Many of these prophecies yet to be fulfilled have to do with the second coming of the Messiah. Throughout the Bible's progressive revelation of God to man are a number of prophecies that God will send a Redeemer, a virgin-born Messiah, who will reconcile us to God. Ultimately, this Messiah will set up the Kingdom of God on Earth. In this book I will attempt to tie these messianic prophecies together and reveal how they are coming to pass in our generation. I trust it will help you to understand that "the days are at hand, and the fulfillment of every vision" that Jesus the Messiah is coming soon.

PART I

Countdown to Armageddon

"And there shall come forth a rod out of the stem of Jesse, and a Branch shall grow out of his roots: And the spirit of the LORD shall rest upon him, the spirit of wisdom and understanding, the spirit of counsel and might, the spirit of knowledge and of the fear of the LORD; And shall make him of quick understanding in the fear of the LORD: and he shall not judge after the sight of his eyes, neither reprove after the hearing of his ears: But with righteousness shall he judge the poor, and reprove with equity for the meek of the earth: and he shall smite the earth with the rod of his mouth, and with the breath of his lips shall he slay the wicked. And righteousness shall be the girdle of his loins, and faithfulness the girdle of his reins. The wolf also shall dwell with the lamb, and the leopard shall lie down with the kid; and the calf and the young lion and the fatling together; and a little child shall lead them."

Isaiah 11:1-6

CHAPTER 1

Longing for the Messiah

Pagan societies of history found inspiration by looking back to their ancient glories and their legends of a "golden age." Jewish prophets, through their inspired prophecies, introduced a revolutionary idea that the "golden age" lies in the future and will begin when their Messiah-King comes to Earth. The messianic ideal developed among the Jewish people as a response to a longing for a restored sovereignty. Their loss of political independence, combined with a desire to return in triumph to their land of promise, nurtured a strong faith in the prophecies that God would ultimately send His Messiah-Redeemer.

The word "Messiah," the English translation for the Hebrew word moshiak, means "anointed one" and refers to the act of anointing with oil, as in consecrating a king or priest. The word appears several times in the Old Testament in reference to an anointed one. The first time the word is used as a title is in 1 Samuel 2:10: "He will give strength to His king, and exalt the horn of His *anointed.*" The second reference to the "anointed" is found in the great Messianic Psalm of David, Psalm 2. David speaks about the "kings of the earth" who "set themselves, and the rulers take counsel together, against the Lord and against His anointed," *Moschiak.* Then he goes on to say: "I have set My King on My holy hill of Zion. I will declare the decree: The Lord has said to Me, You are My Son, today I have begotten You" (vv.6-7), which reminds us of John 1:14: "And the Word became flesh and dwelt among us, and we beheld His glory, the glory as of the only begotten of the Father, full of grace and truth." Also 1 John 4:9: "In this the love of God was manifested toward us, that God has sent His only begotten Son into the world, that we might live through Him."

The longing for the "Messiah" became stronger in the hearts of God's chosen people during the inter-biblical period, while first the Greeks and then the Romans ruled the promised land, just before Jesus Christ was born.

Even though the writers of God's Word used the precise word *Moshiak* only a few times, Jews searched the Psalms and Prophets for the many promises of the coming King-Deliverer. By the time Jesus was born, faithful Jews referred to their "Messiah" much more frequently; in the New Testament, which was written in Greek, *Messiah* translates into *Christos*, Christ. By the time Jesus began to minister throughout Judea, Galilee and Samaria, the idea of the coming Messiah was widespread. Andrew, a future apostle, along with another man, heard John the Baptist refer to Jesus as the "Lamb of God." The two men followed Jesus one day. Then Andrew went to his brother and told him, "We have found the Messiah" (John 2:41). The Samaritan woman at the well told Jesus, "'I know that Messiah is coming' (who is called Christ). 'When He comes, He will tell us all things'" (John 4:25).

Who is this Messiah? Why was His coming so important to the Jews of old? Who is He to the Christians? How will His coming affect the lives of all those on Earth?

The Need for a Messiah-Redeemer

From the time that God drove man from the Garden of Eden, humankind has sought the meaning of his life and his universe. Each of us has a spiritual vacuum deep within that causes us to realize that something is profoundly wrong with our spiritual lives. We sense a deep alienation from our fellow man as well as from our Creator. Yet, despite this alienation, every person in every culture has what Ecclesiastes 3:11 calls "eternity in their hearts." This "eternity" causes us to want to believe in a Creator God and to form some kind of religious system that will put us in touch with our Creator.

This spiritual alienation occurred when our original parents, Adam and Eve, rebelled against the only commandment God gave them. They were created by God with a free will, placed in a perfect paradise where they could enjoy beauty and bounty. They had only one prohibition. God chose to test their love and obedience by telling them they could eat of any tree in the garden except the Tree of the Knowledge of Good and Evil, for "in the day that you eat of it you shall surely die" (Genesis 2:17).

Into this garden paradise came Satan in the form of a serpent. He deceived Eve by telling her that if she ate of the forbidden tree she would reach a greater spiritual evolution: "You will be like God, knowing good and evil" (Genesis 3:5). This desire to be "like God" was the very reason why Satan was "cut down to the ground." He had said in his heart: "I will ascend into heaven, I will exalt my throne above the stars of God;...I will be like the Most High" (Isaiah 14:12-14). Satan was created by God as the most beautiful angel in heaven, yet he rebelled against God and recruited as many as one-third of all created angels, the "sons of God," to defy the Most High God. These became the demon spirits who will ultimately be cast into the "everlasting fire prepared for the devil and his angels" (Matthew 25:41).

Eve, using her God-given free will, believed what Satan told her and ate of the tree and gave some to Adam to eat. When Adam and Eve disobeyed God's single command they died spiritually that day to God's promise of everlasting life. They died physically in less than a thousand years instead of living eternally as they were created to do.

The spiritual future of humanity looked hopeless after the Fall. God had created man and woman in perfection, placed them in an ideal environment for a wonderful, rewarding life of purpose, love, pleasure, and granted them the joy of walking with God "in the garden in the cool of the day" (Genesis 3:8). Yet, despite every advantage, the first time they were faced with a decision about obedience they failed God. That initial rebellion has been repeated billions of times throughout history. Today we have many cults, such as the New Age movement, that tell us that we can "be like God." Satan, the first rebel, continues to offer the same disastrous advice he gave Eve.

The whole course of man-made religion is to create the false ideal of transcendence based on some short cut to experience the divine without obedience to the revealed Word of God. The ultimate question each one of us has to answer is: "Who is going to rule your life?" We will either accept that we are a creation of God and worship Him, or we will rebel against God and worship ourselves as the god of our own lives. As the great poet, Milton, said in *Paradise Lost*: "Either in the end you will say to God, 'Thy will be done,' or in the end He will say to you, 'Thy will be done.'" This choice is so fundamental that it literally determines your eternal destiny.

The Bible reveals that of all our sins, pride is the greatest because spiritual pride is the fundamental rebellion against God. It is the one sin that, unless we repent, prevents us from ever asking God to forgive us of our continual rebellion against Him. The sins of the flesh and spirit are by-products of the basic spiritual rebellion that demands we do it our way at all costs. It is this spiritual pride that is the toughest sin for us to repent of and seek forgiveness for. However, if we repent, God stands ready to transform our lives so that we can once again have joyful communication with Him and find fellowship with other believers as part of His Church, the Body of Christ on Earth.

The Promise of A Messiah

After discovering their terrible rebellion, God revealed His tremendous grace to Adam and Eve. Even though the immediate consequence of their sin was severe (see Genesis 3:16-19), God promised to send a Redeemer who would defeat Satan's plans and destroy his "seed." In the brief prophecy, "I will put enmity between...your seed and her Seed; He shall bruise your head, and you shall bruise His heel" (Genesis 3:15), is the promise of the virgin birth. The words "her Seed" do not appear elsewhere in the Bible. A child is always called the "seed" of a man, never the seed of a woman.

Thousands of years later the prophet Isaiah continued this theme when he prophesied that a special sign would be given to Israel when "the virgin shall conceive and bear a son" (7:14). Despite the attempts of some liberal scholars to reduce the meaning of this virgin birth prophecy, the original word used by Isaiah is *almah*. While *almah* does not refer primarily and solely to the virginal status of a girl it does clearly refer to a young unmarried girl, one who has not previously engaged in sexual relations. The Septuagint translators, who in 285 B.C. were much closer to the nuances of the original Hebrew language of the Bible, translated *almah* into the Greek *parthenos*, which clearly indicates a virgin. This Septuagint version was used by Jesus, His disciples, and the Jews of the first century. Prior to the prophecy being fulfilled and the Gospel account being recorded, these Jewish Bible scholars understood the prophecy to mean that the Messiah would be born of a virgin. The baby Jesus was born to the virgin Mary in fulfillment of these two separate prophecies— Genesis 3:15 and Isaiah 7:14.

After being expelled from the Garden, Adam learned to live and toil "in the sweat" of his face as he cultivated the soil of a world that also suffered from God's curse: "Thorns and thistles it shall bring forth for you" (Genesis 3:18). All of creation was damaged because of sinful rebellion. Even the animals that God brought to Adam to name began to kill each other for food. The good news, however, is that in the Millennium of Messiah's rule the curse will be lifted, animals will once again become non-violent and "the wolf and the lamb shall feed together, the lion shall eat straw like the ox" (Isaiah 65:25).

Messiah as Kinsman-Redeemer

God's original plan was that mankind would "fill the earth and subdue it; have dominion over the fish of the sea, over the birds of the air, and over every living thing that moves on the earth" (Genesis 1:28). But, in rebelling against God and choosing instead to listen to Satan, Adam and Eve handed over dominion of our planet to God's adversary, the enemy of our soul, the "prince of the power of the air, the spirit who now works in the sons of disobedience" (Ephesians 2:2) during our rebellion.

When Satan came to Jesus in the wilderness, he took Him to a high mountain and offered to give Him all the kingdoms of the world if Jesus would fall down and worship him. He had this right because Adam and Eve sold it all to the devil. Notice that Jesus did not dispute his claim. We are living in enemy occupied territory until Christ returns to defeat Satan, recovering dominion of this planet and setting up the Kingdom of God under His Messiah reign.

In a sense, Adam mortgaged our planet to Satan. When Christ returns in glory, at the end of the "times of the Gentiles" (Luke 21:24), He will redeem God's creation from Satan, having already paid for it with His precious blood.

The word *redemption* refers to the act of buying something out of the market. The biblical book of Ruth clearly illustrates this principle of redemption. When Naomi returned to Bethlehem from Moab after the death of her husband and two sons, she brought her daughter-in-law Ruth with her. Naomi's husband had sold his family property so she had no property of her own, no more sons, and no grandsons. Naomi contrived, in a perfectly acceptable, legal and moral way, to see to it that she would be cared for in her old age and Ruth would have a husband and sons to carry on the family name. She did this by invoking two laws: the law of redemption, and the law of levirite marriage. A kinsman-redeemer of Naomi's husband had to intercede on her behalf to regain the lost property. The one who came to their rescue was a near relative named Boaz. He was not the closest relative, however, so he legally approached a man who was more closely related and offered him the chance to buy back the property for Naomi. The man said yes in accordance to the law of redemption; but when he heard that he also had to marry the widow of the son of his relative he stepped aside. Then Boaz, like Jesus Christ, stepped forward to redeem and restore the lost property. He also married Ruth, and they became parents of a boy who years later had a grandson who became King David.

One day Christ our Kinsman-Redeemer will not only reclaim what Adam lost, He will also take His Church to Himself as His Bride. In the oldest book in the Bible, Job declares that he knows "that my Redeemer lives, and He shall stand at last on the earth; and after my skin is destroyed, this I know, that in my flesh I shall see God, whom I shall see for myself, and my eyes shall behold, and not another" (Job 19:25-27).

Ancient Jews looked for their hope in the one who would be anointed, the Messiah, the Redeemer, when they lost political independence and their land of promise. The children of Israel have a strongly developed sense of God's justice that inspires a belief that their Messiah-Redeemer will ultimately right all wrongs: "'There is hope in your future,' says the Lord, 'that your children shall come back to their own border'" (Jeremiah 31:17).

As a Sacrificial Lamb

When Adam and Eve lost their innocence and their direct daily communication with God they also lost their guiding light for spiritual behavior. God in His mercy provided them with a system by which they could atone for their sins, the sacrifice system. The first sacrifice was made by God when He killed the first animal ever slain in order to make "tunics of skin, and clothed them" (Geneses 3:21) to cover their nakedness. This first sacrifice was necessitated by mankind's rebellion and the need for a covering for sin, an atonement.

Abel, second born son of Adam and Eve, brought the first acceptable offering to God, when he gave God the best from his flock of sheep. His sacrifice acknowledged his personal responsibility for sin, for "without shedding of blood there is no remission" of sins (Hebrews 9:22). Obviously, the blood of animals could not take away a person's sins, but by regularly bringing his sacrifice to the high priest to offer to God, sinful mankind was reminded that he was out of step with his Creator. Also, he was constantly reminded that one day the Lamb of God would be slain as the ultimate sacrifice for all his sins. One day in heaven we will hear the song: "You are worthy...for You were slain, and have redeemed us to God by Your blood out of every tribe and tongue and people and nation, and have made us kings and priests to our God; and we shall reign on earth" (Revelation 5:9-10).

The Character of the Messiah

A great prophecy of Isaiah reveals much about the character of the coming Messiah: "For unto us a Child is born, unto us a Son is given; and the government will be upon His shoulder. And His name will be called Wonderful, Counselor, Mighty God, Everlasting Father, Prince of Peace. Of the increase of His government and peace there will be no end. Upon the throne of David and over His kingdom, to order it and establish it with judgment and justice from that time forward, even forever" (Isaiah 9:6-7).

Jesus the Christ (Messiah) came once as a suffering servant to die for lost sinners. However, His return will not be as a suffering servant but as the King of kings and the Lord of hosts to destroy the works of the devil and clean out the pollution of sin throughout the world.

Isaiah gives four outstanding characteristics of the coming Anointed One, the King, the Messiah: "For unto us a Child is born, unto us a Son is given....And His name will be called Wonderful, Counselor, Mighty God, Everlasting Father, Prince of Peace" (Isaiah 9:6). These names identify the deep need the people had, and still have, for a leader who like Joshua would lead them to a place of rest. But this time the rest will be forever, such as is spoken of in the book of Hebrews (4:9).

Wonderful Counselor

In the title "Wonderful Counselor" (peleh ya'ats) "Wonderful" means a marvelous, wonder-filled or miraculous thing. This name Wonderful is most appropriate to the coming Messiah because His reign will transform a sin-sick world into the most marvelous planet we could ever dream of and will fill the inhabitants of His kingdom with wonder. Counselor, ya'ats, appears twenty-four times in Scripture, including this passage from Isaiah. A Counselor is one who advises and deliberates about weighty matters. The Messiah is the Wonderful Counselor, the great spiritual guide both to the Church and the nation Israel. Jesus is the one person in history who is supremely qualified to be the Wonderful Counselor to humanity.

Mighty God

Mighty God (El Gibbot) clearly declares that Messiah is not simply an elevated leader of men. The person of the Messiah is uniquely God. The Hebrew word Gibbot means one who is mighty, powerful and a strong champion of man. El literally indicates that this one is the Almighty God, not just a representative of God. This is only one of many verses in the Bible that clearly identifies the person of the Messiah with that of God. (See John 1:1 and Romans 9:5.)

Everlasting Father

The description "Everlasting Father" seems very unusual at first glance, but upon closer examination we see that it identifies the Messiah as the eternal Father-Creator. He always was and He will always be. John 1:1 calls Him the Word that was in the beginning with God and "all things were made though Him, and without Him nothing was made that was made" (v.3). The book of Hebrews states that God "has in these last days spoken to us by His Son, whom He has appointed heir of all things, through whom also He made the worlds" (1:2).

The Bible differentiates between the roles of Jesus Christ the Son of God, the Holy Spirit, and God the Father in the Trinity. The prophet Isaiah declares in his description of the promised Son that He is the "Everlasting Father." There was no time frame in which He was created; He precedes time. "In the beginning was the Word, and the Word was with God, and the Word was God. He was in the beginning with God" (John 1:1-2). It also declares that He will be manifested to the world in a later period of time following the lifetime of Isaiah (700 B.C.).

Prince of Peace

The title Prince of Peace, proclaims that the promised Messiah will finally defeat the dreaded scourge of bloody warfare, which has cursed man's existence since Cain killed Abel. The name "Prince" declares that Christ will bear the crown of David and will truly reign upon the earth as the

Royal Sovereign of this universe. Unlike earthly princes whose careers are often marked by continuous warfare, the Messiah's reign will usher in that eternal peace which mankind has longed for throughout all generations. Isaiah tells us that "of the increase of His government and peace there will be no end" (v. 7). The Messiah's kingdom will increase to include all of His created universe without the violence of war. This world has experienced thirteen years of war for every single year of peace during its four thousand years of recorded history.

Finally, when Christ—Messiah—returns to set up His kingdom, mankind will enjoy a world where the weapons of war will never be heard or seen again. Wonderful Counselor, Mighty God, Everlasting Father, Prince of Peace.

In the next chapter we will examine Daniel's prophetic revelation of the future Gentile world empire that will prepare the way for the coming Messiah.

CHAPTER 2

Daniel's Dream of World Empire

One night, more than two thousand years ago, the greatest emperor in ancient history, Nebuchadnezzar of Babylon, lay on his bed wondering about the future of the Earth, his place in history, and the empires that would succeed him. When he fell asleep, God gave him a most unusual dream of a great image of a man composed of different metals. When Nebuchadnezzar awoke, the dream had left him and he could not remember it. It disturbed him so much that he called the wisest men in his kingdom to come and tell him the forgotten dream and its meaning. Of course, the magicians and priests could not do this. They pleaded with the king to tell them his dream and then they would give its meaning. But the king could not. Nebuchadnezzar threatened to destroy all the wise men in the empire because they failed to do what he wanted.

Among those facing death was Daniel, a young captive from Jerusalem who along with other noble youth was taken to Babylon to serve the king. These young men were chosen because they were without "blemish, but good-looking, gifted in all wisdom, possessing knowledge and quick to understand, who had ability to serve in the king's palace, and whom they might teach the language and literature of the Chaldeans" (Daniel 1:4). Not only did Daniel have these virtues, but he was also devoted to God Almighty, following His commandments and praying to Him daily. When Daniel got the bad news he went to the king and asked him not to kill all the wise men yet but to give him a little time and he would tell the king the dream and its interpretation. Daniel went home and told his three friends, Shadrach, Meschach and Abed-Nego to pray with him concerning the dream so that they would not perish with the other wise men in the kingdom.

The young men did pray, and God revealed the dream and its interpretation to Daniel. Daniel went before the great king and told him what God had revealed, giving the glory to the Lord for the revelation. He told the king that his dream was of a great metallic image. Its "head was of fine gold, its chest and arms of silver, its belly and thighs of bronze, its legs of iron, its feet partly of iron and partly of clay" (Daniel 2:32-33).

The amazing dream symbolized the course of Gentile rule in the world for the next twenty-six hundred years. The image's four parts represented four world empires that came into being in the exact prophesied order within the first five hundred years of the prophecy. Although more than two thousand years have passed since the fourth kingdom, no ruler has succeeded in establishing another world power equal to the greatness of that fourth empire Rome. Charlemagne, Frederick Barbarossa, Genghis Khan, Napoleon, Adolph Hitler, and Stalin all tried and failed to take over the world.

The four empires which Daniel predicted were: (1) the gold head—the Babylonian Empire; (2) the silver chest and arms—the Media-Persian Empire; (3) the bronze belly and thighs—the Greek Empire; (4) the legs of iron and feet and toes of iron and clay—the Roman Empire.

The Empire of Pure Gold, Babylon

The image's head of pure gold in Nebuchadnezzar's dream, Daniel said, symbolized Nebuchadnezzar and the Babylonian Empire. The gold head spoke of the enormous wealth and power of this first great empire that controlled the entire known world, a position which could have belonged to the people of God had they not thrown it away.

After centuries of deep apostasy, God finally took His promise of world sovereignty away from Israel; the promise had been conditional. He had warned them repeatedly through Moses, Solomon, Isaiah, and Jeremiah that they would suffer terrible consequences if they continued to defy His commandments. He would punish Israel for worshiping false gods and for unconfessed sins. God especially condemned Israel's weakness of seeking protection by allying with evil nations like Egypt rather than trusting in God's care. The Jews would halfheartedly pay attention to God's messengers and, for a time, turn back to Him. But they could not believe that God would ever allow a pagan nation such as Babylon to conquer them, their promised land, and their divine sanctuary even though they continually lived in open sin and apostasy.

Finally, God gave up on His people. He gave them the news in the following way: He told His prophet Jeremiah to make yokes and bonds "and send them to the king of Edom, the king of Moab, the king of the Ammonites, the king of Tyre, and the king of Sidon" with a message that said, "Now I have given all these lands into the hand of Nebuchadnezzar the king of Babylon." The message continued, "I also spoke to Zedekiah king of Judah according to all these words, saying, 'Bring your necks under the yoke of the king of Babylon, and serve him and his people, and live!'" (Jeremiah 27:3,6,12). God was going to allow the province of Babylon to rise up and overpower the Assyrian empire in 608 B.C. and conquer all the nations of their known world. At the time of his dream, Nebuchadnezzar had indeed become emperor of the dynamic Babylonian empire and was rapidly conquering all other kingdoms in his path.

Not only did Jeremiah accurately predict the fall of these nations, he also prophesied the exact duration of the Babylonian empire as lasting seventy years. This seventy-year time span was the number of years Israel had missed keeping the Sabbath year during 490 years. God included the law of the Sabbath of the Land and the law of Jubilee with the laws He gave Moses: "When you come into the land which I give you, then the land shall keep a sabbath to the Lord. Six years you shall sow your field, and six years you shall prune your vineyard, and gather in its fruit; but in the seventh year there shall be a sabbath of solemn rest for the land, a sabbath to the Lord" (Leviticus 25:2-4).

The leaders and people of Israel ignored God's command from 1096 B.C. when Saul became king until 606 B.C. when Babylon devastated the land of Israel. As 2 Chronicles 36:20 and 21 explains: "Those who escaped from the sword he [Nebuchadnezzar] carried away to Babylon, where they became servants to him and his sons until the reign of the kingdom of Persia, to fulfill the word of the Lord by the mouth of Jeremiah, until the land had enjoyed her Sabbaths. As long as she lay desolate she kept Sabbath, to fulfill seventy years."

The Empire of Silver, Media-Persia

The silver chest and arms of the image in Nebuchadnezzar's dream indicated that the empire after Babylon, that of Media-Persia, would be even stronger in force, just as silver is harder and less malleable than gold, but would be less valuable than the Babylonian kingdom.

In October, 538 B.C., King Belshazzar of Babylon held a feast for "thousands of his lords," his wives, and concubines. He commanded that the gold and silver vessels which had been taken from Solomon's Temple be brought to the banquet hall so his guests could drink wine from them. As they drank and "praised the gods of gold and silver, bronze and iron, wood and stone," the fingers of a man's hand suddenly appeared and began to write some mysterious words on the wall. The king became so frightened that "the joints of his hips were loosened and his knees knocked against each other" (Daniel 5:6). He called for the "astrologers, the Chaldeans [wise men], and the soothsayers...saying...'Whoever reads this writing, and tells me its interpretation, shall be clothed with purple and have a chain of gold around his neck; and he shall be the third ruler in the kingdom'" (v. 7). Needless to say, none of these great, wise men could tell the king what he wanted to know.

Daniel, now an old man, had been forgotten after Nebuchadnezzar's death by everyone except the queen mother. She came into the banquet hall and told the king to call on Daniel, he would know what the words meant. Daniel was sent for. He stood before the king and said: "O

King, the Most High God gave Nebuchadnezzar your father a kingdom and majesty, glory and honor....But you his son, Belshazzar, have not humbled your heart" (vv. 18,22). Then Daniel gave the interpretation of the words on the wall: "This is the inscription that was written: MENE, MENE, TEKEL, UPHARSIN. This is the interpretation ...God has numbered your kingdom, and finished it;...You have been weighed in the balances, and found wanting;...Your kingdom has been divided and given to the Medes and Persians" (vv. 25-28).

That very night in October of 538 B.C., Darius the Mede led his rebel army under the great brass gates spanning the Euphrates River that cut through the center of the mighty city of Babylon. The city walls were more than thirty stories high, designed to keep out invaders. But the enemy forces dammed and diverted the river and made their way right to the center of the city along the empty river bed. Jeremiah had prophesied precisely how God would deliver the evil kingdom of Babylon to its doom: "The bars of her gate are broken...his city is taken on all sides; the passages are blocked, the reeds they have burned with fire" (Jeremiah 51:31-32).

Daniel was promoted to the third place in the kingdom as the king promised, despite the bad news he delivered and, "That very night Belshazzar, king of the Chaldeans, was slain" (Daniel 5:30).

When the Media-Persian Empire of Darius rose to power, God rose up a new Persian king, Cyrus, to issue a decree in 536 B.C. that allowed the Jews to return to Israel—seventy years after the people were carried into captivity: "The Lord stirred up the spirit of Cyrus king of Persia, so that he made a proclamation throughout all his kingdom and also put it in writing, saying, '...He [God] has commanded me to build Him a house at Jerusalem which is in Judah. Who is there among you of all His people? May the Lord his God be with him, and let him go up!'" (vv. 22-23).

Despite this freedom to go home, less than 1 percent of the ten tribes who had been conquered by Assyria 115 years earlier, and less than 5 percent of the tribes of Judah and Benjamin in Babylon took advantage of the offer. In a curious historical parallel, many Jews today who (since 1948) could return to Israel choose to remain integrated into the thriving commerce of wealthy countries and stay settled in their comfortable lifestyles. Some of those Jews who chose to remain in Persia in their Jewish communities were the ones which Haman of Persia later attempted to destroy by his evil plan (see Esther 5). God's miraculous deliverance of these Jews occurred because the Jewish girl who became Queen Esther intervened with her husband, King Xerxes, on behalf of her people.

But undoubtedly it was God's will that some of His people stay behind, because years later a Jewish cupbearer-counselor to Persian King Artaxerxes, Nehemiah, felt God's call to fill another need in Jerusalem. Although more than forty thousand had returned to Judah under Cyrus and rebuilt their homes and the Temple, they had neither the heart nor the leadership to rebuild the walls of the once nearly impregnable city. Nehemiah appeared before his king to ask permission to return to Jerusalem to rebuild the walls of the burned city. King Artaxerxes willingly allowed his servant Nehemiah to lead a mission to rebuild the walls of the city. Not only did he give permission, he also provided a great amount of the materials to complete the task. Why do you suppose this Persian king responded so willingly?

One day, while comparing some chronological charts, it struck me that King Artaxerxes was not the Gentile pagan King of Persia, but rather a Jewish king, the son of Queen Esther. He was probably taught to love God and Israel at his mother Esther's knees. Therefore, not only did God use Esther's obedience to save her people from the attack by Satan during the days of Haman, but God also allowed her marriage to King Xerxes to produce a Jewish son, Artaxerxes, who would later play a significant role in God's plans to restore Jerusalem.

Artaxerxes signed the decree to rebuild the walls of Jerusalem on the first day of Nisan, 445 B.C. (the twentieth year of his reign), which fulfilled Daniel's prophecy: "Know therefore and understand, that from the going forth of the command to restore and build Jerusalem until Messiah the Prince, there shall be seven weeks of sixty-two weeks; the streets shall be built again, and the walls, even in troublesome times. And after the sixty-two weeks Messiah shall be cut off" (9:25-26). This decree made on March 14, 445 B.C., began the sixty-nine weeks of Daniel's seventy-weeks vision. It was fulfilled to the exact day on Palm Sunday, A.D. 32, when "Messiah the Prince" was "cut off" as Jesus was rejected by the leadership of Israel.

A well-established Jewish community remained throughout Babylon, which today includes Iraq, Iran, Afghanistan, and Syria. Historical records reveal that in the first century up to ten million Jews lived in the lands east of Jerusalem. Other fascinating historical references indicate that Jews also entered China in ancient times. Also, some Jewish gravestones of the ten tribes, dating back to five hundred years before Christ, have been located north of the Black Sea in present day Russia. These large Jewish communities produced a rich literature (such as the Babylonian Talmud) and were a fertile ground for the spread of the gospel by first-century apostles.

There is an interesting historical parallel between the emperors of Assyria and Media-Persia and Russian leaders of our century. When the Assyrians conquered the known world they took whole populations from fallen countries such as Israel and transferred them to remote areas throughout the Assyrian kingdom. Then they moved "people from Babylon, Cuthah, Ava, Hamath, and from Sepharvaim, and placed them in the cities of Samaria instead of the children of Israel" (2 Kings 17:24). Stalin, in the 1950's moved the Estonians from the Baltic region to Siberia. The tactic was designed to break the people's independent spirit and help integrate them into a homogeneous empire. Leaders of the Media-Persian empire in 538 B.C. had exactly the opposite population policy. King Cyrus allowed the Jews to return to Israel, just as today Mikhail Gorbachev is allowing national population groups to return to their traditional areas from which Stalin evicted them.

History records that the Media-Persian empire had enormous armies, such as King Xerxes' great army of more than a million that attacked Greece. It was said that it took one entire day for that assembled army to pass before the king's throne which was set on a high hill. Yet this huge empire lacked the nobility and impact which Babylon exerted. This second of the world empires lasted only two hundred and seven years. In 331 B.C. the Media-Persian Empire was destroyed by the spectacular invasion of the swift armies of Alexander the Great, the third world empire of the image.

The Bronze Empire, Greece

The third part of the image, "the belly and thighs," were of bronze, which is much less valuable than pure gold or pure silver. The Greek Empire would lack much of the luster and magnificence of the Babylonian and Media-Persian empires, but because bronze is also much stronger than gold or silver, Alexander and his four successors would be awesome in their ability to destroy their enemies. His army would cut through the ancient kingdoms as a knife through butter. Never again in history would an army move so quickly and decisively to destroy superior numbers of armies. In a supplementary vision, recorded in Daniel 8, the prophet predicted that this empire was like a rapidly moving male goat that destroyed the Media-Persian ram. History records that the aggressive Alexander exacted revenge on the Persians for Xerxes' earlier attack on Greece with brilliant military strategies using revolutionary new tactics.

Alexander, a pupil of the philosopher, Aristotle, believed that Greek culture could unify the world. He founded a new city in each country of his empire that would serve as a model for the furtherance of Greek culture. Public buildings, gymnasiums, open-air theaters, the spread of Greek names, Greek dress, and a common language all indicated the power of this great third empire.

After conquering the ancient seaport of Tyre in 332 B.C. Alexander moved on, intending to destroy the city of Jerusalem because the Jews had unwisely resisted his demands. Josephus reports that as he approached the city, intending to exact his vengeance, the high priest of the Temple came out in his beautiful white robes to meet the conqueror. Alexander was shocked as the priest told him that God had revealed to the prophet Daniel, some three hundred years earlier, that a great king would arise from Greece and subdue the entire world. When he showed Alexander the exact prophecies in the ancient Scriptures about his career, Alexander was so moved that he worshiped in the Temple and gave orders not to destroy Jerusalem or the country (Antiquities 11.5).

When Alexander built Alexandria in Egypt (331 B.C.) he encouraged Jews to settle there, giving them privileges comparable to those of his Greek subjects. Several years later under the Greek Ptolemy II, Jews in Alexandria translated the Hebrew Old Testament into Greek. It is said that this Greek king had an enormous love of knowledge and desired a copy of the Hebrew Scriptures in his own language. He arranged for a group of seventy Jewish scholars in Egypt to translate the ancient Hebrew texts. The resulting translation was later called the LXX, or Septuagint, the word for seventy. Previously, only a few educated priests and scribes could read the Scriptures. The Septuagint is the translation that Jesus and the apostles quoted from in the New Testament. Greek is also the language the writers of the New Testament used to record God's messages.

Daniel had prophesied that, at the peak of the male goat's power, "The large horn was broken, and in place of it four notable ones came up toward the four winds of heaven" (Daniel 8:8). When he died at the age of 33, Alexander lamented because there were no more countries to conquer. Since he had no heir to succeed him, the Greek empire was broken into four divisions led by Alexander's four generals, exactly as the prophet Daniel had told Nebuchadnezzar.

Two key areas would later impact Israel by continually contesting each other for supremacy in the Promised Land: (1) the Syrian area north of Galilee which was ruled by the Greek General Seleucus I, and (2) the land of Egypt led by Greek General Ptolemy I. Just as Poland has suffered repeatedly as a weak land power between the two giant military powers of Germany and Russia, so it was Israel's unhappy fate to lie on the playing field between the two strong Greek empires of the Seleucids and the Ptolemies.

Daniel had further prophesied that one horn would later arise out of the Seleucid Greek kingdom and persecute the Jews. This part of the prophecy was fulfilled when King Antiochus IV, known as Epiphanes ("God made manifest"), set out to destroy Judaism in retaliation of a political-religious disagreement with Rome.

The disagreement came about when, in 71 B.C., Antiochus attempted to invade Egypt. The rising Roman nation sent a senator to tell him that Rome would not allow him to alter the balance of power in the Mediterranean by conquering agriculturally rich Egypt. When Antiochus refused to answer the senator's question about whether he would withdraw his armies from Egypt, the senator silently drew a circle around him in the sand with a sword. He told Antiochus that he must give Rome his reply to their demand before he could leave the circle. Even though the fourth mighty empire of Daniel's prophecy was not yet a world power, Antiochus feared Rome's growing might. He angrily consented to withdraw his armies. In vengeance, he told his troops to kill tens of thousands of Jewish men, women and children as the army retreated from Egypt through Jerusalem.

Later, on Chisleu 24, 168 B.C., Antiochus stopped the daily morning and evening sacrifices. He then angrily sacrificed a pig on the Temple altar in June, 167 B.C. to profane it and show his contempt for the Jewish God. An old Jewish priest named Mattathias and his three sons led an apparently hopeless rebellion against the overwhelming force of the Seleucid armies. God intervened and allowed the Jews to miraculously defeat the invading armies. On Chisleu 24, 165 B.C., three years to the day after Antiochus stopped the daily sacrifice, the Jewish army threw the Seleucid army out of the Temple mount. The next morning at dawn, Jewish soldiers under the leadership of Judas Maccabaeus—"the Hammer"—cleansed the ruined Temple and erected a new altar on which to resume the daily sacrifice. (This series of events is part of the amazing biblical anniversaries explored in *Armageddon – Appointment With Destiny*. History tells us that the Jews searched the Temple and discovered a small vial containing one day's supply of holy oil for the candelabra that had escaped destruction by the enemy. Miraculously, God allowed this oil to last for eight days in the Temple until more sanctified oil could be prepared. This deliverance of the Temple from the defiler became known as the Feast of Dedication. This "Festival of Lights"—Hanukkah was celebrated by Jesus (see John 10:22).

From that time in 165 B.C. Israel recovered a strong measure of its independence. The descendants of the Maccabees became known as the Hasmonean Dynasty and ruled Israel for one hundred years in peace, using a variety of foreign alliances, until Rome invaded Jerusalem.

The Empire of Iron, Rome

The fourth part of the metal image in Nebuchadnezzar's dream was composed of two strong legs of iron, the Roman Empire. As iron "breaks in pieces and shatters all things...that kingdom will break in pieces and crush all the others" (Daniel 2:40). While the legs were composed of iron, the feet and toes were partly iron and partly clay. God revealed to Daniel that the fourth world empire would be as strong as iron and, with her incredible military and police forces, would trample all nations of the world under its overwhelming force. Though it would possess tremendous strength and would annihilate other nations, it would be of less refinement and value than the previous three empires.

This fourth empire transformed the known world with Roman institutions, law, and language. Much of the civilized world today still practice the laws derived from the Roman empire, speak languages based on Latin, and form governments and armies that trace their lineage and traditions back to ancient Rome. This great empire turned its nations into one enormous military machine that was unstoppable and ruled the known world far longer than any other.

Exactly as the dream foretold, the empire divided into two legs following Emperor Constantine: the Western Empire based in Rome and the Eastern Empire based in Constantinople (Istanbul, Turkey). The Eastern Empire became known as the Byzantine Empire and continued until its defeat by the Turks in A.D. 1453, while the Western Empire ceased to exist as a major force in A.D. 476 when the barbarians defeated Rome.

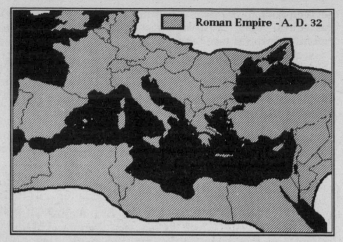

The Revived Roman Empire

The last part of Nebuchadnezzar's dream was: "You watched while a stone was cut out without hands, which struck the image on its feet of iron and clay, and broke them in pieces. Then the iron, the clay, the bronze, the silver, and the gold were crushed together, and became like chaff from the summer threshing floors; the wind carried them away so that no trace of them was found. And the stone that struck the image became a great mountain and filled the whole earth" (Daniel 2:34-35).

This phase of the Roman Empire, the unusual feet with ten toes of partly iron and partly clay, is the final form of the Roman Empire which is yet to come. This Revived Roman Empire will consist of a confederation of ten nations based on the old empire. This confederation will be composed of both strong and weak nations—part iron and part clay, partly authoritarian and partly democratic.

During the past fifteen hundred years many have tried and failed to revive the glories of Rome. Yet God tells us that in the days immediately preceding the return of Jesus Christ to set up His kingdom this confederacy will be formed. One of the most startling features of the world since the rebirth of the nation Israel in 1948 is the rapid formation of the

Revived Roman Empire in a reunited Europe. In 1948 NATO, the North Atlantic Treaty Organization, was formed to defend Europe against threats from the massive conventional armies of Communist Russia. In 1957 the Treaty of Rome accelerated the move to bring together many nations of Europe in a confederation of economic and trade relationships, the European Economic Community. In 1990 the E.E.C. dropped the word "Economic" from its title and is now the European Community (EC). In 1990 it included twelve member states with many more nations lined up to submit applications, a potential colossus of economic, political and military power in Europe.

In June, 1990, members of the EC met in Dublin to discuss future moves toward full integration of their economies. Surprisingly, the nations also announced that their previous plan to achieve economic and monetary union by December 31, 1992, would now be enhanced. They now agree to a plan that calls for a European Political Union that will involve the creation of a European Defense Army, together with a common European Foreign Policy. The prophet Daniel told us that the leader of a revived Roman Empire will make a treaty with Israel for seven years. For the first time in two thousand years a united Europe will be able to fulfill this specific prophecy within a few years.

The E.C.U. is the monetary unit which this alliance has created to take its place as one of the world's leading currencies. As the deadline for the 1992 plan approaches, many nations are very concerned that they may be left out of the preferential trading status of this new "super state." They are scrambling to make whatever arrangements they can to obtain treaty rights with the EC. Also in 1990, for the first time in a thousand years, the major nations of Europe joined together under the auspices of the Western European Union to coordinate a military response to Iraq's invasion of Kuwait. At the present time the EC has no military committee capable of implementing this armed response so they were forced to use the Western European Union. It is probable that this crisis will accelerate the demand for a permanent military structure with a joint multinational command to be used in future crises.

As further proof of European unity, the world witnessed the joining of West and East Germany on October 3, 1990, creating a massive financial and technological power base that will be the engine for a revived Europe. The United States, up until now the mightiest nation in the world, is faced with serious economic problems that will curtail her future ability to influence world events. The U.S. also finds that changed perceptions in Congress about the need for defense against Russia are creating serious problems in adequately funding armed forces, which is necessary to exert true world power. The ultimate result is that Europe is increasingly being perceived by other nations as the future major center of world power in the 1990s.

By 1993, an organization will be operating in Europe and the Mediterranean along the lines of the Roman Empire during the first century. It is almost as if God has set back the hands on the clock to the historical situation as it existed two thousand years ago. Today, as then, Rome was allied with or had conquered all of Europe and the nations surrounding the Mediterranean but was unable to conquer the Parthian Empire, the area of present-day Iraq, Iran, Afghanistan, and Saudi Arabia.

Today in Europe we witness the willingness of nations to surrender their national power to the Executive Commission of the European Community. Since 1978, citizens can directly elect their members to the first international European Parliament which meets in Strasborg, France. The Bible tells us that this ten-nation confederacy of the Revived Roman Empire will eventually be led by a charismatic, brilliant man who will be given sovereignty of the world. Daniel (9:24-27) confirms that this end-time leader will come out of the Roman empire.

Daniel, in another example of a prophecy within a prophecy, tells us that "the people of the prince who is to come shall destroy the city and the sanctuary" (v. 26). Note that this prophecy was fulfilled specifically when the armies of Rome burned the city of Jerusalem and destroyed the sanctuary on the ninth day of Av, A.D. 70. against the order of General Titus. The second part of this prophecy foretells that the coming Antichrist, "the prince who is to come," will come out of the Roman Empire. Therefore we can expect that the coming Antichrist will lead the Revived Roman Empire.

Other prophecies prove that the Antichrist must be Jewish and from the tribe of Judah. Otherwise, Jews would never accept his claims to being the Messiah. Jesus said, "I have come in My Father's name, and you do not receive Me; if another comes in his own name, him you will receive" (John 5:43). This passage proves that the Antichrist will present himself as the Messiah to the Jewish people just as Jesus of Nazareth did.

The final world emperor, who will be the Antichrist, will rule the ten-nation confederacy based in Europe. Daniel declares that "his power shall be mighty, but not by his own power" (Daniel 8:24). In other words he will receive supernatural power from Satan to enable him to achieve his spectacular results in politics, economics, and war.

In this same passage Daniel tells us that this man will come forth "in the latter time of their kingdom" (v. 23) and that "when the transgressors have reached their fullness, a king shall arise, having fierce features, who understands sinister schemes." During a terrible period of sinfulness, this arising king who is satanically possessed, totally and deeply involved with the occult, will be in control. The prophet's words that he "shall prosper and thrive" indicate that this world leader will bring the world to economic prosperity—at least initially. Daniel goes on to say that "he shall destroy many in their prosperity."

The Antichrist's success will "magnify himself in his heart" and lead to his great blaspheming of God. Daniel also declares that in his subtlety he shall destroy "the mighty, and also the holy people" (v. 24).

Like all antichrists who have come before him, this last Antichrist will despise his Jewish people because they bear God's Holy Name and are His Chosen People. "He shall even rise against the Prince of princes," yet he will meet his doom when he battles the armies of heaven and "shall be broken without human hand" (v. 25) when the Messiah returns and casts him into the Lake of Fire.

Twenty-six hundred years ago, God, in a dream to a pagan king, set the scene for the return of the Messiah.

In the following chapters we will examine the prophetic roles which America, Russia, Iraq, and the European Community will play in this great final drama.

CHAPTER 3

Russia's Appointment With Destiny

Even those who have only a casual interest in the Bible wonder how the world's nations fit into the events of the last days. What roles will the United States and Canada play in the Battle of Armageddon? In the judgment of the nations? Also, how does the powerful USSR fit into Bible prophecy?

The first thing we must realize is that biblical prophecy focuses on a nation's relationship to Israel in the end times and on the unfolding kingdom of God. The Lord declared that Israel is the spiritual center of this world and He has set the Promised Land at the center of the nations. In the prophetic song that Moses sang to the people of Israel, which they were to "write down...for yourselves,...teach...to the children of Israel" and put "in their mouths, that this song may be a witness for Me" (Deuteronomy. 31:19), he sang: "When the Most High divided their inheritance to the nations, when He separated the sons of Adam, He set the boundaries of the peoples according to the number of the children of Israel. For the Lord's portion is His people; Jacob is the place of His inheritance" (32:8-9). Therefore, if we are to understand clearly God's plan for our country and the rest of the world, according to Bible prophecies, we must see Palestine as the center of His plan.

Why Is America Not Prominent in Bible Prophecy?

Bible prophecy says nothing about America being the world super power in events leading up to the Battle of Armageddon. I believe the reason for this is that the North American continent will not be economically able to participate as the major super power for much longer.

As a Canadian and friend of America who appreciates what the United States has done in protecting the West from Russian threats, I wondered at the sad state of financial affairs when the United States was forced to go, "cap in hand," to beg funds from Germany and Japan to help in the Persian Gulf crisis. While the reasons for this action were that these countries must "bear their share" of expenses for this war, and also that many objected to taking U.S. money from needed welfare projects for defense, the primary reason was that the United States was not financially able to fund a massive war effort.

Waste, hundred-billion-dollar deficits, and the Savings and Loan crisis have eroded the economic ability of America to continue as the world's leading super power.

A huge amount of the 300 billion dollars spent annually on the defense of our nation is wasted in ways that seriously affect our ability to win wars. For example, both the American and Canadian military are overstaffed at the command level. Lars-Erik Nelson, in the *Toronto Star*, stated that each of the two hundred and forty-eight squadrons of U.S. Air Force fighter planes, missiles and support aircraft is commanded by a lieutenant colonel. He asks, "How many lieutenant colonels does the U.S. Air Force employ?" The unbelievable answer is "12,500 lieutenant colonels." This helps to explain why 150 billion dollars is spent each year on personnel expense.

The waste does not stop at personnel. Reports also reveal overspending in supplies. Media revealed that the Pentagon spent three thousand dollars on a screwdriver that could be bought at a local hardware store for six dollars. A recent book, *The Pentagonists*, reported that $14,835 and sixty-three man hours of engineering went into a piece of coat hanger wire three inches long.

Every year the Defense Department budgets billions for new and experimental weapons while admitting that our current ammunition supply levels in Europe and America would last no more than a month in an all-out war. The amounts of ammunition and missiles needed in a modern war are almost beyond imagination. The Gulf war used over ten days' worth of sophisticated weaponry that would be required in a European war —— (Fortunately, the Persian

Gulf war showed that much of our high technology can be devastatingly lethal.)

These greedy and wasteful practices may leave our military without adequate funds for troop training, ammunition, and armaments needed to defend our own country from an aggressor, much less participate in a war the size of the prophesied Armageddon.

Another drain on the American economy is the bail-out of Savings and Loan institutions. The Savings and Loan problem is only the tip of the iceberg. During the next few years, headlines will reveal that an equally disastrous situation exists in the banking and insurance industries. These crises will further erode our ability to project power internationally.

These facts may explain why the North American continent will not be a significant influence in the Middle East events of the last days. But do we appear in any Bible prophecies of this period or are we completely out of the picture?

Many Bible scholars believe that Ezekiel mentions our role in the war of Gog and Magog. In chapter 38, the prophet describes the reaction of a group of nations to an attack by Gog (Russia): "Sheba, Dedan, the merchants of Tarshish, and all their young lions will say to you,'Have you come to take plunder? Have you gathered your army to take booty, to carry away silver and gold, to take away livestock and goods, to take great plunder?'" (Ezekiel 38:13). "Tarshish, and all their young lions" is believed to refer to the British Commonwealth countries and America that are descended from the British "lion." Ezekiel's quote sounds like a diplomatic protest at the UN.

The United States could take a passive role in the coming war of Gog and Magog. The next questions is, What is Russia'a role in the coming events of Bible prophecy?

Russia in Bible Prophecy

Russia is the "Gog and Magog" of Bible prophecy. In order to fully understand the role Russia will play in the last days we must look at her history as well as her present day situation. Her place in prophecy is described by Ezekiel: "Then you will come from your place out of the far north, you and many peoples with you, all of them riding on horses, a great company and a mighty army. You will come up against My people Israel like a cloud, to cover the land. It will be in the latter days that I will bring you against My land, so that the nations may know Me, when I am hallowed in you, O Gog, before their eyes" (Ezekiel 38:15-16).

Over a thousand years ago the city-state of Muscovy had a strong psychological need to invade her neighbors in order to provide a buffer zone of defense against their enemies. This need began to increase with Peter the Great, the czar of Russia who died in A.D. 1725. Peter transformed his medieval country into a powerful military-political force in Europe. When he died he left a Political Will and Testament to the Russian leadership that is fascinating in light of the events of the past two hundred and fifty years. While some scholars doubt its authenticity, it has been a blueprint for Russian expansionist aims and strategies from the time of the czars to the current leader, Mikhail Gorbachev.

The 1890 edition of *Bohn's Standard Library* recorded several points of this Testament of Peter the Great:

"1. The Russian nation must be constantly on a war footing to keep the soldier warlike and in good condition. No rest must be allowed, except for the purpose of relieving the State finances, recruiting the army, or biding the favorable moment for attack. By these means peace is made subservient to war, and war to peace, in the interest of the aggrandizement and increasing prosperity of Russia.

"3. No opportunity must be lost of taking part in the affairs and disputes of Europe, especially in those of Germany, which from its vicinity is one of the most direct interest to us...

"8. We must keep steadily extending our frontiers northward along the Baltic, and southward along the shores of the Euxine [Black Sea].

"9. We must progress as much as possible in the direction of Constantinople and India. He who can get possession of these places is the real ruler of the world. With this view we must provoke constant quarrels at one time with Turkey and at another with Persia. We must establish wharfs and docks in the Euxine [Black Sea], and by degrees make ourselves masters of that sea as well as the Baltic, which is a doubly important element in the success of our plan. We must hasten the downfall of Persia, push on into the Persian Gulf, and, if possible, re-establish the ancient commercial intercourse with the Levant through Syria, and force our way in the Indies, which are the storehouses of the world...

"13. When Sweden is ours, Persia vanquished, Poland subjugated, Turkey conquered—when our armies are united, and the Euxine and Baltic are in the possession of our ships...We must make use of one to annihilate the other; this done, we have only to destroy the remaining one by finding a pretext for a quarrel, the issue of which we cannot be doubtful, as Russia will then be already in absolute possession of the East, and of the best part of Europe.

"14. ...When these countries are fully conquered, the rest of Europe must fall easily and without a struggle under our yoke. Thus Europe can and must be subjugated."

This basic strategy which was outlined centuries ago by Peter the Great is still being followed today. Some people have jumped to the conclusion that the Communist government of Russia has changed its fundamental goals and strategies in view of the current softening toward the Western world. They should consider what is actually taking place in the Soviet Union today. While it is true that there is a change of tactics, and while there are many in Russia who genuinely wish to change the country into a democracy, there is another side to the apparent relinquishing of power in the largest country in the world. The Soviet leadership in the Communist Party, army and KGB are allowing these surface changes to occur so that the West will be lulled into complacency. They hope the West will pour out the most massive financial and technical aid in history.

Russia's Regrouping and Replanning

In the mid 1980's, Moscow Center, the planning department of the KGB, Russia's massive intelligence agency, was forced to develop a new plan. For over twenty years their initial plan to weaken and divide the West proceeded according to plan. The West was disarming and giving away or selling technology which Moscow desperately needed. Despite worsening economic and political problems during the 60's and 70's, the USSR began to believe that victory could still be achieved. Then, as the moment of conflict approached, an unexpected and unwanted political event occurred: The United States elected a most unusual man to the office of president. In the following eight years, Ronald Reagan transformed the weak, vacillating power of the West into a revived military and political colossus with the renewed moral capability of defending itself.

As America rearmed with a new commitment to pay the price of a protracted struggle for freedom, Soviet intelligence planners despaired to see their long-laid plans of world domination begin to fade. Renewed military expenditures, a vision of Strategic Defense Initiative, modernized nuclear weapons and an enormously increased nuclear equipped navy and air force combined to destroy Moscow's confident plans of early success. A radical change of plans was needed because the challenge was immense. These new plans were elegant yet simple in their ultimate execution to once again bring Russia into the limelight as the strongest military power on Earth today.

These steps include: the genial era of glasnost; a democratic breakthrough in Eastern Europe; and a quiet, massive buildup of Soviet military power.

The Genial Era of Glasnost

The new initiative adopted by the Soviet Union involved Mikhail Gorbachev, the new KGB candidate for general secretary, and a policy called "perestroika." It involved a massive propaganda campaign designed simultaneously to deceive the West as to Russia's true ntentions. Glasnost was designed to encourage western ations to invest enormous sums of money and technology in the revival of the inefficient communist economies of astern Europe and Russia. Despite the well-known fact that his "glasnost" would be the fifth time since 1917 that ussia has pretended to reject communism and liberalize self, the West once more lined up to buy into the "big lie" of Soviet reformation and democracy. Just as she has after each previous period of glasnost, Russia will again follow p with a brutal renewal of dictatorship, just as Lenin's communist doctrine requires.

The latest show of glasnost followed extensive iscussions on disarmament in Geneva in the early 1980's. he West immediately started to disarm while Russia talked bout future arms cuts (which will not take effect until 1993 to 1995). Russia convinced most western analysts, through a well-publicized demonstration of destroying several housand obsolete tanks and old submarines, that a true hange of heart and mind had occurred in the leadership of he Soviet Union. No one in the West questioned why a peaceful" Russia continued to support the dictatorships in Cuba, Afghanistan and Angola to the tune of sixteen billion dollars per year. This was at a time when the country could ot produce bread or cigarettes for its own unhappy itizens.

No one asked why Gorbachev, the "great man of peace," ontinued to imprison huge numbers of political iscontents in Russian concentration camps, in despicable onditions. Nor have they questioned why Russia continues to spend more than ten billion dollars per year to produce he most sophisticated titanium double-hulled ballistic uclear submarine in the world. This Delta class submarine s a first-strike naval weapon that can dive deeper, faster, and nore silently than anything produced by America. They are ow producing new submarines every seven weeks.

Just as the KGB anticipated, the prospect of real world eace and freedom caused the rapid evaporation of Western olitical will to support the long range planning, cquisition, and support required for an adequate defense orce.

A Democratic Breakthrough in Eastern Europe

For the past few years the world has watched as Eastern Europe fought to throw off the shackles of communist dictatorship. Many have given Gorbachev credit for allowing it to happen. While this is partly true, there is another side to the revolution—a hidden side.

The initial stages of this revolution were planned in Moscow by Gorbachev and the KGB as a first step in implementing their plan. In 1988 they decided to get rid of the corrupt, hard-line Stalinist leadership of their Eastern European allies. These included Honecker in East Germany and the brutal Milos Jakes of Czechoslovakia. These old style leaders were resisting Gorbachev's reforms at every turn and were severely criticizing glasnost and perestroika as a betrayal of true "Marxist-Leninism." They needed to be replaced with "reform communists." However, at the end of the revolution in Czechoslovakia the government of President Vaclav Havel set up a special parliamentary commission to determine the facts behind the headlines.

The following information uncovered by the parliamentary commission was reported in the May 30, 1990, edition of the London Times as well as on a BBC-TV documentary. The initial stages of the Czech revolution was rigged by the KGB and its Czech counterpart, the StB (the Czech secret police), under the tactical direction of StB General Alois Lorenc. The operation was code named Operation Wedge. It was planned to coincide with the anniversary of the November 17, 1939 murder of a Czech student by German invaders. The StB infiltrated groups of Czech dissident with secret police agents. Their mission was to induce violent demonstrations that would provoke extreme police brutality by the hard-line Milos government. The purpose was to provoke public identification of Milos Jakes with the hated Nazis. They hoped the result would be the leadership of Zdenek Mlynar, a respected Czech who just happened to be a friend of Mikhail Gorbachev.

Three days before the demonstrations were set to take place, the chairman of the KGB, General V. Gruschenko went to Prague to personally oversee the operation with General Teslenko, the KGB chief in Prague. During the very violent demonstration on November 17, the cameras were rolling to feed the footage to the Western media who sent it back to Czech broadcasters. One of the police infiltrators was a young man who pretended to be a student named Martin Smid. He led the demonstrators into a police trap where 561 of them were severely beaten. The "murder" of this "student" by the police led to an overwhelming public outrage that ultimately became the spark of the "velvet revolution" that overthrew the communist government. This "student" later turned up alive as Lieutenant V. Zivcak at the secret StB police headquarters.

The Czech parliament determined that, while the secret police and Gorbachev had planned a "revolution from the top," the pent-up anger of the people had exploded, producing a far-ranging "revolution from below," which fortunately totally overthrew the communist party. While Gorbachev tried to tinker with the governments of Eastern Europe, he inadvertently started a landslide that wiped away all the Soviet inspired communist regimes. The dynamic nature of these counter revolutions in Europe should have warned the Gorbachev government that they were playing with fire when they began to unleash similar forces within Mother Russia. Now that the Russian KGB and Gorbachev have embarked on the same road within Mother Russia as they did in Eastern Europe, there is an extreme danger that Moscow Center will lose control of the process.

There is another area of influence that came into play in the democracy movement in Eastern Europe, one that has been under-reported and generally ignored by Western media. That influence was the fact that a great deal of the planning and logistics of these street demonstrations came from the Christians of Europe, meeting in the basements of churches. For decades these believers had been in desperate prayer for their countries. It is not accidental that, at this time in these last days, the Lord should move to open up these countries to the gospel of Jesus Christ in an unparalleled way. Bibles are now flowing into these countries and into Russia as never before in history. Literally millions of copies are being distributed in nations where the mere possession of a Bible a short time ago meant a term in a concentration camp. When Czech President Havel made his inaugural speech he spoke at length about his faith in Jesus Christ and the power of God that had been manifested in his nation's deliverance.

How ironic to hear a leader of a formerly communist nation speak freely about his faith in Christ and then find that our so-called "free press" in America chose to censor his religious remarks from all accounts in the media.

A Massive Buildup of Soviet Military Power

Russian strategic and conventional forces have expanded at a tremendous rate under glasnost and perestroika. Despite a great deal of negotiations and treaty-making, Russia continues to arm for war. Before softening her approach to disarmament talks, Russia was spending at least 28 percent of her gross national product on defense, but she could not stay ahead of America's high technology defense industries. So, the Kremlin decided to change gears and discuss disarmament seriously. As a result of agreements between the two nations, America began to withdraw large forces from Europe and other parts of the world. Thirty-eight thousand left in the spring of 1990, and more than fifty thousand troops left in the fall of 1990 for Desert Storm operations. The U.S. also withdrew six hundred of its most effective M1A tanks from Germany. This leaves the European NATO forces at their most vulnerable level in forty-five years. In addition, while the United States has increased its ICBMs by twelve, Soviets have expanded by one hundred and forty in the last year. Russia is better prepared to launch a surprise attack on Europe or Israel than they were four years ago.

Russia, however, did make some moves toward disarming. They began to scrap certain types of obsolete missiles, old tanks and rusty submarines, while cameras dutifully recorded every scrapped weapon. At the same time, the Soviets began to replace these obsolete weapon systems with more sophisticated technologies that use fewer missiles to deliver greater destruction at much improved accuracy rates. For example, the Russians would destroy an obsolete large 2-megaton missile that had an accuracy rate of only five hundred yards, but replace it with a smaller .5-

megaton warhead with an improved accuracy of thirty yards to target center.

While this show of disarmament looks good on paper, the net result is that the Russians—since disarmament talks began—now have higher destructive capacity missiles with much better reliability levels. Despite five years of peace talks under Gorbachev, according to the exhaustive study *Soviet Military Power 1990*, the USSR spent more on defense in 1990 than they did under Gorbachev's predecessors.

Intelligence reports indicate that the Russians both knew about and supported Iraq's invasion of Kuwait. They stood to gain a great deal by pinning down much of the West's military force in the Saudi Arabian desert.

Every day a Soviet Aeroflot plane takes off from New York City loaded with every issue of the latest American-Canadian technical, aviation, electronic magazines and books. The plane carries translator interpreters and computers that translate the material into Russian for distribution throughout the Soviet intelligence community.

Recent Soviet fighter aircraft are technically identical to closely copied American and European aircraft. Each recent American advanced fighter plane has been duplicated exactly by Russia's KGB Technical Intelligence Directorate. Since 1958, the Soviets have released aircraft very similar to ours. Since 1984, Russia has not developed any new types of fighter planes. (Neither has America.)

A massive transfer of armaments is also occurring as both the U.S. and the USSR begin to ship enormous quantities of weapons to Third World countries. As major weapons systems fall under the strategic and conventional arms treaties, the two superpowers are creatively selling their excess weapon production to these other countries. As an example, the Saudi Arabian air force has just received a new Russian missile capable of hitting Israel. These sales accomplish a number of national objectives:

1. They lock in an ally's policy through continued arms sales.

2. They produce hard currency for Russia and sales to the U.S. to support continued military production lines.

3. They keep defense plants running with trained staff so that they do not have to be mothballed or transferred over to consumer production. In other words, the military-industrial capacity to remobilize remains unimpaired.

4. The result is well-armed allies with training by both superpowers to engage in regional wars if the need arises.

Consider surveillance techniques used by the Soviets (as well as other countries). At present, not only are the Soviets set up to eavesdrop on all telephone conversations, but they can also eavesdrop, through a computer program that uses your phone as a radio microphone, on any conversation within a room that has a telephone, and you will not even know it is being done. Even phones in government offices are accessible unless they are equipped with special security systems. Huge groups of human analysts and translators work with computers to analyze the most interesting calls.

Every phone, teletype, satellite transmission, fax message, radio phone and overseas mail message is continually analyzed by the KGB and by our own National Security Agency. Radio traffic from pilots is analyzed to the point where files are kept on each pilot and his family. As an example, the Israelis used this kind of intelligence information to talk to Syrian pilots during the 1982 Lebanon War to distract them during battle engagements.

Satellite photo analysis enables NATO to identify terrorist leaders and drug lords as well as individual army units. Despite official denials, current photo resolutions are such that even documents in a man's hand can be read from satellite cameras in space.

For the past twenty-five years the Soviets have consistently spent over ten times the money the U.S.A. has each year on their Strategic Defense Initiative in the development of space weapons. Their primary motivation in sidetracking American efforts, is that they know a lot of the Strategic Defense Initiative can work, and they fear the American advantage in its technical capacity of high -speed computers and high-energy physics. Soviet high-energy particle beam weapons can send a lightning bolt of laser-directed energy across the sky to destroy targets. In early

April, 1990, the Soviets used a new blue laser device to blind several Canadian pilots who challenged Russian penetration of Canadian air space. The laser beam focused on the pupil of the pilot's eye for less than one-tenth of a second, resulting in instant blindness.

The Soviet Union consistently outproduces the United states in every major weapons system used in modern warfare:

Weapon Type	Russia Outspends the U.S.A.
Submarine launched ICBMs	3.5 to 1
Battle tanks	3.8 to 1
Surface-to-air missiles	6.4 to 1
Self-propelled artillery	8.6 to 1

While the United States Congress has hindered funding of the America Strategic Defense Initiative, the Soviet Air Force has fielded almost ten thousand SAMs—surface to air missiles, each capable of intercepting a multi-warhead ICBM. Meanwhile, the FBI and CIA have both reported to Congress that the Soviets have recently launched the most aggressive intelligence operations against the U.S.A. and NATO in forty-five years.

It took the United States over a hundred days to bring sufficient armaments and men into Saudi Arabia to withstand an attack from the limited forces of Saddam Hussein. How long would it take to assemble a military force large enough to withstand the much more awesome Russian army divisions in Europe? Yet American military strategy calls for keeping only enough forces in Europe to hold on until a huge army can be ferried from American bases in the continental United States in the event of war.

Our experience in the Persian Gulf has revealed that, because Congress has chosen to spend money on other priorities, we do not have enough fast transport ships or large military transport planes to move the enormous amounts of modern weapons and manpower our armies would require.

In World War II the U.S. had the world's largest Merchant Marine and Canada had the third largest. Recently we were forced to beg and borrow ships from other countries to ship essential arms to Saudi Arabia. We took more than fifty "victory" World War II ships out of mothballs to assist in the Gulf war. The tragic result could be that the Russian army would be eating breakfast on the English Channel while American and Canadian troops were still trying to board the few ships and planes available to transport them to the war front in Europe.

In view of these foregoing facts, is it possible that the Union of Soviet Socialist Republic could once more be considered a threat to world peace? It would be very tempting for Russia to try to grasp victory from the jaws of defeat by using their current overwhelming military force while they still have it.

Cold War Revival?

If you are tempted to point to recent events in Eastern Europe as proof that Russia has mellowed, remember that the long-range strategy of Russia has always been to neutralize Europe. Isn't this precisely what is being accomplished today? When you hear Mikhail Gorbachev talk about Russia belonging to "a common European home" from "the Urals to the English Channel," you need to think carefully about where these developments will ultimately lead. Could this current build-up of armaments in Russia and the cosmetic softening of the communist hard line eventually lead to a cold-war revival?

The demand for freedom within the republics of the USSR is causing great alarm among the Soviet General Staff and could easily become an excuse for a military coup that would reestablish totalitarian power. The hatred that is growing toward Gorbachev's failed and half-hearted reforms could easily lead to a resurgence of hard-line communism. While there is a great reservoir of democratic spirit within the oppressed nations of Eastern Europe who were conquered by Soviet tanks, there is no deep-seated tradition of democracy or free enterprise within the republic of Russia. Except for a few months of parliamentary freedom in 1917, most of their history has been dictatorial. In the event that Gorbachev is overthrown, most commentators expect his replacement will be a military or KGB candidate. According to an Associated Press report (September 27, 1990) speculating about an imminent army coup, Chief of

Staff General Dmitri Yazov assured the new Soviet Parliament that "no army should use arms against its own people." Yet, the people of Moscow and Leningrad fear that the military, upset by the soaring crime rate, growing shortages of food, and escalating ethnic unrest, will be tempted to ally themselves with hard-line KGB and old Communist Party elite to overthrow Gorbachev's reformers. Even the Communist Youth newspaper, *Komsomolskaya Pravda*, reported concern about military plotting to take over power stations, television and radio stations, and railway terminals. The military moved brutally to put down democratic movements in Georgia and the Baltic despite Gorbachev's claims of innocence.

The Soviet thaw is definitely reversible. In only one day a tragic reversal occurred on Tiananmen Square in Beijing; democracy was crushed in Czechoslovakia by Soviet tanks in 1968, Hungary in 1956, Germany in 1955, and Russia itself in 1917. A brutal dictator, who is willing to kill thousands, and several well-equipped army divisions, can easily put down a democratic revolution. Successful revolutions, such as those we recently saw in the Philippines, East Germany, Romania, and Poland, come about only when a great movement for democracy from the people occurs at the same time the dictatorship lacks the nerve to react.

Whenever concern about a possible military coup is raised, some commentators—including Russian generals—claim that "there is no tradition of military coups in Russia." However, they conveniently forget that the Communist party came to power in the 1917 October Revolution, through a military coup against the democratically elected government of Prime Minister Kerensky. A group of 184 dedicated Bolshevik soldiers won by successfully attacking key installations and the Winter Palace.

As the fifteen republics of the USSR continue to disintegrate into rebellious entities, there is a growing danger that, at some point, military and KGB forces will intervene and reestablish dictatorial and military control. A case in point is the fact that not too long ago Gorbachev secretly moved four elite paratroop units and two divisions into critical areas surrounding Moscow and Leningrad under the pretense that they were there to assist farmers in the potato harvest. Potato pickers, however, do not generally need bulletproof flak jackets and special issue AK-47 submachine guns such as these soldiers wore. Other elite commando regiments, that specialize in capturing command and control headquarters, have been moving around Moscow in special night maneuvers. Colonel Sergei Kudinov of the Ryazan paratroop division, and a member of Shield—an organization of former and current military officers, accused Gorbachev of secretly bringing in these troops on Ilyushin 76 military transport planes with tons of provisions.

The Soviet military has set up a separate economy within Russia where they own and operate mines, farms, factories, etc., with total control from top to bottom. As a result, the military is the only part of the Soviet economy that is still functioning with a degree of discipline and efficiency. If the current unrest continues—and it more than likely will, it is quite possible that the army and KGB could argue that they are the only ones who know what to do to bring about unity. They could claim that they are the true saviors of Mother Russia as they set about militarizing the whole society. Even if the other fourteen republics should successfully break away, the largest republic—Russia— would still retain the bulk of the population, land and military-industrial assets of the Union. The Magog of the Bible could succeed in unloading a great number of its intractable "nationalities" problems if the USSR breaks up. It will still be the world's strongest and largest military power. Remember that Germany, with far less population, land, resources, and military power, almost conquered the world between 1939 and 1945.

Consider the enormous power Gorbachev holds in his hands. The thought has occurred to some: Could Gorbachev be the Antichrist? Or, is he the "Gog" of Ezekiel's prophecy of the coming war of Gog and Magog?

Where Does Gorbachev Fit in Prophecy?

Whenever a great power arises, those who are concerned about Bible prophecy ask the question, "Is this the Antichrist?" Is Gorbachev the Antichrist? A careful study of Scripture relating to the Antichrist indicates that he is different in character from Gorbachev in many ways.

First, Jesus told the Jews, "I have come in My Father's name, and you do not receive Me; if another comes in his own name, him you will receive" (John 5:43). This statement indicates that the Antichrist will present himself to the Jewish people as the Messiah. One who is not Jewish could never hope to be accepted as Messiah. No "secret Jew" could be received as Messiah. Gorbachev is not Jewish, he is a Russian Gentile.

Second, Daniel prophesied that the kingdom of the Antichrist will be the revived Roman empire. Further, he says that "the people of the prince who is to come shall destroy the city and the sanctuary" (Daniel 9:26). The people and empire that destroyed Jerusalem and the Temple in the first century was the Roman Empire; therefore, the "prince who is to come," the Antichrist, must come out of the Roman-Mediterranean world. He must lead the ten-nation revived Roman Empire and he must be a Jew. All of these factors eliminate Mikhail Gorbachev as a candidate for the role of Antichrist.

The second question has to do with Gorbachev being "Gog," the leader of Magog. When we look at the character of the leader of the nation known as Magog we find that he will be a master politician who is capable of gathering together a great number of allies. The nation that leads the alliance is called Magog, which was the name of one of the grandsons of Noah who, after the flood, settled in the area north of the Black Sea in present-day Russia. The context indicates that Ezekiel was referring to a country known in his day. Ezekiel 38:15 says that the armies will "come from your place out of the far north." Jewish commentaries say that the word means the "northernmost extremity of the civilized world." Jewish historian Flavius Josephus, in his book *Antiquities of the Jews*, says that the descendants of Magog are the Scythians (1.6) who were the Russian tribes that expanded northward, eastward, and westward from their central base in the Caucasian regions north of the Black Sea. The *Yerushalmi Megillah* (3.9) also specifies Magog as the nomadic tribes north of the Black Sea in today's Russia.

The War of Gog and Magog

The coming Russian-Arab invasion of Israel is called the War of Gog and Magog in Bible prophecy. Ezekiel 38 lists the nations that descended from the sons and grandsons of Noah. Most of Magog's allies are descended from Japheth, one of Noah's three sons. The leader, Gog, is identified as "the prince of Rosh, Meshech, and Tubal" (v. 3) which we believe refers to Moscow and Tobolsk, a city in Russian Siberia. Meshech, Tubal and Gomer are also sons of Japheth. Ashkenaz, Gomer's son, settled in Eastern Europe, primarily in the areas of Germany and Poland.

Verse 5 of this same chapter in Ezekiel says that "Persia, Ethiopia, and Libya are with them [Rosh, Mesheck, and Tubal], all of them with shield and helmet." Jewish commentaries on Ezekiel describe Persia as being those lands now called Iran, Iraq and Afghanistan. It is amazing to observe that each of these modern nations is allied with the Soviet Union in their hatred of Israel.

Ezekiel goes on to record God's command to Magog-Russia: "Prepare yourself and be ready, you and all your companies that are gathered about you; and be a guard for them" (Ezekiel 38:7). This reference is an indication that Russia will not only organize this great alliance of nations but she will also provide their weapons. The magazine *Jane's Defence Weekly* lists the armaments of all these nations in great detail. It is intriguing to witness that each of these enemies of Israel is armed primarily by Soviet-produced weapons including SAM missiles, AK-47 assault rifles, M-72 tanks and MiG-23 to MiG-29 fighter planes.

Gog, the leader of Magog, is described as a very strong leader who has the undisputed power to declare war on his own directive, without recourse to committees and counselors. The prophet says that God will control his mind: "On the day it shall come to pass that thoughts will arise in your mind, and you will make an evil plan: You will say, 'I will go up against a land of unwalled villages; I will go to a peaceful people, who dwell safely, all of them dwelling without walls, and having neither bars nor gates'" (Ezekiel 38:11).

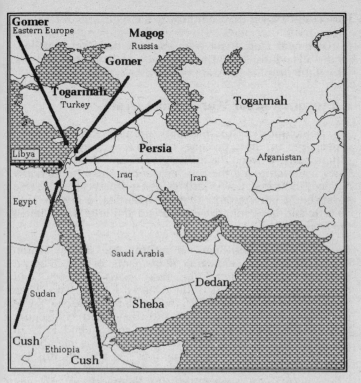

The War of Gog and Magog
The Coming Russian – Arab Invasion

The subsequent account describes that this Russian leader decides to raise a huge confederacy of nations to attack Israel without referring to other leaders. It is interesting in this regard to note that as of May 1, 1990, Gorbachev received exactly this kind of dictatorial power from the new Soviet constitution, which he engineered. Despite all of the democratic reform talk, Gorbachev has amassed more dictatorial power as president than even Marshall Stalin possessed. This new constitution literally gives the president the power to declare war and send troops to attack nations on his own decision, without action from the Communist Party, the Politburo or the new Soviet

Parliament. Never in recent history has a politician received such totalitarian power. However, this does not prove that Gorbachev is Gog. If he was replaced, the next president would also have the same unique constitutional powers, which the prophet Ezekiel predicted he would have.

A Provocation for War Against Israel

Some question Russia's motivation for attacking Israel, especially in her present condition. First we must differentiate between the military, KGB, and the Communist Party leadership and the Russian people. Despite the many changes in Russia, power still resides exclusively with these government party groups that are historically deeply anti-Semitic and have supported terrorism and four wars against the Jewish state.

The rising anti-Semitism within the Soviet Union expresses itself in emerging movements of the "Pamyat National Patriotic Front." The name means "memory," and these people are violent in their hatred for the Jews. They blame Jews and Masons for all the problems of Russia. Some members have beaten up Jews and desecrated synagogues and Jewish cemeteries. Others have approached Russian Jews and told them, "I have taken a vow as a member of Pamyat to kill a Jew...You are my Jew." As a result, Russian Jews who have always thought of themselves as Russians who would live forever within the Soviet Union are now fleeing to Israel at a rate of over three thousand per day.

This tragic hatred of the Jew throughout Russia and Eastern Europe is the mark of civilization unredeemed. We will witness the fulfillment of Jeremiah's prophecy after this Russian exodus is over. Jeremiah declared: "It shall no more be said, 'The Lord lives who brought up the children of Israel from the land of Egypt,' but, 'The Lord lives who brought up the children of Israel from the land of the north, and from all the lands where He had driven them.' For I will bring them back into their land which I gave to their fathers" (Jeremiah 16:14-15).

For years I puzzled over one detail in Ezekiel's great prophecy about the coming war of Magog: Who are "the peoples who are with you" in chapter 38, verse 4? These are in addition to the allies listed. As I considered the overwhelming military power of this Russian-led alliance I wondered why Russia would need all these other nations to come against such a small country as Israel. Why wouldn't Russia simply use twenty-five to forty of her best army divisions, backed up by her overwhelming air power and the threat of nuclear weapons? Even a small nuclear strike with three or four missiles would render the whole country of Israel uninhabitable for hundreds of years.

Is it possible that "the peoples who are with you" indicates that Russia will attack Israel under a United Nations resolution and a UN flag? Possibly Russia will arrange with Arab nations to vote through a series of General Council and Security Council resolutions to send a UN peacekeeping army to Israel to enforce the establishment of a Palestinian state on the West Bank, East Jerusalem and Gaza. Israel could not agree to such a force because her Arab enemies would take advantage of this to ultimately destroy her. Arab nations, apart from Egypt, have never accepted Israel's presence on any part of the British Mandate territory, not just the so-called "occupied territory." This "UN scenario" may ultimately develop out of the recent Persian Gulf crisis.

Two important developments have occurred during the last six months. First, Russia and the Arabs are now calling publicly for the creation of a new United Nations peacekeeping force with a permanent army, navy, and air force in the Middle East to enforce the will of the Security Council.

Second, the Arabs, Russians, and Europeans are now arguing that if it is right for the United Nations to drive Iraq out of Kuwait, it is also right to use such force to drive Israel out of the West Bank and Gaza. The argument, of course, totally ignores the fact that Israel legally reconquered the West Bank and Gaza after being invaded by enemy nations. Israel is therefore not obligated by international law to return them. Equating Israel's possession of these territories with Iraq's brutal unprovoked invasion of Kuwait flies in the face of all justice and international law. Yet this argument is setting the stage for the coming war of Gog and Magog at some point following the Gulf war.

The Gog and Magog of Ezekiel 38 and Revelation 20

Before discussing when the war of Gog and Magog will occur, I feel we should explain the difference between the Ezekiel account of the battle and another reference to Gog and Magog in the book of Revelation. The passage in Revelation says: "Now when the thousand years have expired, Satan will be released from his prison and will go out to deceive the nations which are in the four corners of the earth, Gog and Magog, to gather them together to battle, whose number is as the sand of the sea" (Revelation 20:7-8).

The "Gog and Magog" of this Revelation passage does not occur at the time of the War of Gog and Magog of Ezekiel. A close examination of Revelation 20 clearly reveals that this last battle of history is similar only in the names "Gog and Magog." In the Ezekiel account the war follows in the generation after Israel was reborn as a nation, while in Revelation the war follows the thousand year reign of the Messiah. In Ezekiel, Magog has a long list of specific allies who are destroyed by an earthquake, overflowing rain, fire and brimstone and fighting among themselves. The army in Revelation 20:9 is destroyed when "fire came down from God out of heaven and devoured them."

I believe the War of Gog and Magog (as it is described in Ezekiel) will precede the Battle of Armageddon. In fact, I think the political-military consequences of the defeat of Magog will set the stage for the rise of the kingdom of the Antichrist and will ultimately lead, some years later, to the climactic Battle of Armageddon.

When Will the War of Gog and Magog Occur?

It is important for us to realize that the Bible's prophecy in Ezekiel about the coming War of Gog and Magog is not influenced by the temporary maneuvering now going on in Moscow. The prophet Ezekiel does not declare that "Communist" Russia will come down against the mountains of Israel; rather he says that "Magog," which is Russia, will lead an alliance of nations against the Jewish state. Even if Russia should genuinely repudiate communism it would not change the fact that God has declared that Russia's appointment with destiny will not be postponed.

Despite the great amount of discussion and negotiation in Europe today about disarmament, most of this activity is not scheduled to take place before 1993. For the moment, despite our victory in the Gulf, Russia and her allies remain the most powerful military force in the world today.

In considering this important matter of the timing of the war of Gog and Magog we need to study three scenarios. Will this war take place (1) prior to Daniel's seventieth week of years and the seven-year treaty of the Antichrist with Israel; (2) at some point during the seven-year treaty period; (3) at the end of the seven-year treaty period as part of the Battle of Armageddon? (The Antichrist's seven-year treaty and the Great Tribulation will be discussed at length in a later chapter.)

I consider scenarios (2) and (3) unlikely. They demand that the forces of Russia, Eastern Europe and the Arab nations attack Israel during the time when the Antichrist is reigning as the false messiah and while he is committed, by his "covenant" (Daniel 9:27), to defend Israel against her enemies. The detailed description of Ezekiel 38 and 39 does not mention the Antichrist, the Revived Roman Empire, its armies, the treaty nor the Jew's expectations that the Antichrist will protect them from the invading armies of Magog. I find it inconceivable that the Antichrist would not be mentioned if this attack occurs during the period when he is sworn to defend Israel. Even if he betrayed Israel you would expect to find Ezekiel referring to him.

There is another reason why the battle of Magog in the Ezekiel passage could not take place during or at the end of the seven-year treaty period. All the details of the Battle of Armageddon as described in Joel 2, Zechariah chapters 12 to 14, and the book of Revelation, differ from the methods, armaments, participants, and ultimate outcome of the battle of Magog described by Ezekiel. Ezekiel 39:12 says that it will take "seven months" for Israel to bury the dead "in order to cleanse the land" of Israel because of massive casualties—85 percent of the invading army is killed. They will be burning "the weapons, both the shields and bucklers, the bows and arrows, the javelins and spears" for seven years for fuel! It seems unlikely that, if this took place as part of the Battle of Armageddon, it would take seven months to cleanse the land of bodies or that the Jews would have to use Russian weapons for fuel for seven years during the miraculous prosperity of Christ's Millennial rule.

Some scholars conclude that this attack by Magog must take place during the seven-year treaty with the Antichrist because they believe that Ezekiel 38:11 refers to a time when Israel "appears" to be at peace. The prophet declares that Gog, the leader of Magog, will say, "'I will go up against a land of unwalled villages; I will go to a peaceful people, who dwell safely, all of them dwelling without walls, and having neither bars nor gates'" (38:11). This passage refers precisely to Israel's present military situation where she is dwelling safely because of her strong defense in cities that have no walls or defensive bars. The prophet had never seen a city without walls. Ezekiel lived in a time when every city and village in the world was surrounded with huge defensive walls for military protection. However, modern artillery, bombs, and missiles make walls and bars militarily irrelevant. Israel now relies on swift counterattack and mobile defense rather than on walls surrounding even her West Bank settlements.

My conclusion is that Ezekiel's vision does not require Israel to live in total peace with her Arab neighbors prior to this prophesied attack, but rather that she "dwell safely," not expecting immediate attack. This description could easily apply to conditions existing today following the war in the Gulf.

Russia's Appointment With Destiny

I believe that the war of Gog and Magog will precede the seven-year treaty and create the preconditions that will allow Antichrist to consolidate his revived Roman empire in Europe. When this devastating battle is concluded, God "will send fire on Magog and on those who live in security in the coastlands. Then they shall know that I am the Lord" (Ezekiel 39:6). With the Russian-Arab armies nearly destroyed ("You shall fall upon the mountains of Israel, you and all your troops and the people who are with you; I will give you to birds of prey of every sort and to the beasts of the

68

field to be devoured" [39:4]), the world's military-political balance of power will be profoundly altered. The Russian Empire will disintegrate into independent nations and republics, just as most of the USSR republics (that were incorporated into the Russian Empire by either the czars or communist dictators) are demanding. Ezekiel prophesied, "Every man's sword will be against his brother" (38:21). This indicates civil war. Smaller republics such as the Baltics could be released without too much concern; but releasing the Ukraine and the six southern Muslim republics to independence sends shivers down the spines of Soviet leaders.

With fifty-two million people, the Ukraine is the second largest republic and is the breadbasket of the USSR. The six Muslim republics, including Azerbaijan, provide 38 percent of the manpower for the vast Soviet armies. During the ethnic civil warfare last year between the Azerbaijan and Armenians, the Azerbaijani rebels overran four military bases including one with a number of nuclear warheads. For three days the area was convulsed in bloody war as Russian special commando units fought to recapture these nuclear bombs from Muslim extremists. As a result of this incident and several other unpublished conflicts, the Soviet General Staff has taken the extraordinary step of removing all nuclear missiles and atomic artillery shells from the six Muslim republics and taking them back into the Slavic republic, Russia.

The war in the Gulf and the situation in Russia suggest that the coming Russian-Arab invasion of Israel could follow within the next several years. One of the questions that may occur to readers concerns the reason for God's prophetic judgment of Russia and these Arab nations. In the first place, they will invade Israel in an attempt to annihilate the Jewish people from the face of the world. Additionally, these nations have persecuted the Jews for centuries. Several millions of Jews and Christians were slaughtered by the Communists of Russia of the past seventy-three years. Though God works on a different timetable than we do, He never forgets those who persecute His people. As Genesis 12:3 declares: "I will bless those who bless you, and I will curse him who curses you."

The Lord told Ezekiel that the ultimate reason for

destroying the awesome assembly of nations that attack Israel concerned the nation's view of God: "Thus I will magnify Myself and sanctify Myself, and I will be known in the eyes of many nations. Then they shall know that I am the Lord" (Ezekiel 38:23). When the battle is over and the Lord has miraculously delivered the Jews from their enemies, the nations and Israel will all know that it was the Lord who saved them. I believe that there will be few atheists alive from that point on in history. Pharaoh's soldiers knew that the Lord was the God of Israel as they drowned in the waters of the Red Sea. The world's citizens will also witness the overwhelming supernatural power of God's hand in a manner that cannot be denied. We do not know if God will delay the rapture until the War of Gog or Magog, we may still be here to witness it. This supernatural intervention may open the door to the last great evangelistic harvest of the age of grace. That is the prayer of many Christians. It might be the only thing that will awaken the people of North America and Europe from their spiritual sleep.

Israel will experience a renewed religious revival and the rebuilding of the Temple following the end of this war. The miraculous delivery from certain annihilation may motivate Israel to begin the rebuilding of the Temple as the Bible prophesied. In the book *Armageddon – Appointment With Destiny* I explore the possibility of the Ark of the Covenant's rediscovery following this War of Gog and Magog. God says in Ezekiel: "I will set My glory among the nations" at the conclusion of the battle. This "glory" may refer to the lost Ark of the Covenant which the Ethiopians claim is protected in an underground temple in northern Ethiopia. "So the house of Israel shall know that I am the Lord their God from that day forward" (Ezekiel 39:22). The Lord reveals that a huge group of exiles will return, presumably from Russia: "Now I will bring back the captives of Jacob, and have mercy on the whole house of Israel" (v. 25).

These are the fascinating roles which the Bible indicates will be played by the United States and Russia in the great unfolding prophecies leading to the coming of the Messiah. In the next chapter we will explore the role of Europe's rising superpower in God's tremendous prophetic plan for the last days.

CHAPTER 4

Europe: The Fourth Riech, Kingdom of Antichrist

On December 31, 1992, a powerful new superstate will arise in Europe that will transform the world's delicate balance of power in ways most of us have not foreseen. This new trans-national confederacy was prophesied thousands of years ago as one of the final signs of the coming Messiah.

Nebuchadnezzar's dream of a great metallic figure, which symbolized the four great gentile empires of the future, had legs of iron and feet and toes "partly of iron and partly of clay." Daniel interpreted the legs as being the fourth great empire, the Roman Empire. The final form of the Roman Empire as symbolized by the feet and toes of part iron and part clay will be a confederation of ten nations, some strong and some weak. They will join to form a European "Superstate" that will precede the coming of Messiah to establish His Kingdom forever.

Such an organization began in Europe in the 1950's with the forming of the Common Market. As a two-thousand-year era of anarchy and continual inter-state warfare ended, the world watched in amazement as a new era began. For the first time in history a group of proud countries that had fiercely guarded their national independence volunteered to abdicate their sovereignty to an appointed—not elected—council made up of representatives from their European neighbors.

The Common Market: The Embryo of the Revived Roman Empire

Up until 1990 the aims of the Economic European

Community (the Common Market), was to (1) integrate their economies, (2) coordinate social developments, and (3) bring about political union of the democratic states. Presently the twelve member nations include Belgium, Denmark, France, West Germany, Greece, Ireland, Italy, Luxembourg, Netherlands, Portugal, Spain, and the United Kingdom.

The Common Market confederation agreed that a single European market would remove all barriers to free trade and free movement of capital and people. The completion of this economic program is scheduled for December 31, 1992. However, no one anticipated the rapid political and economic collapse of Eastern Europe. This collapse now clears the way not only for total economic freedom, but also for a military and political Superstate unlike anything ever witnessed in history.

Already the European Community (EC) produces 20 percent of the world's wealth and over five trillion dollars in gross national product. As one measure of its rising power, Europe today has a million scientists to America's 750 thousand.

Despite the current euphoria in Europe over the many political changes, Europeans are not ready for the challenges of becoming a superpower. The problem of reconciling the vastly different dreams and ambitions of these ancient European nations will stretch the negotiating abilities of the wisest diplomats and politicians.

Every European magazine and newspaper wages a daily campaign to sell the concept of a unified state by 1993. The greatest minds and most influential forces on the continent are working to shift all power to a group of trans-national political bodies, including the European Parliament and the Executive Commission in Brussels. Although there is an elected group of 518 representatives to the European Parliament in Strasborg, it is acknowledged that this is the weakest of the EC governing bodies. It lacks the power to make laws, raise taxes, or choose the all-powerful Executive Commission. The real power belongs to this unelected Executive Commission composed of seventeen appointed representatives from the twelve nations.

The irony of our time is that, at the same moment Eastern Europe is fleeing dictatorship, the EC is embracing a totally undemocratic form of totalitarian government that will have profound consequences for the future of the world. The stage is being set for the rise of a charismatic leader who will find the tools of totalitarian control already in place for the Kingdom of the Antichrist. It is interesting to note that Jean Monet, the founder of the European Economic Community, was recently reburied in Paris near the tomb of Napoleon, another leader who dreamed of a "United States of Europe."

Adding to the huge wave of support from Western Europe is the release from Russian domination of many Eastern European nations. The first six of these nations, with a population of more than 120 million, including Hungary and Poland, have begun negotiations to join the European Community.

At the same time these nations are enjoying renewed hope of a "European home" there is a growing fear that the rise of Germany's colossal power will overshadow the new alliance. Many feel that Germany will now accomplish the domination of Europe through peace, negotiation, and money, which she failed to do through two World Wars.

Since their defeat in World War II, and the revelation of the horrible Holocaust, old German leaders have suppressed their pride and ambition. Now, however, a new generation of Germans has taken the levers of control in the fatherland as well as in the European Superstate organizations. These new leaders do not feel guilty or intimidated by memories of the horrors of World War II. They are ready to assume the political and military responsibility that goes with the awesome economic power accumulated over the last four decades. Germany has the largest trade surplus per capita of any nation in the world. She is already the economic engine of a revived Europe, with mighty banking houses, exporters, and enormous corporations. Any list of the twenty major banks of the world will show a majority of German banks (the balance are Japanese). Only twelve years ago, America would have dominated the list. Today 82 percent of the all new investment pouring into Eastern Europe is coming from Germany. As one example of economic power where America used to dominate, Airbus—the new European multinational manufacturer of airplanes—has captured 30 percent of the world market.

When the reunification of Germany began, the Soviets initially demanded that Germany detach itself from NATO and become neutral. As they reconsidered their position they realized that a neutral Germany was a much greater danger to Russia. They finally acquiesced to NATO's demands because they determined that a powerful reunited Germany could best be checked by her position within the Western alliance with Germany remaining a partner in NATO.

Many Europeans who fear German domination now hope that Britain will fulfill her historic role of balancing German power. As French President Francois Mitterrand said, "We must create this united Europe with Germany but not be dominated by it." While the French and Germans have both pushed for the new Superstate, the French have always feared that Germany would overshadow them. While Margaret Thatcher remained as prime minister, the United Kingdom tried to keep a certain distance from the rising European Superstate. However, Prime Minister John Major wants to solidify his relationships with Europe and will now remove all obstacles to the total reunification of the ancient Roman Empire.

The Revived Roman Empire

The European Community has three levels of government: (1) Executive Commission; (2) National Governments; and (3) Regional Governments. By January 1, 1993, the EC will have:
    One European citizenry
    One high court
    One central bank
    One common currency
    One passport
    One center of economic control.

The president of the Executive Commission, Jacques Delors, is the most powerful man in Europe today. As a member of the Executive Committee he is unelected, powerful, brilliant, and fanatical in his intent to unite

Europe for the first time in two thousand years. The thirteenth floor of the executive building in Brussels contains the inner sanctum—the secretive operations center of the Executive Committee that directs all governmental operations in the EC. Using his power as president, Delors is rapidly pressing forward his plan for the total integration of these European states. In the minds of many Europeans, Jacques Delors is the man of the hour. Recently he declared in an interview: "My objective before the end of the decade is a real Federation of Europe." He described this federation as having "powerful supranational institutions, legislators, executives with the levers of power being exercised not in Bonn or Paris or London but in the home of the Super Institutions. This is the great hope for peace in Europe and without it I think we could be moving into possibly a dangerous world."

While there is some opposition from national movements in France, Britain, and Germany to the rising Superstate, Jacques Delors cleverly appeals to regional feelings of voters against their national state governments. He has promised three levels of government—regional, national, and European—which he says will empower the regions against national powers. By appealing to the smaller ancient regions, such as Provence and the Rhineland, Delors is attempting to create a new Superstate with regions much like Medieval Europe during the Crusades and the Holy Roman Empire. People forget that the national states of France, Germany, etc., are less than two hundred years old, but the regions have an identity that can be traced back to the provinces of the Roman Empire. Thus we are witnessing a simultaneous movement: a growing regional autonomy and, at the same time, the development of a huge trans-national Superstate on the continental level.

Europe is now involved in the greatest voluntary transfer of sovereignty in world history. The ceding of power by these nations to an unelected Executive Commission is unprecedented. Yet, this incredible situation was predicted by the ancient prophets of the Old Testament. Daniel declared that the nations would transform themselves into a Superstate first, then the Antichrist would arise to take over political, economic, and military power. The revival of the Roman Empire in the form of these nations in our generation gives the strongest proof that we will witness the fulfillment of the rest of the prophecies concerning the coming of the Messiah.

The Kingdom of the Antichrist

This European-Mediterranean Community will be the base for the rise of the Kingdom of the Antichrist. Some students of prophecy suggest that the Antichrist's kingdom will consist of thirteen states (currently there are twelve) not ten. Some believe that from these thirteen states three will be "plucked out by the roots" and the remaining ten will submit to the Antichrist. However, Daniel 7 makes it clear that (1) only "ten horns" arose from the Roman Empire (2) "and there was another horn, a little one [the Antichrist] coming up among them"; (3) "before whom three of the first horns were plucked out by the roots" (v. 8). This means that the Antichrist will arise from among the ten nations but will not be one of the ten. Also, he will pluck out three of the original ten. The problem arises when we try to rework prophecy to fit the existing arrangement of twelve EC members, then add one more to make thirteen so that three can be "plucked out by the roots." Events are rapidly changing, and I am certain our Sovereign God is quite capable of rearranging the membership of the final European Superstate to fulfill the prophecy to the precise letter and number.

Using this initial base of ten nations, the Antichrist will present himself as the new Caesar who will have the answers to all the economic and political needs of the world. After obtaining political power, one of his major acts will be to consolidate his power by establishing a Seven Year Treaty with the state of Israel to provide protection for the Jewish state. Daniel 9:27 says: "Then he shall confirm a covenant with many for one week." This "week" of seven years will begin with the making of a treaty with Israel. During the first three and one-half years of the treaty "week," the Antichrist will produce a great deal of peace and prosperity which will cause the nations, including the Jews, to accept him as the great leader the world yearns for. Daniel 8:25 says: "Through his cunning he shall cause deceit to prosper under his hand; and he shall magnify

76

himself in his heart. He shall destroy many in their prosperity."

The Antichrist will appear to fulfill some of the prophecies concerning the Messiah. Some Jews will accept this counterfeit as the true Messiah. Jesus said, "I have come in My Father's name, and you do not receive Me; if another comes in his own name, him you will receive" (John 5:43). Many will accept the Antichrist as the Messiah. This indicates, along with the prophecy that the Antichrist will enter into the Holy of Holies in the rebuilt Temple, that this man must be a Jew. No Jewish believer would ever accept a Gentile as a candidate for the Messiah. He must come from the tribe of Judah and line of David.

"But in the middle of the week," when the Antichrist "shall bring an end to sacrifice and offering," religious Jews will know that he is a counterfeit Messiah. They will rebel against him and when he demands public worship of himself and his statute, they will flee to the wilderness to escape his power. While many teachers point to a verse which indicates that some Jews will flee at that time to Petra in Jordan, it is highly unlikely that all Jews could hide there. Petra is not large enough to accommodate the huge population of Israel. Jesus, in Matthew 25, describes His judging of the sheep and goat nations of the Tribulation on the basis of how these nations treat tribulation believers, both Jew and Gentile, during that terrible time. I believe that Jewish and Gentile "tribulation saints" who respond to the message of the 144 thousand witnesses of Revelation 7 and the two witnesses of Revelation 11 after the Rapture will flee to North America and other countries to escape. Hopefully, the Judeo-Christian tradition of liberty and freedom will cause our citizens to provide protection to those who flee the Antichrist. Many will flee from the mark-of-the-beast system the Antichrist will impose throughout his kingdom during the last three and one-half years, called the "great tribulation" (Revelation 7:14).

The Antichrist will be empowered and possessed by Satan while assisted by the False Prophet (see Revelation 16:13-14). This prophet will display supernatural powers while he is in direct sight of the Antichrist, which will cause many to believe that the Antichrist is the true Messiah.

However, we must remember, since Satan is not omnipresent, his power is limited. The false prophet will not accept worship as such, but will direct men to worship the Antichrist, who will be possessed by Satan: "A king shall arise, having fierce features, who understands sinister schemes. His power shall be mighty, but not by his own power" (Daniel 8:23-24). The devil will finally display his hatred of men as he attempts to destroy all who refuse to worship him.

The Antichrist will seek the assistance of the world's false religious system, "the great harlot" of Babylon (Revelation 17:1), during his rise to supreme power. After the Rapture, all religiously minded people from Catholic, Protestant, Orthodox, and New-Age type churches will join together in the end time religious apostasy. With all true believers taken to Heaven, these "religious" people will unite quickly and lend their vast organizational powers to the Antichrist to assist in his rise to world power.

However, the Antichrist and the "ten horns which you saw on the beast...will hate the harlot, make her desolate and naked, eat her flesh and burn her with fire" (Revelation 17:16). Satan has no desire to share his worship with anyone, not even an apostate church. After the Antichrist and Satan destroy the false church, he will demand that all men everywhere worship him directly. His method of enforcement will involve the "mark of the beast."

The Mark of the Beast

"And he [Antichrist] causes all, both small and great, rich and poor, free and slave, to receive a mark on their right hand or on their foreheads" (Revelation 13:16). By this system the Antichrist will control his subjects. Revelation 13 goes on to say that "no one may buy or sell except one who has the mark or the name of the beast, or the number of his name" (v. 17).

Due to the following explanation: "His number is 666" (v. 18), many speculate that the actual mark will involve the use of the number 666. However, 666 was recorded so that tribulation believers on Earth during this terrible period will know with absolute certainty that the Antichrist is the false messiah. His miracles and deception will be so diabolically effective "so as to deceive, if possible, even the elect" (Matthew 24:24). None of the Church will be deceived, however, because the Church will be in heaven celebrating the marriage supper of the Lamb (Revelation 19:9) when this system is introduced. The mark may involve a brand or implanted device which may include the number 666.

It is important to realize that the Greek text does not spell out the number as we do in English, but rather it uses the three Greek letters that convey the number 666. The Bible does not actually claim that 666 is the actual mark, though it is possible.

This man's name in the Greek or Hebrew language will be equivalent numerically to the number 666. There are only two numeric languages in the world—Greek and Hebrew—that use letters of their normal alphabet to express numeric data. Latin uses only a few numeric letters, such as those found in Roman numerals. In Greek (and Hebrew) every single letter of the Word JESUS has a numeric equivalent. (See diagram 1.)

Numeric Value of Names of Jesus

JESUS = ΙΗΣΟΥΣ = 888

Other Names of Jesus :

CHRIST	= 1480 (8 x 185)	
LORD	= 800 (8 x 100)	
SAVIOUR	= 1408 (8 x 176)	
EMMANUEL	= 25600 (8 x 3200)	
MESSIAH	= 656 (8 x 85)	

I = 10
H = 8
Σ = 200
Ο = 70
Υ = 400
Σ = 200

Jesus = 888

Diagram 1

The sum of the numerical letters that compose the name JESUS add up to 888. All the names of Jesus—Emmanuel, Savior, Christ, etc., in Greek, are numerically composed of numbers that are divisible by 8. This is why so many early Roman churches were built on eight-sided foundations, including the original church where the Dome of the Rock exists today. Since this system was known to every Greek-speaking child in the first century, it is more than probable that the prophet John used the same system to predict the identity of the Antichrist, the First Beast of Revelation 13. In other words, the Antichrist will have a public name in Greek (or possibly Hebrew) that numerically equals 666. Attempts to find such names by applying the numeric system to English and Latin names are futile and inconsistent with the Greek language of John and the Greek audience he was addressing.

The increasing use of the number 666 by financial, governmental, and electronic systems suggests that we are quickly approaching the day of implementation of this hateful system of totalitarian control. However, don't be deceived; until the Antichrist appears and demands worship as god, the mark of the beast belongs to the future. The actual mark may involve the number 666 or it may be some other symbol which Revelation does not describe. It will be implanted on the forehead or the right hand. Modern electronic scanning technology can now detect miniature data encoding devices at a distance. While these tiny (1/4 inch long) devices are designated to implant with a syringe beneath the skin of an animal, they could easily be adapted for human use. Such passive coil devices can hold over forty-five billion bits of data, including complete medical, governmental, and financial records. The scanner's invisible electronic field induces a current in the implant to cause it to read out its data, just like a bar code device in a store.

Justification for its introduction to the general public could include the search for missing children or the identification of bodies. It could initially be used by governments to identify social assistance recipients who could then make cash withdrawals from automatic tellers. Some have proposed that such an implant would safely allow the homeless to withdraw from automatic tellers immediate cash from their social account every few days, thus eliminating the threat of robbery of large cashed checks. However, the technology is introduced. At some future point the Antichrist will utilize the "mark of the beast" as history's ultimate totalitarian police state control system.

I suspect that once the technology is in place, the Antichrist of the Revived Roman Empire will simply give everyone in his dominion a short period of time to report to some government place to swear allegiance to his worship. Those who fail to report will not receive the mark that will allow them to buy or sell. Those who resist his worship will have the option of martyrdom or fleeing to the mountains, as believers did in the Middle Ages. Fortunately, those who accept the invitation of Christ—the Church, will not endure the wrath of God during that terrible period. When Jesus said that "he who endures to the end will be saved" (Matthew 10:22), He was talking about those "tribulation saints" who will endure these last days of unparalleled horror as Satan develops his plan for man's destruction.

The "week" of seven years will conclude with the climactic Battle of Armageddon when the Messiah will return to save Israel and the tribulation believers. Christ will destroy the Antichrist and his armies. Daniel ended his interpretation of Nebuchadnezzar's dream by identifying the "stone" that "was cut out without hands, which struck the image on its feet of iron and clay [the Revived Roman Empire] and broke them in pieces." He told the king that "the God of heaven will set up a kingdom which shall never be destroyed; and the kingdom shall not be left to other people; it shall break in pieces and consume all these kingdoms, and it shall stand forever" (Daniel 2:34,44). The return of Christ will end the rise of the Fourth Reich, the kingdom of the Antichrist.

In the next chapter we will talk about the rise of Babylon and the war in the Gulf. We will examine how the Gulf War has set the stage for the coming Russian-Arab invasion of Israel.

CHAPTER 5

The Rise of Babylon
The War in the Gulf

Babylon was the most powerful empire the ancient world had ever seen. Yet the Lord prophesied its destruction after it burned Jerusalem and the Temple. Though the city and empire crumbled centuries ago, the Lord said that Babylon would rise once again as a major power in the generation before the return of the Messiah. This amazing empire was destined to rise and fall three times in history.

In a previous chapter we studied Nebuchadnezzar's dream about a metallic man which Daniel told him represented four great Gentile empires. The first of these great empires, indicated by the gold head of the image, was that of Nebuchadnezzar's own Babylonia, which would soon be overthrown by the Medes and the Persians. This overthrow, which occurred in 538 B.C. was the first of a three-fold rise and fall of Babylon. The second overthrow has just been completed, and the whole world watched it happen on television. The third and final overthrow is still to come. That will occur when Isaiah's prophecy will be fulfilled: "Babylon, the glory of kingdoms, the beauty of the Chaldeans' pride, will be as when God overthrew Sodom and Gomorrah" (Isaiah 13:19).

At this writing it seems impossible that Babylon could ever rise again to become a notable world power. But Bible prophecies tell us that the ancient city of Babylon will rise again from the desert to take its place on the stage of world history. This will happen as we approach the Great Tribulation and the return of the Messiah.

Ancient Babylon

The ruins of Babylon, capital of Babylonia, is situated about twenty miles from Iraq's present-day capital of Baghdad. This wonder city of the ancient world, which was built around the Tower of Babel, had fifty-six miles of walls, thirty stories high and over eighty feet thick. The walls extended thirty-five feet below ground and were encompassed with deep moats filled with water diverted from the Euphrates River to prevent access. One hundred very ornate gates of brass, many of them emblazoned with figures of bulls and dragons and faced with glazed tiles, opened into the city. The banks of the Euphrates River, which divided the city into two almost equal halves, were flanked by brick walls with twenty-five gates opening into the streets of the city. One of the stone bridges crossing the Euphrates was a half mile long, thirty feet wide and had drawbridges that could be removed at night.

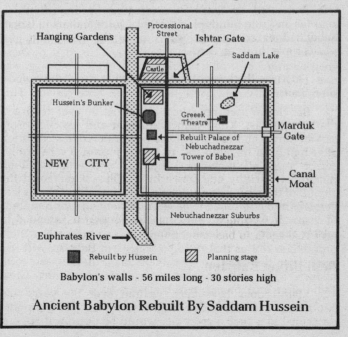

Babylon's walls - 56 miles long - 30 stories high

Ancient Babylon Rebuilt By Saddam Hussein

Within the walls of Babylon were the famous hanging gardens, a huge seventy-five-foot high artificial mountain, considered by the ancients as one of seven wonders of the world. These magnificent gardens could be seen for fifty miles across the flat landscape. The series of terraces held trees, vines and flowers and were watered by a system of wells and fountains. King Nebuchadnezzar had the gardens built for his queen who came from a mountainous area and hated the flat plains of Mesopotamia.

Also within the city was the great temple of Marduk (Bel) that adjoined the Tower of Babylon (Babel). The temple contained a golden image of the god Bel and a golden table, which together weighed about fifty thousand pounds—of solid gold. This lavish use of gold, costing more than $320 million in our dollars, was characterized as the "head of gold" in Nebuchadnezzar's dream, described by Daniel (chap. 2). The temple of Bel contained other images of Bel and Ishtar, lions, and a human figure made of gold. The city was dedicated to Satan as indicated by its fifty-three temples and one hundred and eighty golden altars to Ishtar. Nebuchadnezzar's palace was one of the most exquisite edifices ever built on earth.

This was the ancient city of Babylon, the "glory of the Chaldeans."

Babylon was also the most brutal nation ever to arise in the Middle East. King Nebuchadnezzar and his successors carved out an enormous military power that defeated nation after nation in its rapid rise to world supremacy. Its armies swept away all previous kingdoms and established an incredibly wealthy and powerful empire. It remained the capital of the empire even during the reign of the Medes and Persians and continued to be an important city for hundreds of years. If Alexander the Great had lived he intended to restore the city to its former glory.

Rebuilding Babylon

Many books have been written over the years that confirmed a future rebuilding of Babylon. One prophet described that such a great city would be destroyed "in one hour." In 1865, J.A. Seiss wrote an extensive discussion of Babylon's future. He stated: "I conclude then, that such a great commercial city, different from all that now exist, will yet be, and that it will be old Babylon rebuilt."

In a fascinating article about the rebuilding of Babylon, Subhy Haddad reported that the governor of Babylon, Gita Suheil had declared: "[Saddam Hussein] has signed an open check to reconstruct the ancient city and revive the marvelous shape it had before the Persian aggression which destroyed it more than twenty centuries ago" (Philadelphia Inquirer, October 10, 1986).

A curious book entitled Babylon was published by the Iraqi government in 1982. It requested other governments to provide assistance to Iraq in its gigantic rebuilding project. The book states Hussein's position: "The archaeological survival of Babylon is a patriotic, national and international duty." To commemorate the new city the government minted an official seal of the Babylonian Festival with Hussein's face superimposed over that of ancient King Nebuchadnezzar's.

It is more than ironic that the modern nation of Iraq, under the savage rule of President Saddam Hussein, has chosen the image of ancient Babylon and its King Nebuchadnezzar to symbolize its vainglorious desire to rule the Middle East today. Every village and city in Iraq displayed billboards depicting Hussein shaking hands with King Nebuchadnezzar, who has been dead for more than twenty-five hundred years. In this display of imperial envy, Saddam Hussein reveals his lust to re-establish the former Babylonian Empire and dominate his Arab neighbors.

City Construction Already Underway

Could this ancient city of Babylon be rebuilt in our day? The startling answer is yes. Though it was buried for centuries by desert sandstorms, German archaeologists discovered the old ruins in 1898. For the first time in history an ancient capital will be rebuilt from ashes as a functioning city. Saddam Hussein embarked on this amazing construction project in 1978 and has poured over $500 million into Japanese and Korean construction firms to accomplish his purpose. Hussein has offered $1.5 million to any engineering company that can create the special water system, using the old methods, to provide waters for a rebuilt hanging gardens. To the people of Iraq, a rebuilt city of Babylon symbolizes their desire to see a Babylonian Empire rising from the oil-rich deserts and protected by their powerful military. The city has truly become the center of the nation's pride, especially since their terrible defeat in the recent Gulf war.

Today, despite the Iran-Iraq War and the Persian Gulf War, Hussein continues to expend enormous efforts to recreate the wonders of the glorious kingdom of Babylon. Thousands of laborers are rebuilding the Temple of Marduk, the throne room, the Grand Processional Way, and a new beautiful Saddam Hussein palace. The palace has a Swiss-built underground nuclear bomb shelter for President Hussein.

Over sixty million bricks have been made to place in the walls of Babylon. They are engraved with a dedication "To King Nebuchadnezzar in the reign of Saddam Hussein." The fabled Ishtar Gate, taken to Berlin years ago, has now been reconstructed in Babylon. Plans exist for a complete tourist city that will feature amusements, playgrounds, theaters, religious activities, and a commercial thoroughfare. Incredibly the main hotel will be built in the shape of a giant pyramid with a pagan shrine on the roof. Plays celebrating the pagan gods are now performed each year during the Babylonian Festival. At the last festival, several openly honored the pagan gods of Babylon, including Ishtar. The official theme says it all: "From Nebuchadnezzar to Saddam Hussein, Babylon undergoes a renaissance." However, the renaissance is one which the prophets warned will lead to certain destruction.

"The Abundance of Her Luxury"

In the book of Revelation, John saw a vision of the fall of Babylon. He quotes the angel as saying that "the merchants of the earth have become rich through the abundance of her luxury" (Revelation 18:3). Since Iraq's defeat in the Persian Gulf War it is difficult for us to see how Babylon could become so wealthy in "gold and silver, precious stones and pearls, fine linen and purple, silk and scarlet, every kind of citron wood, every kind of object of ivory, every kind of object of most precious wood, bronze, iron, and marble; and cinnamon and incense, fragrant oil and frankincense, wine and oil, fine flour and wheat, cattle and sheep, horses and chariots, and bodies and souls of men" (18:12-13). However, as part of the cease fire agreement, Iraq may be forced to spend less of her huge oil revenues on armaments. This could result in an enormously wealthy commercial city that, according to prophecy, will also be a center for witchcraft. The rise of pagan rites in Iraq, together with the rebuilding of Babylon, should make Christians very aware that the Messiah will soon come.

Hussein's Goals for Iraq

Hussein has often compared himself to King Nebuchadnezzar and has clearly declared that his great goal is to recreate the ancient Babylonian Empire in all its glory, wealth, and military power. His vision has so affected the various layers of Iraqi society that it is more than probable that this drive would continue even if Saddam were killed or exiled. In considering Hussein's inner motivation regarding this idolization of the dead King Nebuchadnezzar, we should remember his 1979 speech, quoted by David Lamb in the *Los Angeles Times* (October 12, 1990). Hussein declared: "What is most important to me about Nebuchadnezzar is the link between the Arab's abilities and the liberation of Palestine. Nebuchadnezzar was, after all, an Arab from Iraq, albeit ancient Iraq. Nebuchadnezzar was the one who brought the bound Jewish slaves from Palestine. That is why, whenever I remember Nebuchadnezzar, I like to remind the Arabs, Iraqis in particular, of their historical responsibilities. It is a burden that should not stop them from action, but rather spur them into action because of their history."

This astonishing speech reveals that of all the qualities which might impress Saddam Hussein, the one he wishes to emulate is the fact that Nebuchadnezzar "liberated" Palestine—an Arab code word that means to "kill the Jews."

The goal which Hussein has set for himself and Iraq is the duplication of history and the taking of "bound Jewish slaves from Palestine." This satanically inspired desire motivates many Arab leaders. Despite enormous problems facing Arab nations, tragically, their most enthusiastic goal is the elimination of Israel.

In 1977, President Hussein wrote and published a book in Iraq and Switzerland called *Unser Kampf* (Our Struggle). The book was totally ignored in the West, just as *Mein Kampf* (My Struggle), by Hussein's hero Adolph Hitler, was ignored. In *Unser Kampf*, Hussein declared that Iraq had three main goals that would motivate and guide their activities:

1. "We believe in a policy of international tension and preparation for war." He argued that this situation would help produce a stronger sense of belonging. "We believe that in times of tension, the Arabs find their unity again."

2. "Divide Europe, the United States and Japan over their oil policies." Hussein believed that Iraq could play each of these nations against the other to achieve his goal of divide and conquer.

3. Achieve the "expulsion of the Jews" and create "the establishment of a Palestine state in place of Israel." This third goal became the most important in Hussein's plan for the recreation of the Babylonian Empire, with himself occupying the place of King Nebuchadnezzar.

The Butcher of Baghdad

King Nebuchadnezzar's Babylon was known as a brutal and awesome empire. Saddam Hussein's reputation is running a close equal. Hussein was born into a poor landless peasant family near the village of Takrit on April 28, 1937. He was hated by his stepfather and went to live with his uncle at the age of 10. His uncle, Khayrallah Tulfah, had been kicked out of the Iraqi army for attempting a pro Nazi coup against the British. This led to an abiding hatred for both the British and Zionists, which was passed on to young Saddam.

Despite poor grades, Saddam's charisma won him the position of high school class president. After six years of school, Hussein tried to enter the Baghdad Military Academy but was refused because of his academic record. He went to Egypt and studied politics and law. When he returned home his uncle had become the mayor of Baghdad and proved helpful to Saddam in his attempts to rise to a position of power in the Baath Socialist Party.

Hussein Studies Brutality

Hussein spent a year and a half working 9:00 to 5:00 each day in the torture and interrogation center of the Iraq Intelligence Division. Many witnesses have testified that, over the years, he has personally tortured many Iraqi and Kurdish dissidents.

In the mid 1970's Hussein rose to a position that was second in command behind the president. He remedied his lack of military experience by appointing himself lieutenant-general of the Iraqi army. The fact that he never attended one day of army boot camp or completed any military training may explain some of his more bizarre military moves in the Persian Gulf war. If any military leader achieved some measure of success during the Iraq-Iran war, Hussein had him executed for fear he would be a threat to his regime. Six days after he became president he personally executed twenty-one of his close friends and cabinet members.

Hussein's personal brutality is legendary in Iraq. Last year a cabinet member in the economics department delivered a rather poor report on the state of finances in Iraq. Hussein asked him to step out into the hallway to discuss the matter. Once in the hall, Saddam took out his pistol and calmly shot the man in the head

A few years ago the wife of a cabinet member called the ministry to inquire if her husband would be home for dinner. Hussein sent her a message that her husband would be home shortly. An hour later, several army officers delivered a box to her door. To her horror, the box contained her husband's body, cut up into more than a hundred pieces.

Reliable reports confirm that Hussein personally ordered chemical attacks on Kurdish villages in Iraq as well as the regular use of chemical weapons against Iran. Over the years, death squads have been sent out to kill Iraqi dissidents throughout the Middle East and Europe. Amnesty International interviewed hundreds of Kuwaiti refugees who had escaped the savage Iraqi killers whom Hussein sent in to subdue the population. The report specified forty-eight methods of torture and execution the Iraqis were using to destroy those who fell into their hands. Hussein's teams mutilated their victims, applied electric shock to their organs, and often engaged in mass rape in an attempt to break their spirits. They tortured and killed little children in order to force their parents to reveal hiding places of foreigners or resistant Kuwaitis.

When Saddam Hussein invaded Kuwait, his former ally, on August 2, 1990, some one hundred and twenty of Iraq's senior military officers opposed the action. In response, Hussein ordered the torture and execution of these loyal officers for opposing his betrayal of Kuwait. He personally tortured a number of them. Although he claims 100 percent support from his oppressed people, according to a special report by Dennis Eisenberg from Jerusalem, Hussein told Yasir Arafat that "he doesn't trust a single man, woman or child in Iraq" (Toronto Sun, September, 1990).

Iraq Attacks the USS Stark

The CIA reported that they had strong documentation that President Saddam Hussein ordered the missile attack on the USS Stark on May 17, 1987. Despite Iraqi public apologies at the time of the attack, columnists Jack Anderson and Dale Van Atta published CIA documents reporting that both Iraq and Arab sources confirmed that "the strike was no accident" (April, 1990). The intelligence report added, "The CIA has collected evidence that...Hussein may have paid a $35,000 reward and allowed the use of a late model Mercedes Benz to the Iraqi pilot responsible for the 'accidental' missile attack in 1987 on the USS Stark."

Hussein Fears Assassination

Hussein's reign of terror is so despised by his own people that, during Desert Shield he was forced to turn to Yasir Arafat to obtain a special group of a thousand PLO terrorist bodyguards to protect him against assassination attempts. More than ten thousand PLO terrorists, flown in from their headquarters in Tunis and Lebanon, are now operating from a secret army base in Baghdad. Hussein often stays at this base near the capital under the protection of his Arafat-supplied guards. His passion for security rose to such a level that he hired three Saddam Hussein "doubles" who appeared at various locations in the country, complete with a retinue of security men. These look-alike actors were intended to fool potential hit teams who might try to get revenge for the thousands of Iraqis and Kurds he has killed. It has been reliably reported that Hussein now displays the same elusive behavior Noriega did in that he moves his location five to seven times every night to minimize opportunities for his many enemies to assassinate him. After the last failed attempt to assassinate him, he ordered his security men to "drag the bodies away and burn them."

President Hosni Mubarak of Egypt reported that Hussein told him that "when I am killed, the largest part of me which will remain will be the size of my little finger." Many of those who interviewed him during the Persian Gulf war commented on the eerie calm Hussein showed. American intelligence confirmed that he was taking heavy tranquilizers from three doctors in an attempt to calm his nerves.

Babylon on the Move

For more than ten years, Iraq, which is in the most turbulent area in the world, amassed huge quantities of armaments. The country rose from a modest Middle East power to become the dominant military force in the region. Hussein used his nation's $100 million dollar a day oil revenues to build his armed forces into a formidable military machine that was rated the fourth most powerful in the world. For five years before the Gulf War, Iraq, with only seventeen million people, was the largest arms importer in the world. Hussein invested over $50 billion in weapons and military infrastructure. He bought sophisticated armaments from Russia, the United States, and many European countries.

Despite some half-hearted attempts to restrict Iraq's access to the most dangerous military technologies, including missile guidance and nuclear triggering devices, Iraq succeeded in developing a very high technology military strike capability. It was said that "Saddam Hussein never saw a weapons system he didn't like." Before Operation Desert Shield turned into Operation Desert Storm and Allied Forces began bombing military locations in Baghdad, Iraq had at least seventeen chemical and biological warfare labs and five nuclear research sites. His appetite for modern weapons of mass destruction was unequalled in the Third World.

Russia's Secret Agenda in the Middle East

While presenting herself as a good world citizen and "peace-loving" member of the United nations, the truth is that Russia, the Gog and Magog of the Bible, continues to maneuver behind the scenes to achieve her long-term aim of political-military control of the Middle East. During the war in the Gulf, Russia publicly stood on the side of the United States and the UN allies against Iraq's naked aggression. However, behind the scenes, Russia did everything in its power to plan this war and assist Iraq in its plans to conquer Kuwait and Saudi Arabia. While this claim may seem unlikely at first glance, I challenge you to consider the evidence.

Russia, for two decades, was Iraq's main arms supplier. This nation sold Hussein every kind of weapon in the Soviet arsenal except nuclear warheads. In turn, Iraq provided the Soviets with desperately needed Western hard currency. Iraq refitted Soviet SCUD missiles to dramatically increase their range from 250 miles to more than 600 miles. The trade-off involved a smaller warhead, either conventional or chemical-biological, with a potential for a very small tactical nuclear (.2 megaton) warhead.

According to the August 22, 1990, *New York Times* (Op-ed page), top Soviet tactical tank warfare expert, Colonel General Albert Makashov, entered Iraq on July 17, 1990, just two weeks before the Iraqi army invaded Kuwait. General Makashov remained in Iraq throughout the crisis, working daily with eight thousand Soviet military advisors in the country. Whether it was in Czechoslovakia in 1968 and again in 1989, or in Afghanistan in December, 1979, the Soviet pattern is always the same. A few days or weeks before military action commences, the Soviet General Staff will send in their top military or intelligence specialist to look things over "on the ground." Then they launch an attack. Eight thousand military advisors, who worked side by side with tank units, infantry and intelligence units, were still in Iraq for months after the August 2, 1990, invasion. The British Broadcasting Corporation reported in February, 1991, that Russian military advisors were still providing sophisticated maintenance for Soviet MiG-29 jets and top-secret electronics systems.

The already high level of Soviet military shipments to Iraq increased 200 percent in the period from early January, 1990, through the Kuwait invasion in August. United States photo-reconnaissance satellite pictures revealed that critical Soviet military shipments were being sent to Iraq over the Russian border as late as August 7, 1990, five days after Russia agreed to abide by the UN arms embargo.

When the world began to watch, the Russians sent desperately needed spare parts to Iraq through special arrangements by way of countries such as Yemen, Sudan and Jordan.

During January, 1991, the Allied Maritime Intercept Force boarded a Soviet freighter in the Red Sea, the *Dimitri Furmanov*, that was trying to smuggle 106 tons of Russian armaments and special electronic gear to Iraq through Jordan. Despite a false manifest, the illegal cargo was destined for Saddam Hussein's troops. The Soviet newspapers admitted that the Russian military had tried to smuggle tons of contraband military equipment despite Russia's vote for the United Nations embargo. This type of operation was not done by some captain at a low level. It was approved at the highest level of the Soviet general staff with Gorbachev's knowledge. Did Gorbachev denounce this shipment when it was discovered and call for military heads to roll? No. This important news was ignored by thousands of media personnel. It was mentioned only once and was never followed up by commentators even though secret Russian assistance to Iraq's war effort was the most important background story of the Gulf War. It was ignored because it did not fit the agenda of the Western news media, which was committed to the fiction that Russia has truly abandoned its goals of dominating the West.

An Ally in the Gulf War?

President Gorbachev asked President Bush to provide Russia a forty-eight hour advance warning before the UN forces launched Operation Desert Storm against Iraq. While the U.S. refused to do this, President Bush did call Gorbachev one hour before launching the air attacks. Immediately after Bush's call, Russia sent a secret message by military satellite from Moscow to the Russian embassy in Baghdad; American intelligence intercepted the message. The Soviet ambassador rushed an emergency message to Saddam Hussein to warn him of the impending attack. Fortunately, Iraqi bureaucracy interfered with the transmission and forced the ambassador to wait until morning and go through proper channels by talking first to the Iraq foreign ministry.

When President Bush launched the ground war phase he informed each of the allied member nations of the timing. However, having learned a lesson from Gorbachev's betrayal, Bush waited until thirty minutes before the attack to inform Gorbachev. He kept Gorbachev on the phone for twenty-eight minutes, leaving the Soviets only two minutes to warn Iraq.

A further indication that Russia remained close to Iraq during Operation Desert Storm is shown by the fact that on January 25, 1991, the Soviet general staff offered to the press a detailed critique of Allied bombing damage in Iraq. They claimed that 90 percent of the air sorties missed their targets. How could the Russian's have offered this detailed intelligence assessment unless their military advisors were still conducting daily intelligence assistance to Saddam Hussein? When Iraq threatened Turkey because it provided America with access to Turkey's air bases, President Bush asked Turkey to move troops to provide protection against an Iraqi attack. Turkey moved 180 thousand NATO troops to the Turkey-Iraq border to protect the bases and provide pressure on the Iraqi army to draw off forces from the Kuwait theater of operations. Russia promptly ordered over 200 thousand troops from the Soviet southern command theater to move up to the Russian-Turkish border to intimidate Turkey. News media totally ignored this threatening military maneuver.

In light of all these facts it is impossible to believe that Russia was not aware of Iraq's plans to invade her neighbor. Although American intelligence agencies knew of Russia's involvement, the pressing political need to keep this broad-based United Nations coalition together prevented the administration from publicly confronting the Soviets about the disturbing facts. For example, the allies were criticized for bombing Jordanian truck convoys traveling to Baghdad which American intelligence said contained Soviet military supplies. White House spokesman Marlin Fitzwater admitted that we had targeted "cargos of military significance." When challenged about the Soviet nature of these "cargos of military significance," the American administration sources tried to protect the Russians by claiming that "nothing significant is going from the Soviets to Iraq. We don't think Mikhail Gorbachev would let that happen" (*U.S. News and World Report,* February 18, 1991). This is one of the bigger lies presented to the public during the war in the Gulf.

Chemical-Biological Weaponry

Russia, of course, was not the only country that contributed to Iraq's tremendous armaments build-up. In all, more than two hundred companies from many nations also helped. Hussein called on Western technical assistance to develop a number of biological warfare weapons, including botulism, anthrax, and the plague. United States intelligence agencies reported that these weapons could have been operational in military quantities within six months of Iraq's attack of Kuwait. The deadly anthrax disease, which is fatal to both cattle and humans, is one of Iraq's main weapons. There is no known antidote for anthrax. One failed anthrax experiment at a secret laboratory near Basra, Iraq, brought about the deaths of more than three hundred cattle. A terrible experiment with anthrax germ warfare on a small uninhabited British island during World War II has left the island still poisoned fifty years later.

According to the Pentagon, most of Hussein's weapons complexes were either destroyed or badly damaged in air attacks. The most important of these complexes was located at Samarra, north of Baghdad. Engineers who fled Iraq declared that the Saad-16 Chemical Research Armaments Center was the most advanced they had ever seen. German companies (sixty-three of them) contributed in a major way to the development of Iraq's nuclear, chemical and biological programs. As one example, Germany supplied the TH-2 and T-2 mycotoxins that are essential to the manufacture of certain biological weapons. The Taji Complex, which was also destroyed, was capable of producing advanced artillery and chemical weapons including cyanide, somar, Sarin, and Tabun.

Lieutenant General Stanislav Petrov, commander of Soviet chemical warfare, claims that prior to Operation Desert Storm, Iraq had between two thousand and four thousand tons of poisonous weapons as well as biological agents such as Siberian plague and cholera. He also stated that Iraq could possibly have various exotic African disease germs and botulin toxin—the most lethal bacteria known. Petrov says that "one hundred grams of such a substance could bring death to hundreds of millions of people." He went on to say that if there is a strike on the storage sites the consequences are unpredictable (*Los Angeles Times*, January 29, 1991).

A particularly worrisome development is a new gas that uses prussic acid, which Hussein claims will eat away the material in all existing gas masks, rendering soldiers and civilians vulnerable to other chemical agents.

The "Supergun"

Iraq acquired the most powerful artillery in the world with over thirty-five hundred heavy artillery weapons, including the awesome G-5 155-mm howitzer, a towed artillery gun designed by Gerald Bull and built in South Africa and used by both sides in the Iran-Iraq war. The G-5 cannons destroyed whole units of the Iranian mass-advance armies, killing as many as twenty thousand soldiers in one savage encounter in the Faw Peninsula Battle.

Mr. Bull, a brilliant Canadian armament and ballistic expert, worked with the Iraqi government to provide the most advanced weapons available in the world today. He had worked with both American and Canadian defense industries who were on the leading edge of ballistic missile research. He developed an obsession to create a "Supergun" with an enormously long barrel that would allow the firing of a shell or satellite with precise accuracy and great velocity. Using a sabbot missile with a rifled barrel would greatly magnify its velocity and ultimate power.

This advanced but experimental technology was rejected by the U.S. Defense Department due to other commitments to companies that manufacture standard missile launch systems. Gerald Bull then turned to other countries for business—Israel, South Africa, Iran, and most of all, the growing military power, Iraq.

Over the past six years, Bull's armaments firm, Space Research Corporation, arranged contracts with a multitude of high technology armaments firms in the U.S. and Europe to supply Iraq with the newly designed Supergun, which bears the code name "Babylon." Four of the guns—two small ones called "Baby Babylon" and two large ones—were secretly brought into Iraq and set up in two underground complexes. Although many commentators initially denied that Iraq had received these Superguns, a special report from London by the Independent News Service confirmed on November 16, 1990, that "Iraq is believed to have three 'Superguns' manufactured by British firms."

Several large shipments of parts for additional Superguns were seized in Britain, France, Germany, Greece and Turkey. In mid-September, 1990, twelve barrel segments were embargoed in Jordan. Naturally, Iraq claimed that these barrels were not really parts of a Supergun assembly, but were simply oil pipeline. As one customs official commented with some humor, "This may be the world's first rifled oil pipeline." Despite Iraq's sporadic denials, Hussein has boasted several times that he now has a secret weapon that can "burn half of Israel." Knowledgeable intelligence agents believe that this Supergun would allow Hussein to deliver chemical, biological or conventional warheads against Israel in the future. Although Israel did not retaliate to conventional missile strikes from Iraq, a chemical attack could still provoke Israel to consider a nuclear strike.

One especially devastating weapon Iraq still has is the recently designed fuel-air explosive that could be delivered to its intended target with great accuracy by the new Supergun. This weapon disperses a thin cloud of very high octane aviation fuel over a two-square-mile area. A secondary precision detonator ignites this explosive gas cloud which then produces an extremely powerful explosion that destroys everything within two square miles. Those who have witnessed tests of this new weapon claim that it is as devastating as a small nuclear bomb. It would be especially devastating to areas where there are oil refineries, pumping stations, cities, and command bunkers.

As a postscript to this section, on March 22, 1990, a bullet ended Gerald Bull's life. Apparently he had made a fatal mistake in his last choice of clients for his deadly merchandise.

Nuclear Weaponry

Although Iraq had signed the Nuclear Non-Proliferation Treaty against developing its own nuclear armaments, Article 10 of the treaty allowed Iraq to withdraw its compliance with the terms of the treaty if it deems that its "supreme" interests are endangered.

For at least fifteen years Iraq has conspired with a large number of Western high technology companies to thwart customs restrictions designed to prevent nuclear technology getting into the hands of Third World countries. Billions of dollars have been spent in setting up advanced nuclear labs and reactors. With an abundance of oil, Iraq's only purpose in obtaining nuclear capabilities must be the creation of nuclear weapons which would transform it in one short moment into a superpower capable of devastating Israel or any other enemy.

In August of 1989 an enormous explosion occurred at a secret underground weapons lab at Al-Quaqua. This lab was trying to develop high melting-point explosives and rapid detonation explosives. These particular explosives are used only in the production of nuclear implosion devices. Iraq purchased three hundred tons of yellowcake in the early 1980's, one of the basic raw materials used only in the production of nuclear weapons.

In March of 1990, British and American authorities announced that they had seized forty nuclear triggers known as high speed capacitators. However, in May, Saddam Hussein held one of these devices in his hand and revealed that they had already imported a number of these highly secret devices that are needed to control the sophisticated electronic triggering sequence for a nuclear bomb. The attempt to import forty nuclear bomb triggers, along with the importation of Swiss gas centrifuges that refine Uranium 235, proves that Iraq is working twenty-four hours per day on her own "Manhattan Project."

The much criticized attack Israel made in 1981 on Iraq's 70-megawatt nuclear reactor facility at Osiraq set back Hussein's nuclear warhead project by more than four years. While several nations publicly condemned Israel at the time for its action, many world leaders were secretly very thankful that Israel hindered Hussein's development of nuclear weapons. Unfortunately, this French-built reactor had already produced enough plutonium to create one or two very primitive weapons. If Israel had not bombed the Osiraq reactor, the United Nations forces in Saudi Arabia would have been sitting ducks for a lightning nuclear attack.

Another very unpleasant scenario involves the Iraqi creation of a warhead that could be filled with radioactive waste products from their nuclear reactor program, such as strontium 90 and thorium. Such a dirty weapon could be fired at an enemy target with either a modified Scud-B missile or the new Supergun. When the warhead exploded in the air, deadly radioactive material would float down on the target city or oil field, making the area uninhabitable for hundreds of years until the radioactivity finally decays. During World War II, nuclear scientists in the Manhattan Project suggested that bombs composed of radioactive material be dropped on Germany and Japan, which would poison their cities for decades. The idea was rejected in favor of more selective targeting of cities and bases with the newly developed nuclear bombs. Whether the world wants to admit it or not, we are now two minutes to midnight on the doomsday clock. The foregoing information proves how modern Babylon is contributing to the rapid approach of the end times.

When we consider the devastating destructiveness which many nations now possess we must realize that we are very close to that event described in the Bible as the great Battle of Armageddon. The twenty-four elders sitting before God, as described in the book of the Revelation of Jesus Christ, sang about the Lord God Almighty who "should destroy those who destroy the earth" (Revelation 11:18). Surely, the world is quickly approaching the time when only the coming of the Messiah, the Prince of Peace, will save mankind from the evil course we have embarked upon.

The Gulf War—Setting the Stage for Gog and Magog

The Persian Gulf War only set the stage for the coming war of Gog and Magog. Now that the war is over, Russia will regroup and begin to plan for the coming Russian-Arab invasion of Israel as described by the prophet Ezekiel. After the Iraqi failure, the Russians will conclude that they must invade the Middle East with their own troops along with their Eastern European allies and the Arab nations.

One of the most significant developments of the Gulf crisis was the American utilization of United Nations Security Council resolutions to provide legal justification to expel Iraq from Kuwait territory. The Russians and Arabs now feel they have clout to demand that the United Nations use their power to pass similar resolutions demanding that Israel give up the West Bank, East Jerusalem, and Gaza to the Palestinians and the PLO.

Watch for Canada, the United States, and nations of Europe to betray Israel and join in the increasingly strong resolutions against Israel's possession of these territories. Israel must hang onto these territories or commit national suicide. The UN Security Council will probably vote for economic sanctions, an arms embargo, etc., to attempt to force Israel to allow the creation of a PLO state in the territories.

We may ultimately see the UN sending peacekeeping troops to "protect Palestinians." The PLO requested this resolution after they manufactured the tragic Temple Mount riots in October, 1990. Eventually, as Israel continues to say no, it is possible that the Russians and Arabs will use the UN Security Council resolutions as the legal pretext for the coming Russian-Arab invasion of Israel. The Soviets love legal umbrellas for their illegal actions. This invasion will be the next major event in Bible prophecy.

It is fascinating to witness how events in the Persian Gulf War are setting the stage for the coming war of Gog and Magog. As these events unfold, we can be confident that the time for the second coming of the Messiah rapidly approaches.

Babylon Resurrected

Some of the most startling and dramatic of Bible prophecies describe a resurrected Babylon that will rise up in the last days prior to Messiah's coming to set up His Kingdom. Isaiah, Jeremiah, Ezekiel, Daniel, and John all prophesied extensively about the future of this great Babylonian Empire that had so severely oppressed the nation of Israel. Many of their prophecies hold a double meaning concerning Babylon: a fulfillment soon after the prophecy was delivered, and a much later fulfillment, thousands of years in their future.

Some parts of these prophecies that are now being fulfilled involve specific predictions about a great alliance of nations that will arise to stand against the power of Babylon in the final generation. Others describe the destruction by fire of the city of Babylon in such a supernatural fashion that the fire burns forever. The city will never be inhabited again. Several prophecies describe the city as being destroyed supernaturally in one hour and the merchants of the world weeping for the loss of their profits. We know that these prophecies refer to something that has not yet happened because Babylon was not destroyed in that manner when the Media-Persian Empire conquered them in 538 B.C.

Iraq's Plan to Conquer Saudi Arabia

Iraq's attempt to attack and conquer its virtually defenseless neighbor Kuwait was the first stage in Hussein's plan to reestablish the Babylonian Empire. It took only six hours on August 2, 1990, for the million regular army Iraqi soldiers to roll over the twenty-thousand-strong forces of Kuwait. Then Hussein paused to assess reaction from the world, and especially from America, to this attack. Meanwhile he began to prepare his forces for the second stage of Project Babylon. This plan, which he had worked out with his Soviet advisors, called for a two-week halt to let the world react and acquiesce to his occupation of Kuwait. If America had not moved her troops to defend the Kingdom of Saudi Arabia, Hussein would have launched Stage Two: the active involvement of Jordan and Yemen.

A lightning attack on the vital oil fields of Saudi Arabia would be reinforced with an attack by Jordan's Arab Legion on the western provinces of Saudi Arabia—including Mecca and Medina, the two holiest cities in Islam. Yemen would move its army north to occupy the two southern provinces of Saudi Arabia while Iraq would occupy the rest of the kingdom, the United Arab Emirates, and Bahrain. Iraq's planners felt they could conquer the whole Saudi Arabian Peninsula. The political genius of the plan was that they would then call a special meeting of the Arab League and announce that this was simply an internal matter for the

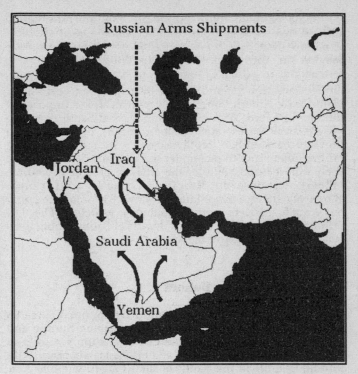

**Hussein's Plan To Conquer
The Middle East's Oil Fields**

"Arab Nation" to resolve. They would claim that this did not involve Western nations and they were simply rectifying the obsolete colonial borders imposed on the "Arab Nation" by the hated colonial powers at the end of World War I.

Does this explain the vote against the use of force which Yemen cast in the United Nations? Does this give you an insight into the underlying motives of King Hussein of Jordan who stood to benefit enormously if Iraq won its monstrous gamble? The PLO and Yasir Arafat bet their futures on the huge victory by Saddam Hussein and his Arab allies. Hussein promised Arafat that they would use the newly conquered territory and oil wealth to accomplish their mutual long-term goal of the "liberation of Palestine" and the elimination of the Jews from the Middle East. Now you can see Arafat's motivation for standing with Iraq.

The military genius of the plan was simply that the rapid occupation of Saudi Arabia by Iraq, Jordan, and Yemen would leave America and Europe with an almost impossible military problem. Without the land mass of Saudi Arabia to set up army bases, attack zones, supply depots, and to provide the strategic depth necessary to build up a half-million-man army to reconquer the kingdom, it would have been almost impossible for the allies to provide a credible military response to the Iraqi conquest. You cannot effectively attack a major land power with a force based only on aircraft carriers and amphibious vehicles. The UN military forces needed the vast deserts of Saudi Arabia to be successful in the counterattack.

How Russia Would Benefit

In two weeks time Iraq would have captured some 65 percent of the world's exportable oil, leaving Europe and Japan—with less than one-hundred-days supply of oil—at the mercy of Saddam Hussein and his Russian backers. With Middle East oil in the hands of their long-time client Iraq, Russia would have benefitted in two ways. First, as the world's largest producer of oil, the Soviet Union would immediately benefit by selling oil at a hundred dollars a barrel, solving many of their most pressing financial problems overnight, at no risk to them. Second, Russia could reverse the disasterous losses they suffered in Eastern Europe in the previous three years by controlling the economy of both Western Europe and Japan. With only three months supply of oil, both areas are vulnerable to oil blackmail and coercion.

Remember, the Russians are world champion chess players. This gambit by Gorbachev had tremendous potential and little risk. When the gambit failed, the Iraqis paid the price, and the Russians lost very little. But the plan almost succeeded! The failure was caused by Russian and

Iraqi miscalculation. By the grace of God, President Bush moved the 82nd and 101st Airborne Divisions onto the sands of Saudi Arabia within five days of the initial attack on Kuwait. Many advised—and some demanded—the President to "give sanctions a chance," claiming that he did not have the authority to move troops into the Saudi Kingdom. Fortunately for the West, the president acted decisively. In the weeks that followed, both he and Vice President Quayle stated that there was a clear threat to Saudi Arabia which demanded immediate military action to protect the oil wells on the Gulf. President Bush knew the precise dimensions of the Iraqi threat facing the world. How did he know?

An Offer Egypt Couldn't Refuse, But Did

Two years before Kuwait was attacked, President Saddam Hussein approached President Hosni Mubarak of Egypt at the conclusion of an Arab League meeting. Hussein offered Egypt a deal he said they could not refuse. He invited Mubarak to participate in a joint invasion of Saudi Arabia, Kuwait, Bahrain and the United Arab Emirates. Egypt would receive $25 billion and all the future oil the country needed; Jordan would join in and receive the western provinces and Mecca and Medina. Yemen would get two provinces.

Fortunately for the West, Mubarak said no. From that moment Egypt was excluded from the secret planning sessions held by Iraq, Jordan, and Yemen. President Mubarak contacted an American senator who passed on the information to appropriate intelligence authorities. Several intelligence sources in Israel and America confirmed to me that this was true. An article in *Newsweek* Magazine, "The Road to War" (January 28, 1991) reported this vital information in a background analysis to the war. However, by and large it was ignored by the press. Yet this data is crucial in evaluating the entire crisis. Although the warning about Hussein's plan to conquer Saudi Arabia seemed too fantastic to be true, some in President Bush's administration have kept an eye on Iraq. Every year, Western intelligence receives a huge amount of contradictory and threatening information from the Middle East. Most are ignored because threats are common from that area of the world. However, when Iraq's surprise attack on Kuwait occurred, President Bush knew that Stage Two of the plan described by President Mubarak would be launched in less than two weeks unless he moved immediately to "draw a line in the sand."

Drawing a Line in the Sand

President Bush's phrase, "draw a line in the sand," comes from ancient Middle Eastern history. Over two thousand years ago, Roman senators challenged Antiochus Epiphanes with this same threat as he tried to invade Egypt. Rome did not want this mad Syrian king, the first antichrist, to threaten her strategic interests in this breadbasket of the area. King Antiochus refused to give a clear answer to the senators as to whether or not he would obey their order and return his troops to Syria. One of the senators took his sword and drew a complete circle in the sand around the astonished Antiochus and demanded an answer to Rome's demand before the king stepped out of the circle. The Syrian angrily complied and ordered his troops to withdraw. As he led his army home to Syria through Israel, Antiochus was so angry at being thwarted in his ambition to conquer the world that he ordered his army to destroy the Jews in Jerusalem. Over forty thousand innocent Jews were killed by Antiochus Epiphanes and his army.

Saddam Hussein and his SCUD attack on Israel and his rape of Kuwait parallels the earlier incident. History does not repeat itself exactly but spirals on another level, similar, but always different. As Iraqi troops took control of Kuwait they behaved as vicious savages against their Muslim neighbor who had supported Iraq with billions of dollars in aid every year. Within the first few weeks of occupation, the army robbed jewelry stores and stole the complete national reserves from Kuwaiti banks and other financial companies. The amount was more than twenty billion dollars. They then took everything that could be removed from the country. Medicines, computers, automobiles, refrigerators, televisions, radios, were carried back to Baghdad.

Isaiah describes a future attack in which a proud leader, prophetically called "the king of Assyria" would conquer and rob a defenseless country. Assyria was an earlier name for Iraq. "Therefore it shall come to pass, when the Lord has performed all His work on Mount Zion and on Jerusalem, that He will say, 'I will punish the fruit of the arrogant heart of the king of Assyria, and the glory of his haughty looks.' For he says: 'By the strength of my hand I have done it, and by my wisdom, for I am prudent; also I have removed the boundaries of the people, and have robbed their treasuries; so I have put down their inhabitants like a valiant man. My hand has found like a nest the riches of the people, and as one gathers eggs, that are left, I have gathered all the earth; and there was no one who moved his wing, nor opened his mouth with even a peep'" (Isaiah 10:12-14). This unusual prophecy indicates that this proud "king of Assyria" would boast that he had conquered by his own wisdom and strength, that he had expanded the boundaries of his country by invading others, and that he had "robbed their treasuries" and the "riches of the people." Could this prophecy refer to the attack on Kuwait?

Not only did Iraq "gather all the earth" of Kuwait, but in their retreat Hussein's army treated the citizens of Kuwait just as Antiochus and his army did the Jews of Jerusalem. The brutality of the Iraqi soldiers and the secret police was beyond anything the civilized world has experienced. Only people who live in the Middle East were not surprised at Amnesty International's report of rape, torture, the killing of ninety babies ripped out of incubators, and mass murder of thousands of other citizens of Kuwait—totally without cause. As the allied forces entered Kuwait City, Iraqi soldiers were still taking women and children out of their homes and killing them in the street with axes. The demonically inspired Iraqi troops committed numerous mass rapes of the wives and daughters of the Kuwaiti resistance. The details of horrifying tortures of innocent old men, women, and children are beyond anything I could decently report in this book. Most Kuwaiti men over the age of sixteen were taken to secret concentration camps in Iraq. At this writing their fate is still unknown.

If this is the kind of behavior Iraq can unleash against her friendly Muslim Arab neighbor, can you imagine what these people intend to do to the Jews of Israel if they can ever convince the world to force Israel into a corner where she cannot defend herself? When this war is over, the Iraqi soldiers and secret police should stand trial with Saddam Hussein in war crime trials just like those held at Nuremburg.

The Temporary Set-Back of Babylon

The Babylonian Empire, the gold head of Nebuchadnezzar's dream image, only lasted seventy years, from 608 B.C. until its defeat by the Media-Persian Empire in 538 B.C. At that time the city of Babylon was burned, but not destroyed. It continued as the capital of the new kingdom. It is the same with Iraq. Even though the Persian Gulf War is a set-back, Iraq will persevere.

Jeremiah gives a prophetic description of what happened in the Persian Gulf War: "For behold, I will raise and cause to come up against Babylon an assembly of great nations from the north country, and they shall array themselves against her; from there she shall be captured. Their arrows shall be like those of an expert warrior; none shall return in vain" (Jeremiah 50:9). This prophecy gives a number of interesting details that match this recent conflict. First, an "assembly of great nations" comes against Babylon from the "north country." The twenty-eight nations were led by North America and included an assembly of supporting northern European nations. This is the first time in history that a great group of nations has come against Babylon. In the attack on the city in October of 538 B.C., only two provinces were involved—the Medes and Persians.

Next, the prophet comments on the astonishing accuracy of the "arrows"—missiles, fired against Babylon "like those of an expert warrior." Could Jeremiah have seen in his vision the awesome display of Tomahawk cruise missiles and smart laser-guided weapons that hit targets with great precision so that "none shall return in vain"?

Babylon's Final Destruction

Babylon, from the time of the Tower of Babel, has rebelled against the Holy God. Throughout history she has stood as a symbol of Satan's hatred against God and His Chosen People. Despite centuries of spiritual warfare the verdict of God against Babylon remains unchanged. Prophets of the Lord carried many warnings to the city about her wickedness and idolatry. These were all ignored by her rulers and people. But God's Word will be fulfilled.

The prophets Isaiah and Jeremiah record God's final intentions for Babylon: "Babylon, the glory of kingdoms, the beauty of the Chaldeans' pride, will be as when God overthrew Sodom and Gomorrah. It will never be inhabited, nor will it be settled from generation to generation; nor will the Arabian pitch tents there, nor will the shepherds make their sheepfolds there. But wild beasts of the desert will live there, and their houses will be full of owls; ostriches will dwell there, and wild goats will caper there. The hyenas will howl in their citadels, and jackals in their pleasant palaces" (Isaiah 13:19-22). "I will dry up her sea and make her springs dry. Babylon shall become a heap, a dwelling place for jackals, an astonishment and a hissing, without an inhabitant" (Jeremiah 51:37). God's final sentence on that wicked city and the evil rebellion of its inhabitants is: "'Behold, I am against you, O you most proud!' says the Lord God of hosts; 'For your day has come, the time that I will punish you'" (50:31).

Iraq will continue when the dust from this war has settled. We will see the rebuilding of the ancient city of Babylon and the fulfillment of the remaining prophecies about Babylon's role as a major economic power in the Tribulation period. The books of Isaiah and Revelation clearly outline God's ultimate destruction of Babylon for her part in the terrible persecution of Israel and the Tribulation saints.

Watch for Iraq to recover and return to the project of rebuilding mighty Babylon. After her military defeat, Iraq will use her awesome oil revenues to become the major economic power described in the Bible. Although Ezekiel 38 and 39 say that Iraq will participate in the coming

Russian-Arab invasion of Israel, she will still survive to become one of the leading centers of satanic pagan worship in the last days. In that regard, several years ago Saddam Hussein changed an Iraqi law to grant citizenship to Satan worshipers and allow them to build communities near Babylon to worship the devil. He surrounded himself with witch doctors from Africa to cast spells to protect him during the Gulf crisis. Iraq is currently rebuilding many of the ancient pagan temples in Babylon and is allowing the training of priests in pagan festival worship. Babylon is once more becoming an abode of devils, just as the prophets predicted.

Babylon the Great Has Fallen

Babylon will play a terrible role as a spiritual center for satanic worship in the last days. A spiritual war has gone on for thousands of years between the spirit of Babylon and the spirit of Jerusalem. All false religions can trace their rites, beliefs, and origins back to Babylon and her initial rebellion against the Laws of God. The essence of Babylonian religion is the attempt to transcend oneself and become as God.

In the Revelation to John about the latter days are these words: "Babylon the great is fallen, is fallen, and has become a habitation of demons, a prison for every foul spirit, and a cage for every unclean and hated bird! For...the merchants of the earth have become rich through the abundance of her luxury.... Alas, alas, that great city Babylon, that mighty city! For in one hour your judgment has come...For in one hour such great riches come to nothing" (Revelation 18:2,3,10,17).

John says that smoke from the burning of Babylon the Great "rises up forever and ever!" (19:3). If you were to visit Babylon during the hot days of summer you would see huge amounts of warm, sticky asphalt oozing up out of the ground. Ancient builders used this pitch as mortar. Scientists tell us that the entire city is built on a lake of thick oil-based pitch or asphalt, lying eight feet beneath the surface. This pitch is molten and expands through cracks in the clay when the ground becomes hot. It is easy to see what will cause the eternal burning of the city of Babylon so that the "merchants...who became rich by her, will stand at a distance for fear of her torment, weeping and wailing" when they see "the smoke of her burning" (Revelation 18:18).

In the next chapter we will see how the nation of Israel has for centuries longed for the coming of their Messiah.

CHAPTER 6

Israel
Rebirth of a Kingdom

Throughout human history civilizations have arisen, prospered and finally died. This pattern was followed by ancient kingdoms such as Babylon, Greece, Rome, and Egypt. However, one nation has refused to follow the blueprint: The nation of the Israelites. Any historian will tell you that the three greatest influences on world culture have been the Romans, Greeks, and Jews. Yet the original Greeks and Romans are lost to history. Only the Jews can trace their unbroken lineage back four thousand years to Abraham. Only Israel has resurrected her ancient "dead" language and uses it today.

No other nation can equal the glorious and tumultuous history of the Jews. They have survived against the most impossible odds. Nations persecuted them, wars ravaged them, and a holocaust diminished their number. They were cut off from their land and exiled throughout more than a hundred different countries for two thousand years. Yet they have endured as a distinct people to raise the Flag of David on the walls of their ancient Jerusalem.

This tiny nation of Israel, with less than five million people, is half the size of Switzerland, encompassing less than eight thousand square miles. In comparison, the United States is more that 370 times larger than Israel in size. Yet the Jews' claim to this small part of the world is challenged by the twenty-one Arab nations that occupy land five hundred times larger than Israel. They are demanding that the Jews give up almost one-half of its heartland. Why? Who deserves to rule the land of Palestine? Why have the Jews survived against overwhelming odds?

The miracle of Israel's rebirth in Palestine is the strongest evidence of God's intervention in human history. The Bible prophesied that Israel would be restored as a nation, become the central player on the stage of world history, and welcome the return of the Messiah. Witnessing the fulfillment of these prophecies is the greatest indication that our generation will also witness the Messiah's second coming.

In this chapter we will explore from both a historical and biblical perspective Israel's incredible history. We will attempt to understand her roles in the past, the present, and the future as God unfolds His plan leading to the age of the Messiah.

Israel's history can be roughly divided into four sections: (1) God promised Abraham that he would become "a great nation" in a promised land; (2) Solomon finally ruled over all the land God promised; the Jews lost the land; (3) Exiled Jews returned to rebuild their nation, only to lose it again; (4) The rebirth of Israel in the twentieth century.

A Great Nation in a Promised Land

When God told Abraham to leave Ur of the Chaldees, in present day Iraq, and travel a thousand miles to "a land that I will show you, He promised Abraham and his descendants all the land that extended "from the river of Egypt to the great river, the River Euphrates—the Kenites, the Kenezzites, and the Kadmonites; the Hittites, the Perizzites, and the Rephaim; the Amorites, the Canaanites, the Girgashites, and the Jebusites" (Genesis 12:1; 15:18-21). This includes considerably more land than the Israelis occupy today. Even though God said the land was Abraham's to possess, his descendants did not control all of it until Solomon became king nearly a thousand years later.

God also promised Abraham that He would multiply his "descendants as the stars of the heaven and as the sand which is on the seashore" (Genesis 22:17). Abraham's wife, Sarah, became impatient because they had no sons to fulfill God's promise of descendants. She took steps that brought about most of Israel's problems today. She told Abraham to produce a son with her maid, Hagar, so that he would have an heir. Hagar bore a son, Ishmael. But this was not the descendant God had promised Abraham.

A few years later, ninety-year-old Sarah did bear Isaac who became the son of God's promise. As Paul put it in his letter to the Romans, "For they are not all...children because they are the seed of Abraham: but, 'In Isaac your seed shall be called' " Romans (9:6-7).

Later, as Ishmael began to hate and mock Isaac, Sarah made Abraham send the handmaid and her son away. Abraham did not want to send his older son away, but God told him: "Cast out this bondwoman and her son; for the son of this bondwoman shall not be heir with my son, namely with Isaac." But God still cared for Ishmael. He said, "Yet I will also make a nation of the son of the bondwoman, because he is your seed" (Genesis 21:10,13). God did not give Ishmael and his descendants any land. Knowing Ishmael's character, God said, "He shall be a wild man; his hand shall be against every man, and every man's hand against him. And he shall dwell in the presence of all his brethren" (Genesis 16:12). This prophecy has been tragically fulfilled in the thousands of years of violence and hatred between the Arabs, the descendants of Ishmael, and the Jews, the sons of Isaac.

In A.D. 628, an Arab prophet named Muhammed captured the city of Mecca in Saudi Arabia and began to write letters to world rulers explaining the principles of the new Muslim faith. This was the beginning of Islam, a religion that traces its origin to Abraham through Ishmael.

Scriptures tell us that Ishmael and his Arab descendents became a nomadic people who freely roamed throughout Palestine and neighboring countries on lands that now encompass a hundred times the area of modern-day Israel. At no time did the Arabs set up an independent nation or a capital in Israel. However, Arabs now possess twenty-one countries surrounding Israel with fifty times the population of Israel. Not only that, of all the countries in the Middle East, Israel is just about the only one that has no oil!

It is interesting to note that although Egypt is often listed as an Arab nation, it is not. As Max Dimont reported in his excellent book *Jews, God and History*, "Strictly speaking, Egypt, of course, is not an Arab nation, though 90 percent of its people profess the Moslem faith. the vast majority of today's Egyptians are of Hamitic descent [descendants of Ham, the son of Noah], with the Arab Bedouins composing the largest minority group. Only a small minority, the Copts, are true descendants of ancient Egyptians."

In addition to the Arabs who descended from Ishmael, there are other groups of middle eastern peoples whom the Bible describes as being enemies of Israel in the last days, an alliance of nations that will come against Israel and then be destroyed by God. Of this alliance, Psalm 83 says, "Your enemies...have said, 'Come let us cut them off from being a nation, that the name of Israel may be remembered no more.' For they have consulted together with one consent; they form a confederacy against You: The tents of Edom and the Ishmaelites; Moab and the Hagarites; Gebal, Ammon, and Amalek; Philistia with the inhabitants of Tyre; Assyria also has joined with them; they have helped the children of Lot" (Psalm 83:2,4-8).

This prophetic list is fascinating in that it enumerates almost all the nations that today oppose Israel's existence:

Edom—from Esau, Jacob's brother: now Jordan
Ishmaelites—Hagar's son: now Arabs
Moab—Lot's son: now Jordan, east of the Dead Sea
Hagarites—from one of Hagar's twelve sons: now Arabs
Gebal—ancient Byblus: now north of today's Beirut, Lebanon
Ammon—son of Lot: now capital of Jordan
Amalek—descended from Esau: now southern Jordan
Philistines—from Ham: now throughout Palestine, Syria
Tyre—a Phoenician city: now Lebanon
Assyria—founded by Assur: now Iraq, Iran
Children of Lot—from Moab and Ammon: now Jordan

The prophet Ezekiel, in his great vision of the "dry bones," described the hatred of Israel's enemies, Israel's exile and her final miraculous return from the valley of "dry bones" (chap. 37) in the last days before the return of the

Messiah. In Ezekiel 35, significantly placed near the prophecy of the restoration of the captives, the Lord describes the coming judgment of God against these nations. This judgment includes Edom (Mount Seir) in present day Jordan, because of their centuries-old hatred of the Jews: "Moreover the word of the Lord came to me, saying, 'Son of man, set your face against Mount Seir and prophesy against it, and say to it, "Thus says the Lord God: 'Behold, O Mount Seir, I am against you; I will stretch out My hand against you, and make you most desolate; I shall lay your cities waste, and you shall be desolate. Then you shall know that I am the Lord. Because you have had an ancient hatred, and have shed the blood of the children of Israel by the power of the sword at the time of their calamity, when their iniquity came to an end...Because you have said, 'These two nations and these two countries shall be mine, and we will possess them,' although the Lord was there'" (Ezekiel 35:1-5,10). The "two nations" refers to Ephraim and Judah, the two parts of the divided kingdom after the time of King Solomon.

The Promise Fulfilled

Even though God promised Abraham's descendants all that land, it was up to them to take possession of it. Abraham, his son Isaac, his grandsons Jacob and Esau, and Jacob's twelve sons all became enormously wealthy. But they did nothing to possess the promised land. They needed something to shake them out of their complacency and satisfaction. The crisis began when eleven of Jacob's sons sold their young brother Joseph to slave traders headed for Egypt. As it turned out, Joseph did very well in Egypt; so well, in fact, that when God moved to bring about His plan for His Chosen People, Joseph was in a position to implement God's will. There was a famine in Palestine that sent the rest of Jacob's family to Egypt. Their descendants remained in Egypt for four hundred years, still not taking possession of their own land.

Finally, a Pharaoh "who did not know Joseph" (Exodus 1:8) began to feel threatened by the sheer numbers of the fertile descendants of Israel. He feared that they might become so numerous that if war came to Egypt they would "join our enemies and fight against us" (v. 10). In an attempt to weaken the Israelites, the Egyptians made slaves of them and "afflicted them with burdens" (v. 11). "But the more they afflicted them, the more they multiplied and grew. And they [the Egyptians] were in dread of the children of Israel" (v. 12).

About this time Moses was born. His life was saved by Pharaoh's daughter and he was raised as an Egyptian but nursed by his own Jewish mother. Moses left Egypt when he was forty and lived "on the backside of the desert" for another forty years. When Moses was eighty, God spoke to him from a burning bush. God told him that he would lead His people out of Egyptian bondage and into "the land of the Canaanites and the Hittites and the Amorites and the Perizzites and the Hivites and the Jebusites, to a land flowing with milk and honey" (Exodus 3:17). After ten plagues and a miraculous exodus the Israelites finally left Egypt and started north, into the wilderness.

Moses never saw "the land of milk and honey. His successor, Joshua, began the conquest of the Promised Land, which Abraham should have initiated hundreds of years earlier. Even then the Jews did not fully realize God's promise until Solomon's magnificent reign. First Kings tells us that "Judah and Israel were as numerous as the sand by the sea in multitude" and "Solomon reigned over all the kingdoms from the River [Euphrates] to the land of the Philistines, as far as the border of Egypt" (4:20-21).

Despite what God had done for them, the Chosen People refused to obey the laws God gave them to insure their survival and their purity as a people through whom a child would be born, Immanuel, "God with us," their Messiah.

After Solomon died the kingdom began to deteriorate. It split into the southern nation of Judah and northern nation of Israel. Not only did the two nations fight and lose to the people surrounding them, they fought each other. Soon the people of God became weak and helpless and finally fell to more powerful nations. First, in 721 B.C. Israel was defeated by the Assyrians, then in 606 B.C. Judah fell to the Babylonians. For a time the hope of repossessing all the land God had promised had to be abandoned.

The First Return from Exile in Babylon

Even though a great number of the Israelites were transported to Assyria and Babylon, just as the prophets had predicted, the Jews were given another chance to reclaim their land of promise. Cyrus, king of Persia who conquered Babylon, signed an edict in 536 B.C. that gave the Israelites permission to return to Jerusalem. Even though many Jews returned to their land they never regained all that Solomon had reigned over. Instead, when Persia lost world power, the Jews fell under the control, first, of Greece and then of Rome.

During the reign of these two powerful nations the people of God began to hope for a Messiah who would deliver them from their enemies and make of them, once again, a great nation. However when Jesus their Messiah came He was not on a white horse, charging in to conquer Rome as the Jews hoped, rather He came as a baby, born in a stable. But He was the Messiah. This fact was prophesied by the father of another boy, John, who was born a few months before Jesus. John's father, the priest Zacharias, being "filled with the Holy Spirit," prophesied of his own son, "You, child, will be called the prophet of the Highest; for you will go before the face of the Lord to prepare His ways, to give knowledge of salvation to His people by the remission of their sins, through the tender mercy of our God, with which the Dayspring from on high has visited us; to give light to those who sit in darkness and the shadow of death, to guide our feet into the way of peace" (Luke 1:67,76-79). But there was no indication in this prophecy that Jesus the Savior would bring victory to the Jews and restore their promised land to them at this first coming. That remains to be fulfilled when He returns the second time.

Even though they were under the rule of Rome, the Jews lived in comparative peace until their rebellion in A.D. 66 caused their final downfall. In A.D. 70, Jerusalem was burned and both Christians and Jews fled the promised land in the second great dispersion in their history. From then until the Balfour Declaration on November 2, 1917, and all through the Second World War, the story of the Jews was one of exile and persecution the world over.

The Return Under the Balfour Declaration

Toward the end of the nineteenth century the pogroms against the Jews within Russia and the Ukraine forced many Jews, who had lived for centuries within Russian lands, to flee for their lives. Many returned to Palestine; many others to North America. The Russian persecution was only one of many that had taken place against the Jews throughout Europe over the previous centuries. Finally, In 1897, largely because of a book by Theodor Herzl, *The Jewish State*, the first Zionist Congress met in Basle, Switzerland, to plan in practical terms the revival of Israel. Herzl's work caused a furor throughout Jewish communities as it aroused for the first time in modern days an intense longing to actually return to Zion.

The Balfour Declaration came about when Lord Arthur James Balfour, head of Britain's Foreign Office, received approval from the Cabinet for this declaration and released it to Lord Rothschild on November 2, 1917. It read: "His Majesty's Government views with favour the establishment in Palestine of a national home for the Jewish people, and will use their best endeavours to facilitate the achievement of this object, it being clearly understood that nothing shall be done which may prejudice the civil and religious rights of existing non-Jewish communities in Palestine or the right and political status enjoyed by Jews in any other country."

The British agreement was endorsed on July 24, 1922, by the Council of the League of Nations, the United States, and, for a short time, even some of the Arabs. Emir Faisal, the king of an independent Syria and son of an Arab leader, met several times with Zionist leader Dr. Chaim Weizmann. One of their declarations stated that "the surest means of working out the consummation of their national aspiration is through the closest possible collaboration of the development of the Arab state and Palestine (the Jewish Homeland)." Faisal wrote to one Zionist leader, Felix Frankfurter, in 1919, declaring: "The Arabs, especially the educated among us, look with deepest sympathy on the Zionist movement....We will wish the Jews a hearty welcome home....We are working together for a reformed and revised Near East and our two movements complete one

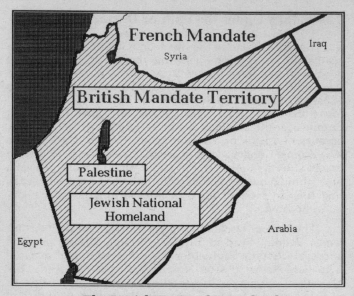

The Jewish National Homeland
The Balfour Declaration – 1917

another. The Jewish movement is nationalist and not imperialist. Our movement is nationalist and not imperialist. And there is room in Syria [which included Palestine] for us both. Indeed, I think that neither can be a real success without the other."

The Zionist Movement

A tremendous number of Jews immigrated to Israel following the Balfour Declaration. The Zionist movement in Europe greatly accelerated the immigration and assisted in establishing new settlements and Kibbutzim. The word *Zionism* was coined to express the ardent desire of the exiled Jews to return to their historic homeland, the Zion of the Bible.

When they returned, where were they to live? When, at the end of World War I the victorious League of Nations

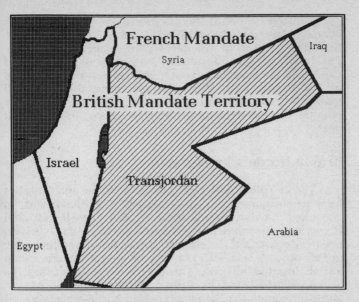

1921 – 35,000 square miles of the Jewish National Homeland were given to Arabs.
[80% of their promised land was lost]

dismembered the autocratic Turkish Empire, which had allied itself with the German forces, they allocated some five million square miles of territory to the two groups of people. The Jews received less than one-fifth of 1 percent of the land—eight thousand square miles. The Arabs won 99.8 percent—five hundred times more land than the Jews got. Out of their huge windfall the Arabs have created twenty-one independent countries with a current population in excess of 200 million.

Of the land apportioned for the Jewish National Homeland in 1917, a further 80 percent was torn out and given to the Arabs in 1921. The British had promised the position of King of Syria to Faisal. In the diplomatic shuffle after the war, the French took over the mandate for Syria and set up their own leadership. In an attempt to placate Faisal, the British offered him the Crown of Iraq.

Winston Churchill tried to please the Arabs further by offering 80 percent of the British Mandate to Faisal's brother, Abdullah, as Emir of this new territory called Transjordan. This totally illegal annexation of 80 percent of the Promised Land helped create the disaster and tension that still exist in the Middle East. When we remember this shameful robbery of land that was promised to the Jews, it certainly puts the current demand of "land for peace" in a different light.

Britain Hinders Immigration

The purpose of the Balfour Declaration and Britain's legal commitments to the League of Nations was to encourage Jewish immigration to the Jewish National Homeland. However, in 1921, 1929, and 1939, Britain drastically changed the rules to curtail Jews from returning to Palestine. A very effective way of preventing continued Jewish immigration into Palestine took place during the Second World War. The British Foreign Office in March, 1939, instructed the British ambassador to Germany to tell the Germans all he knew about the secret methods and routes of escape which the Jews were using to flee the coming Holocaust. They asked the Germans to assist to "discourage such travel." The actual text of the cable read: "There is a large irregular movement from Germany of Jewish refugees who, as a rule, set out without visas or any arrangements for their reception, and their attempt to land in any territory that seems to them to present the slightest possibility of receiving them. This is a cause of great embarrassment to His Majesty's government and as it appears, to the American Government, and the latter have expressed a wish that you should join the American Charge d' Affairs in Berlin in bringing the situation to the attention of appropriate German Authorities and requesting them to discourage such travel on German ships" (March 2, 1939, Foreign Office to Sir Neville Henderson: Treasury Papers, 188/226).

While British authorities used every possible means to turn back the Jews from entering Israel, the doors were thrown wide open to unlimited Arab immigration. A huge number of Arabs flowed into the areas where resident Jewish immigrants were building prosperous farms and businesses. With the severe restrictions of further Jewish immigration, these businesses were forced to hire large numbers of Arab laborers rather than Jews. As a result, Arab populations in Jewish communities such as Jerusalem, Haifa, and Jaffa increased by 90 to 200 percent, while in predominantly Arab towns, such as Nablus and Bethlehem, Arab population increased only between 32 and 40 percent.

Finally, in 1948, the War of Independence resulted in the formation of a Jewish state. Before the Jews became victorious, however, their Arab enemies promised a massacre of the Jews in Palestine. Azzam Pasha, Secretary General of the Arab League, reported in a press conference in Cairo: "This will be a war of extermination and a momentous massacre—like the Mongolian massacres and the Crusades" (*New York Times*, May 16, 1948).

The Egyptian Minister of Foreign Affairs, Muhammad Saleh ed-Din, reported in the Egyptian newspaper, *Al-Misri*, the following: "Let it therefore be known and appreciated that, in demanding the restoration of the refugees to Palestine, the Arabs intend that they shall return as the masters of the homeland, and not as slaves. More explicitly: they intend to annihilate the state of Israel" (October 11, 1949).

Arab Refugees in the Crossfire

During the 1948 war, Arab nations continually appealed to Arab residents of Israel to leave so that invading Arab armies could purge the land of all residents. Because Arab governments were convinced that they would quickly destroy the young Israeli state, they warned Arabs to flee before they attacked. "It must not be forgotten that the Arab Higher Committee encouraged the refugees to flee their homes in Jaffa, Haifa and Jerusalem, and that certain leaders...[would] make political capital out of their miserable situation" (Radio broadcast by Near East Arabic Radio, April 3, 1948).

The Jews, however, encouraged their Arab neighbors to remain and live in peace in the new country. Carl H. Voss in his book *The Palestine Problem Today*, recorded British documents showing that the Jewish Haifa Workers Council issued this appeal: "For years we have lived together in our city, Haifa....Do not fear. Do not destroy your homes with your own hands...do not bring upon yourself tragedy by unnecessary evacuation and self-imposed burdens....But in this city, yours and ours, Haifa, the gates are open for work for life, and for peace for you and your families." Even today the 800 thousand Arabs in Israel have the highest standard of living of any Arabs in the Middle East outside the small oil emirates. The Arabs have the right to vote; there are Arab members of the Knesset (parliament); they also have the right to serve in the military if they so choose. With around 725 Arab schools and colleges, about 90 percent of the Arabs attend schools and have obtained the highest standard of Arab literacy in the Middle East.

In a report by the Arab financed Institute for Palestine Studies in Beirut, Lebanon, the writers concluded that the majority of Arab refugees were not expelled by force in 1948, but fled on their own motivation. A full 68 percent of Arab refugees fled the country, according to the report, without seeing a single Israeli soldier. On April 17, 1950, the Arab National Committee of Haifa wrote a memorandum to the Arab governments that stated: "The removal of Arab inhabitants...was voluntary and was carried out at our request....The Arab delegation proudly asked for the evacuation of the Arabs and their removal to the neighboring Arab countries" (J.B. Schechtman, *The Arab Refugee Problem* [New York: Philosophical Library, 1952]) The International Development Advisory Board report to President Truman on March 7, 1951, stated that "Arab leaders summoned Arabs of Palestine to mass evacuation ...as the documented facts reveal."

Despite many inflated estimates given over the years the best figure of Arab refugees that left Israel at the time of the 1948 War of Independence seems to be approximately 430 thousand. Walter Pinner's book, *How Many Arab Refugees?* (London: MacGibbon and Kee, 1959), did a very careful analysis and determined that this number represented the "genuine refugees." Various Arab organizations often inflated their estimates for politica reasons. United Nations officials estimated, on an individual level, that many of the "refugees" on the relief rolls were fictitious. Local bedouins and residents around the UN camps often claimed refugee status in order to receive significant financial benefits for them and their families. Births were always reported; deaths seldom reported. Families would conceal deaths so they could continue receiving the appointed ration benefits for subsequent resale. United Nations officials claimed they had no observers available to check out false claims and many non-refugees were carried on the rolls. Reports to the United Nations claimed that some Arabs possessed as many as five hundred ration cards.

One factor to remember, regarding the refugee situation, is that the majority of UN officials were in fact Palestinians or Arabs of Syrian, Lebanese, Egyptian or Jordanian background (UNRWA Annual Report of the Director, July 1951-June 1952).

Another important consideration concerning Arab refugees should be noted. Following World War II, there were more than forty million refugees worldwide. The plan for refugees has always been to settle into and rebuild their lives in their new nations. This was done in Poland, Germany, Vietnam, Cambodia and dozens of other nations. This was not the case in Palestine. Only in the case of Arab refugees has the world demanded that common sense, common practice and justice be reversed to force these displaced Arabs to remain in refugee camps after forty years in a hopeless claim that they return. The great majority of Palestinians now living in the camps have been born since 1948.

Throughout this century of vast population movements of refugees, governments and agencies have developed a universal definition of a "refugee" as being a person who was forced to leave his "permanent or habitual" home. However, without debate, a tremendously significant change of definition took place in the case of these Arab "refugees," and these Arabs only. From this point on, an "Arab refugee" would be anyone who had left his "home or habitation" of "only two years prior to 1948 conflict" (Special Report of the Director, UNRWA 1954-55), UN

Document A/2717). This astonishing change in definition vastly increased the number of those who would ordinarily qualify under the universal definition. The underlying reason for this change is that officials recognized that a tremendous number of the so-called "Arab refugees" had only recently entered Palestine, just before 1948 under the rule of Britain, before the British mandate ended.

It is fascinating to note that, between 1948 and 1967, from two and three hundred thousand Arabs chose to move from the West Bank (under the control of Arab Jordan at that time). These Arabs freely chose to move away from what the PLO claims was their "eternal homeland" for economic or other reasons. This indicates that many of these Arabs were not closely connected to that land but had moved into the West Bank shortly before the 1948 War of Independence (Michael Curtis, ed., *Jordan, People and Politics in the Middle East* [New Brunswick, N.J.: Transaction Books, 1971]). This is just one more indication that the Arabs are a nomadic people, just as God had said they would be in His prophecy of Ishmael's descendants.

The Rebirth of the Promised Land

The ancient land of Palestine first became a Jewish nation after Joshua conquered Canaan in 1451 B.C. God's chosen people remained a nation in one form or another for fifteen hundred years until they were defeated by the legions of Rome in A.D. 70. Many fled Roman cruelty to seek sanctuary in other nations throughout the world. Thousands of them, however, despite enormous persecution, remained in the Promised Land; many of the current Sephardic Jews can trace their families back thirteen or more generations. Those who left to live in foreign nations, underwent thousands of years of persecution; yet they never forgot their beloved Jerusalem. They held out hope and continually prayed to return to Israel, their homeland.

In this century, because of years of hatred and oppression, Jews have been forced to abandon their possessions, lands, and money in these countries of refuge to which their forefathers had moved. The have fled to the only place in the world that would still accept them—Israel.

Even those Jews who lived in Arab countries were afflicted with oppression and racial hatred akin to that practiced by the Nazis and Russians, despite the pretty picture commentators often depict of thousands of years of Arab-Jewish peaceful coexistence prior to the creation of an Israel state. If these 800 thousand Jewish refugees could lay claim to compensations, they would far outweigh any similar claims that could be made by Arab refugees who left Israel in 1948.

More Jewish immigrants were created as recently as the Camp David peace talks. When Israel was required to give back to Egypt the Sinai Peninsula, which they had conquered ten years earlier in the 1967 war, the Arabs' long-term hatred toward the Jews was revealed when Egypt insisted that not one single Jew, of the thousands who had lived in Sinai since the 1967 War, could remain in the Sinai. In 1948 more than 850 thousand Jews lived in Arab countries. In 1990 less than twenty-five thousand are left.

In the famous Six-Day War in 1967 against the Arab nations, when Jordan's King Hussein attacked Israel, Israeli forces moved into Jordan and captured the old city of Jerusalem. They penetrated Syria and gained control of the Sinai Peninsula approaches to the Suez Canal. They gave the Sinai back to Egypt in 1977. This occurred despite the fact that the Sinai Peninsula was not the historic possession of Egypt. In fact Egypt, under the control of Britain, acquired the Sinai as part of the Versailles Treaty at the end of World War I.

The Israeli peace was further threatened when, in 1969 the Palestine Liberation Organization was formed. Yasir Arafat, chairman of the Executive Committee, shifted his main guerilla forces to Jordan. Since 1948, Israel has maintained a turbulent hold on a portion of the land which God told Abraham was his possession forever.

Who Owned The Land?

In 1946, the British Mandate Government surveyed Palestine and revealed the following breakdown of land ownership:

70% owned by the British government, in trust for the Jewish National Homeland

8.6% owned by Jews

3.3% owned by resident Arabs

16.5% owned by non-resident Arabs

When the 1948 War of Independence ended, the land owned by the British mandate government was transferred by international law to the new government of Israel. Despite Arab claims to the contrary, the Jews purchased from Arab landowners whatever lands they wanted to sell, often at very high prices.

In the period after the 1967 war, Jewish settlements were built almost entirely on what was Jordanian government land on the Green Line and on former Jordanian army bases along the Jordan River. By design, the settlements in the West Bank and Gaza were normally built on isolated sites far from existing Arab villages to provide military security, not on Arab lands.

From the time Israel again became an independent nation, the PLO has been dedicated to the total destruction of Israel and her Jewish population. During this past year, while promising publicly that it has renounced terrorism, the PLO has launched more than 467 separate terrorist acts against Jews both inside and outside of Israel.

In considering the long-term problem of how they could best make Israel militarily vulnerable, Arab leaders decided that open discussion about "throwing Israel into the sea" and "turning the Mediterranean red with Jewish blood" was not playing well in Western media. Therefore, as a first step in their multi-stage plan, they decided to downplay such bellicose rhetoric and turn to discussing the "need to create a Palestinian homeland." Additional stages will involve a build up of massive forces within Gaza and the West Bank and, finally, the total destruction of the Jewish population.

In the Middle East today, Arab radio stations broadcast two kinds of programs. One, in English, discusses the "reasonable" goal of creating a Palestinian homeland in the West Bank and Gaza that will dwell in peace with Israel forever. The other, in Arabic, talks of the annihilation of

Israel. The Western media, unfortunately, only reports on the "peaceful" broadcast.

In the entire history of the Muslim conquest of Palestine, although the Arabs claim the Temple Mount as their third most holy site after Mecca and Medina, they never set up a significant Islamic school or college there. Jerusalem was never made into a capital, not even a provincial capital, during the entire Arab rule. There was never any evidence of a valid "Arab State."

The Inhabitants of Palestine Before 1948

In his book, *The Innocence Abroad,* Samuel Clemens further described Palestine in A.D. 1863 as "a desolate country whose soil is rich enough, but given over wholly to weeds—a silent mournful expanse ...A desolation is here that not even imagination can grace with the pomp of life and action...We never saw a human being on the whole route."

Estimates set the population of Palestine in 1878 at 141 thousand Muslims settled in all of Palestine (including Israel and Jordan, but more than one quarter of those had moved in to the area within the fifty year period following the conquest by Egypt.

British Consul James Finn, in a 1858 report to the Earl of Clarendon, described the population makeup of Jerusalem: "The Mohammedans of Jerusalem are less fanatical than in many other places owing to the circumstances of their numbers scarcely exceeding one-quarter of the whole population—and of their being surpassed in wealth, in trade and manufacturers by both Jews and Christians."

In his *Travels Through Syria and Egypt in the Years 1793, 1784, 1785,* Count Constantine F. Volney claimed that the population of Jerusalem was less than fourteen thousand; Hebron had nine hundred men and Bethlehem had only six hundred adult men.

The British Consul of Jerusalem, in 1863, reported that the "population of the City of Jerusalem is computed at

15,000, of whom about 4,500 [are] Moslem, 8,000 Jews and the rest Christians of various denominations" (Report of the Commerce of Jerusalem During the Year 1863, Foreign Office report of May, 1984).

The ancient biblical site known as Beersheba had no settled residents, only nomadic Bedouin tribesmen. You can see in the following chart, the comparative numbers of residents of Jerusalem from A.D. 1844 to 1983.

Population Figures for Jerusalem, 1844-1983			
Year	Jews	Moslems	Christians
1844	7,120	5,000	3,390
1896	28,112	8,560	8,748
1922	33,971	13,413	14,699
1948	100,000	40,000	25,000
1967	195,700	54,963	12,646
1983	300,000	105,000	15,000

(These statistics are taken from the Turkish Census of 1844; Calendar of Palestine 1895-96; 1922 Census by British Mandate; Jerusalem—The Old City—1962; Israel Central Bureau of Statistics; Jerusalem Municipality Report.)

The Arabs have claimed that Palestine was always predominately Arab territory. However, the population figures show that this claim is unfounded.

A Palestinian State in the West Bank and Gaza?

The PLO and Arab governments, including Saddam Hussein, have repeatedly claimed that peace would come in the Middle East only if Israel would give in to the Palestinian demand to allow a PLO state on the West Bank. This is absurd because the Arabs could have set up a Palestinian state in the West Bank and Gaza at any time during the Jordanian occupation from 1948 to 1967. Despite

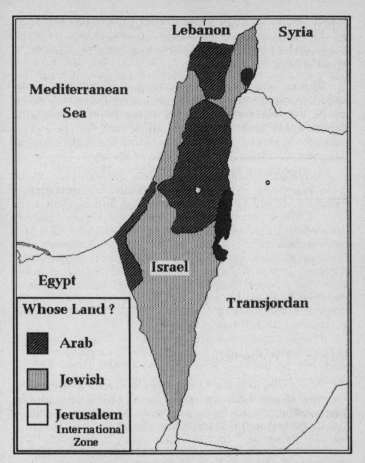

Israel – 1947 U.N. Partition Plan

the fact that Jordan had conquered the West Bank and East Jerusalem from 1948 until 1967, no one ever publicly called for a creation of "a state of Palestine." Not one government, nor any Palestinian group, asked to create a Palestinian homeland. The myth of Palestine had not yet been created.

In fact, according to Bernard Lewis in "The Palestinians and the PLO, a Historical Approach" (*Commentary*, January, 1975, pp. 32-48), "From the end of the Jewish state in antiquity to the beginning of British rule, the area so designated by the name Palestine was not a country and had no frontier, only administrative boundaries; it was a group of provincial subdivisions, by no means always the same, within a larger entity." The Palestine Royal Commission Report (chap. 6, p. 6, par. 11) states that "in the twelve centuries or more that have passed since the Arab conquest, Palestine has virtually dropped out of history."

Until Israel took control of those areas in June, 1967, there had been no public demand that an independent Palestine should exist. The claim that Jordan owned the West Bank is wrong because Jordanian armies illegally invaded and annexed this territory in 1948 after the Arab nations refused to agree to the United Nations' 1947 Partition of Palestine. Only two governments in the world accepted Jordan's illegal annexation. According to noted Yale legal scholar, Eugene Rostow, "The Israelis are now in the West Bank as the occupying power under the Security Council Resolutions of 1967 and 1973....They have a right to remain until full peace is made."

Jordan, A Palestinian State

According to some Arabs, there is already a Palestinian state that is five times the size of Israel. That state is Jordan. Yasir Arafat, in an interview with the Italian journalist Oriana Fallaci in 1970, admitted: "What you call Jordan is actually Palestine." In 1981 King Hussein declared, "The truth is that Jordan is Palestine and Palestine is Jordan." If the Arabs believe that Jordan is Palestine they should concentrate their energies on setting up a "democratic, secular Palestine" in the area of Jordan. The present Jordanian leadership of King Hussein and his minority Hashemite group were imposed by the colonial power of Britain following World War I. Over 70 percent of the population are Palestinian Arabs.

"For the Lord Shall Build up Zion"

According to biblical prophecy, the nation of Israel has been restored, even though it does not yet include all the land God promised Abraham. It is fascinating to realize that a great deal of encouragement for the return of the Jews to Israel has come about during the past three centuries because dedicated Christian Bible scholars believed fervently in the ancient prophecies that God would return the exiles to Zion. In my library are hundreds of old prophecy books written from 1650 to the early 1900's. They clearly reveal that many Christian writers believed that Israel must return to the land before the most important prophecies concerning the Antichrist and the Battle of Armageddon could be fulfilled. The subsequent literal fulfillment of these prophecies about Israel's rebirth encourage us to believe that the remaining prophecies about the Second Coming of the Messiah will also be fulfilled in a literal, common-sense way.

Peter Jurieu, the "Goliath of the French Protestants," wrote in 1687 about his abiding faith in prophecies about the return of the Jews to their Promised Land. At a time when the Jews were dispersed and without support anywhere in the world, he wrote a preface to his book entitled "To the Nation of the Jews." In it he said: "I desire of that People, that they would please to read this book attentively, and without prejudice; especially from the middle of the second Part to the end; they will find nothing there that can irritate them. I confess the hopes they conceive of a Kingdom of the Messiah, which shall be chiefly for them, is built upon express and unquestionable Prophecies; that even their Jerusalem should be rebuilt, and that they shall be again gathered together in their own Land." (*Approaching Deliverance of the Church*, 1687 A.D.).

Today, as Israel retains a tenacious hold on less than eight thousand square miles of soil, the Jews realize that they are surrounded by Arab nations who are committed to their destruction. Therefore, they spend some 30 percent annually on defense (by contrast, the U.S.A. spends about 6 percent). Although many criticize the four billion dollars in loans or grants which America provides Israel each year for military supplies, we have to put this amount in context

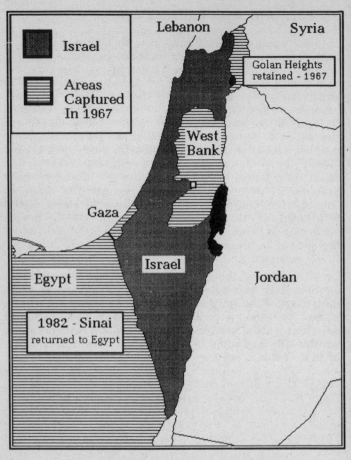

Israel And Land Captured In 1967

with other American defense commitments. For example: the U.S. spends over $120 billion per year defending Europe; some $40 billion in military defense of Japan and the Far East.

This four billion to Israel is described by American military strategists as the best investment the U.S.A. makes.

Israel performs a key role in military defense in the Middle East as well as at the southern end of the defensive perimeter of NATO's military theater. Israel's enormously effective air force and army make the Persian Gulf area more secure without our having to commit half of our available armored units permanently to bases in the Middle East.

Israel also provides America and NATO with tremendous amounts of vital intelligence data on Russia, Arab countries and international terrorism. Vast amounts of technical data, including captured Soviet M-72 tanks, SAM-9 missiles, and MiG-23 fighter planes, has been given to the United States. The Mossad, Israel's secret service, is judged by its competitors to be the best in the world. It has in the past warned Saudi Arabia and Egypt of several planned coup attempts against their leadership. Israel's electronic warfare technology is second to none in the world today. Her sophisticated electronic and human intelligence has proved of immense help to the West on many occasions.

Consider the Arab military threat that Israel always faces, such as Iraq's launching of SCUD missiles into Haifa and Tel Aviv. Combined Arab forces possess more tanks, artillery and soldiers than the entire Warsaw Pact forces in Europe. It is a miracle that tiny Israel with a population of only four million can stand against such an overwhelming array of military force. It is an awesome demonstration of the hand of God.

The words of the prophet Joel seem to refer to this very generation in the Middle East: "Proclaim this among the nations: 'Prepare for war! Wake up the mighty men, let all the men of war draw near, let them come up. Beat your plowshares into swords, and your pruninghooks into spears; let the weak say, "I am strong."' ...come up to the Valley of Jehoshaphat; for there I will sit to judge all the surrounding nations" (Joel 3:9-12).

Yet, Zechariah prophesied, more than two thousand years ago, "Behold, I will make Jerusalem a cup of drunkenness to all the surrounding peoples, when they lay siege against Judah and Jerusalem. And it shall happen in that day that I will make Jerusalem a very heavy stone for all peoples; all who would heave it away will surely be cut in pieces, though all nations of the earth are gathered against it" (Zechariah. 12:2-3).

The rebirth of the nation of Israel occurred on May 15, 1948, despite centuries of persecution, awesome opposition from many countries and threats from Arab forces. Humanly speaking, Israel should not exist, it is impossible. Yet today Israel takes its place among the nations of the world at the United Nations. We are surely living in the days that are prophesied to lead to the most momentous event in human history—the Battle of Armageddon and the coming of the Messiah.

The psalmist wrote of our generation and the rebirth of Zion: "You will arise and have mercy on Zion; for the time to favor her, yes, the set time, has come. For Your servants take pleasure in her stone, and show favor to her dust. So the nations shall fear the name of the Lord, and all the kings of the earth Your glory. For the Lord shall build up Zion; He shall appear in His glory" (Psalm 102:13-16). This extraordinary prophecy that "He shall appear" tells us that God has appointed this time of rebuilding Israel as the time for Messiah's appearance. It even suggests the enormous love the Jews have for biblical history and archeology in the phrase, Your servants take pleasure in her stones, and show favor to her dust." King David declared the Lord's wonderful covenant of the returning Messiah to Israel and to Christians: "For the Lord shall build up Zion; He shall appear in His glory."

In the next chapter we will examine additional prophecies that show how our generation will witness the coming of the King of kings and Lord of Hosts—Jesus the Messiah.

CHAPTER 7

The Signs
of the Coming King

Towards the close of Christ's ministry, His disciples met privately with Jesus on the Mount of Olives, overlooking the beautiful Temple. They asked Jesus a question that has troubled thoughtful men and women through the ages: "What will be the sign of Your coming, and of the end of the age?" The Lord responded by detailing a very specific list of prophecies and events that will mark the final generation before He returns.

On Palm Sunday, the day before this discourse, He had ridden into Jerusalem on a donkey in fulfillment of the prophecy in Zechariah 9:9: "Behold, your King is coming to you; He is just and having salvation, lowly and riding on a donkey, a colt, the foal of a donkey." His disciples and some of the people acknowledged this prophecy and praised Jesus as Messiah, calling out, "Hosanna to the Son of David! Blessed is He who comes in the name of the Lord! Hosanna in the highest" (Matthew 21:9). They desperately longed for a political Messiah who would defeat the Roman armies, not a spiritual Messiah who would reconcile them to God.

After driving the money changers from the Temple He went back to Bethany to spend the night. The next day as He journeyed back to Jerusalem He grieved over the city because the people had repeatedly ignored God's warnings to repent. Christ said that He had often wanted to "gather your children together, as a hen gathers her chicks under her wings, but you were not willing" (Matthew 23:37). Then Jesus added, "You shall see Me no more till you say, 'Blessed is He who comes in the name of the Lord'" (v. 39). This messianic prophecy undoubtedly provoked the disciples to ask the question concerning when these things would happen. Jesus told them: "Take heed that no one deceives you. For many will come in My name saying, 'I am the Christ,' and will deceive many. And you will hear of wars and rumors of wars. See that you are not troubled; for all these things must come to pass, but the end is not yet. For nation will rise against nation, and kingdom against kingdom. And there will be famines, pestilences, and earthquakes in various places. All these are the beginning of sorrows" (Matthew 24:3-8).

Then in verse 12 Jesus says, "And because lawlessness will abound, the love of many will grow cold."

Later in his discourse on the Mount of Olives, Jesus talked about the "abomination of desolation" in a rebuilt Temple. He warned that when this event occurs the Jews should "pray that your flight may not be in winter or on the Sabbath" (Matthew 15:20).

In a parallel prophecy John saw a vision of the coming cataclysm that will precede the coming of the Messiah. In Revelation 6, verses 1 through 8, John describes the four horsemen of the apocalypse that will devastate the world during the coming Great Tribulation period. These four horsemen represent the coming judgments of God on man's sinful rebellion. The white horseman with a bow and no arrows stands for false peace, while the red horseman represents devastating warfare. The black horseman of famine and the pale horseman of death will inevitably follow the approaching conflict of the nations.

In this chapter we will review a series of prophetic warnings given by Jesus and explore how they apply to our generation. Despite the fact that earlier generations looked for the Messiah in their day, we can logically conclude after our examination that these specific prophecies are being fulfilled in our day. In the Gospel of Luke, Jesus said, "When these things begin to happen, look up and lift up your heads, because your redemption draws near" (21:28).

Wars and Rumors of War—the Red Horseman

Despite the call for a "just and lasting peace" in our time, every continent in our world is involved in some kind of civil or international warfare. Nations are rising against nations, and kingdoms against kingdoms. Eastern Europe and Russia are on the verge of what could be the most terrible civil war in human history. In November, 1990, the CIA predicted that Yugoslavia could soon break apart and that civil war would rage within the next few months. At the present time this "rumor of war" has settled into an uneasy peace between the communist-led Yugoslav army and the secession-minded Croatian government. President Franjo Tudjman told the Croatian Parliament that "we were on the verge of civil war and bloodshed with catastrophic consequences" (Times Wire Services, *Los Angeles Times*, January 27, 1990). For the present the two sides have reached an accord. This is the same "Balkan tinderbox" whose ethnic rivalries produced World War I. Additionally, several of the fifteen republics in the USSR are threatening to break away in devastating civil war.

Not only are the individual republics feuding between their minority ethnic populations, many of them are seeking to break away from the control of Soviet Russia. Presently, the only thing preventing the fifteen republics of the USSR from starting a violent civil war is the pervasive presence of the KGB Interior Ministry troops and the powerful Soviet Army Divisions. When the prophesied war of Gog and Magog occurs, the Bible says that "every man's sword will be against his brother" (Ezekiel 38:21). During the last Russian civil war (1918-1922), over twenty million people lost their lives. The fear that the fifteen ethnic republics could break up and capture the massive Soviet armaments, including nuclear and chemical weapons, causes thoughtful world leaders to lie awake at night.

The prospect of a civil war in Russia makes the war in the Gulf look like a war game. With these great armaments in the hands of the various republics, the death toll of a new Russian civil war could be much worse as the "red horseman" of the Apocalypse begins his ride through Asia: "And another horse, fiery red, went out. And it was granted to the one who sat on it to take peace from the earth, and that people should kill one another; and there was given to him a great sword" (Revelation 6:4).

The war in the Gulf set the stage for a vast war throughout the Middle East which will disrupt every nation involved. When the coming War of Gog and Magog ends, all nations will find their futures altered in profound ways. It is quite possible that the casualty list could total in the millions as described by Ezekiel 39. The ramifications of this war will be felt for years to come. America may find that its natural inclination toward isolationism relative to Europe and the rest of the world will once more come to the forefront in both the populace and Congress. When Russia is defeated supernaturally, it is probable that it will result in America withdrawing from the role of "world's policemen."

While world attention has focused on the crises in Eastern Europe and the Persian Gulf, another equally dangerous situation has developed in Asia. The simmering conflict between India and Pakistan over the disputed province of Kashmir is threatening to break out into a full-fledged atomic war between these nuclear armed countries. According to recent reports from Reuters in London, both "the U.S.A. and Soviet governments fear nuclear war between India and Pakistan over the disputed Kashmir region." Intelligence reports indicate that both these countries are prepared to use their nuclear weapons in this conflict. Spy satellites have obtained photographs that show "armed convoys leaving Pakistani nuclear complexes at Kahuta, near Islamabad, and heading for military airfields." The films show "Pakistani F-16 fighter-bombers being loaded with nuclear bomb racks" (*Sunday Times*, May 27, 1990). The Soviets informed the United States that India appeared also to be putting its nuclear weapons on bombers and missiles in preparation for war. Some U.S. government officials reported off the record that "Washington fears a major catastrophe in the subcontinent." Since then the crisis has dropped into the background to a degree, but the underlying conflict remains unresolved. The fact that both these huge nations were willing to go all the way to nuclear war in 1990 remained a secret to most of the world's population. However, the risk of a nuclear tragedy remains unabated.

After years of intense espionage, Chinese intelligence agents have succeeded in stealing the secret of the American neutron bomb from the Lawrence Livermore National

Laboratory where it was developed. On September 29, 1988, the Chinese exploded their first neutron bomb. This is a special advanced type of nuclear weapon that destroys all humans and animals in a target area with deadly radiation while leaving buildings intact. The FBI confirmed that China has the "most aggressive espionage program now in operation against the United States."

Never before in the history of the world has there been so many wars and rumors of wars; and never before has there been so much potential for total destruction.

There Will Be Famines—the Black Horseman

No sooner does one country seem to recover from the devastating effects of famine than another suffers extreme drought and the resulting diseases. According to the *New York Times* (September 30, 1990), forty thousand deaths from malnutrition and disease occur every twenty-four hours, half of which could easily be avoided by using existing medical technology. One of these solutions is the disbursement of ten-cent packages of saline nutrients that effectively combat deadly dehydration; others include low-cost vaccines, vitamins and medical education programs.

The United States House of Representatives heard in October, 1990, that "starvation of apocalyptic proportions is endangering up to 11 million Sudanese, but their government is blocking international food deliveries." The Sudan, north of Ethiopia, is facing famine due to the drought and civil war. However, the military government will not allow relief experts to prevent a famine that threatens to be worse than the one in Ethiopia several years ago.

Unfortunately, population explosion always follows famine. Cho De Sing, the assistant director for the United Nations Population Fund, told the CNN television audience (May 14, 1990) that the world's population is rapidly increasing again. Tragically, this population increase is taking place on those continents least able to afford it—Africa, Asia and Latin America. Yet in wealthy countries of Western Europe and North America the population is steadily falling. The population in Third World countries alone will explode to more than 10 billion by the year 2010, more than double what it is now. This means that 90 percent of all babies born in the next twenty years will be born in countries least able to feed hungry new mouths.

To illustrate this, consider the population figures for these countries:

POPULATION DENSITY

Nation	Number of People per Square Mile
Mongolia	3
Canada	7
United States	68
China	292
India	665
Bangladesh	1970

The reasons for the population explosion are many. Some obvious ones are: (1) China and Africa are abandoning their strong population policies of the 1980s. (2) There is a lack of awareness of ways to control population because of illiteracy, or because such measures have failed in the past where they were tried. (3) There is strong opposition from the Roman Catholic Church toward birth control measures, especially in Latin America.

The United Nations report concluded as follows:

- 100 million new people will be born per year throughout the 90s.

- 512 million are now malnourished in third-world countries.

- 889 million are totally illiterate and unable to engage in industry.

- 1.7 billion live without sanitation or clean water of any kind.

- A population of 6.3 billion is expected by the year 2000.

This figure is over 200 million more people than the 6.1 billion estimate provided by the 1984 United Nations Population report. This, along with the deliberate destruction of the Amazon rain forests will lead to more drought. The erosion of farm land is hindering the growing of food where it is desperately needed, making it even more difficult to feed the people of the world in the future. Truly the "pale horse" of Revelation is rearing its fearful head. "I looked, and behold, a pale horse. And the name of him who sat on it was Death, and Hades followed with him. And power was given to them over a fourth of the earth, to kill with sword, with hunger, with death, and by the beasts of the earth" (Revelation 6:8).

Pestilence—The Pale Horseman of Death

Despite the tremendous advances of medical science we find ourselves faced with the worst disease outbreaks in history. Back in the 1950s we thought that many of the dreaded diseases of the past—malaria, tuberculosis, small pox, etc.—had almost been eliminated from the world. However, in nation after nation throughout the third world, many of these deadly epidemics are making a comeback.

The World Summit for Children reported that every day:

1,400 children die from whooping cough
4,000 children die from measles
2,150 children die from tetanus
2,750 children die from malaria
11,000 children die from diarrhea
6,000 children die from pneumonia

Several of these diseases have become very resistant to antibiotics, leading to the creation of "superbugs." Despite heroic efforts by World Vision and other organizations, a majority of Third World peoples do not have access to clean water or even minimal standards of sanitation. As Christians we have a tremendous responsibility to be our brothers' keepers and to use the resources the Lord has provided to alleviate their needs as much as possible. I encourage you to act now in a practical way to support whichever group you believe is fulfilling Christ's command to care for our brothers.

Among the worst pestilences of today are twenty-five sexually transmitted diseases that are destroying the lives of millions of people throughout the world. Several of these infections are incurable. Many lead ultimately to sterility, severe pain and even death. Our antibiotics are less and less effective with these new strains of mutated diseases.

The Aids Pestilence

AIDS is the first epidemic disease that is 100 percent fatal. Even the dreaded Black Plague in the fourteenth century only killed one third of its victims; two-thirds of those infected recovered.

The terrible killer disease, acquired immunodeficiency syndrome—AIDS—has continued its rampage for almost twelve years now. However, a staggering amount of misinformation about the disease is still being spread. The media and AIDS committees have done a terrible disservice to potential victims of this disease by selective reporting of the facts. While it has been obvious for years that homosexual activity was the major transmitting factor in AIDS, gay groups have tried to disguise these facts in order to protect themselves from adverse publicity and backlash. They have promoted "safe sex" and the use of condoms by the whole population, implying that everyone is equally at risk to catch AIDS. The truth is that AIDS is not an easy disease to catch. You have to expose yourself to it through homosexual activity, shared needles used with intravenous drugs, or transfusions of blood infected with the AIDS virus. Innocent babies are also born with AIDS from their infected mothers. The only noticeable progress in cutting down exposure has been in the careful screening of blood and blood products used in transfusions. Years ago, before the AIDS screening started, thousands acquired AIDS through tainted blood donated by infected donors. In North America, screening has cut the risk of being exposed to AIDS to less than one in three hundred thousand for the average person who does not use intravenous drugs or engage in homosexual activity.

There are continuous attempts by AIDS groups to create panic in the general population by predicting that AIDS is poised to break out into the heterosexual community. However, the statistical breakdown has remained constant for the last ten years with approximately 90 percent of new AIDS cases falling into the admitted homosexual-bisexual male groups. Some 8 percent of new cases prove to be shared-needle drug users or children of infected women drug users. Less than 2 percent of new AIDS cases are heterosexuals who do not seem to fit into any of these categories.

The Canadian Federal Centre for AIDS reported that a woman has only one chance in ten thousand of acquiring the disease if she has normal sexual relations with a man who has AIDS. There are almost no North American cases of a man receiving AIDS from an infected woman unless they already had open infections from other sexually transmitted diseases. The Centre for Disease Control released figures showing that, among college students they studied, only one in two hundred male students and one in five thousand female students were infected by the HIV virus.

It is an entirely different situation in African countries and other Third-World nations. In central Africa, doctors report that 50 percent of those infected with AIDS are women. But within these countries it is common for the average non-religious person to have over a hundred different sexual partners each year. This immoral situation causes the average sexually active partner to have up to five sexually transmitted diseases, including gonorrhea and syphilis. Poor sanitation and poor medical facilities, along with untreated open infections make it possible for the AIDS virus to pass from men to women to men in a manner that would not otherwise occur. These conditions have produced the unusually large number of male and female AIDS victims in Africa.

We are watching the beginning of a death march in Africa beyond anything ever seen before in human history. Despite the government ordered under-reporting of AIDS figures in these nations, the truth is gradually coming out. In the country formerly known as Rhodesia, the official Confederation of Zimbabwe Industry predicted in early July that "the incidence of HIV [the incipient stage of AIDS] will double every ten months, and after a decade, 90 per cent of the work-force could be dying of AIDS-related diseases." The industry group estimated that between 10 and 20 per cent of Zimbabwe's nine million people are already HIV positive. Dr. John Mafson, a medical specialist in Harare, said that between 30 and 50 per cent of hospital patients were testing positive" (Gwynne Dyer, the *Toronto Star*, July 16, 1990). These figures are staggering. They indicate that this one country will see between 20 percent and 50 percent of their population die of this horrible disease over the next few years. Yet these figures are even more astonishing when we consider that Zimbabwe is one of the least affected countries in Africa. You can understand why African governments suppress their devastating figures; they truly do affect their national security.

As you move north from Zimbabwe toward the major countries of Uganda, Zaire, Sudan, etc., the epidemic is even worse. The World Health Organization (WHO) in Geneva released their estimates on AIDS victims between now and the year 2000 for the World Summit on Children in September 26, 1990. In a drastic increase of their previous forecast, WHO now estimates that more than ten million children will contract AIDS from their infected mothers over the next nine years. The true extent of the epidemic could not be determined until these mothers had continued with the disease long enough to pass it on to their fetuses. Presently WHO forecasts that 30 percent of AIDS infected mothers will pass the disease to their babies. The other 70 percent of these children will be orphans at a very early age. This new data has forced WHO to raise its estimate to thirty million deaths from AIDS by the year 2000.

Pollution and Pestilence

Modern technology is producing ever-increasing threats to our fragile environment. Over seventy thousand new chemicals have been produced by our labs and industries in the last forty years. Less than twelve thousand have been tested as to their environmental impact. In 1988, American factories poured four and one-half million pounds of artificial chemicals into our land, air and water, according to the Environmental Protection Agency (EPA). As a result, the EPA estimates that over 50 percent of America's ground water is threatened by these wastes. Oil spills such as the one in the Alaskan Prince William Sound in 1989 by Exxon Valdez, plus the huge quantities Saddam Hussein spilled in the Persian Gulf and torched to pollute the air in

Kuwait, reveal the lack of care we display for the trust God has given to us to care for our planet.

A special report from the Associated Press on April 20, 1990, revealed that the Coast Guard had recorded over five thousand chemical and oil spills in the Great Lakes between 1980 and 1989. The Great Lakes are the major fresh water resource for both Canada and the States.

The Office of Technology Assessment told Congress in October 28, 1989, that there were more than ten thousand toxic waste sites throughout the country that will ultimately require more than $500 billion to clean up.

Global warming, ozone depletion and acid rain continue to ravage the earth while governments conduct study after study, putting off the painful, expensive, and long-term actions that could begin to remedy these problems.

The Lack of Love

"And because lawlessness will abound, the love of many will grow cold" (Matthew 24:12). An unending assault continues on those family values that make our life worthwhile. This is causing the deterioration of the normal bonds of affection which God placed in man to protect the family.

An epidemic of child abuse—physical, emotional and sexual— is afflicting all countries today. Parents can hardly trust their children into the care of anyone, not even close relatives, in this lawless and wicked generation. Just as prevalent is the emotional and physical abuse of elderly parents by their hostile children and the rise of wife abuse.

In a demonstration of a twisted value system, we find the same people marching on Saturday to protect whales and dolphins, then on Sunday holding a rally to protect the rights of a woman and her doctor to destroy the life of her unborn infant. I used to believe that the reason these people supported unlimited abortion was that they truly believed that the unborn fetus was not a living person. When medical evidence began to prove that the fetus can survive out of the womb at earlier and earlier stages in the development cycle, I expected many pro-abortion activists to change to a position where they would refuse to support abortion after the fifth month of pregnancy. Not so. When I listen to these people discuss these questions I realize that they support unlimited abortion on demand regardless of whether the fetus is truly a living human. It has been reliably reported that in a number of cases the aborted fetus has emerged from the womb as a living, breathing baby. Doctors in charge simply abandoned these "aborted" babies to die without food or water. Surely this is an example of love growing "cold" as Jesus prophesied.

Another terrible example of love growing cold was recently reported from Brazil where hundreds of thousands of abandoned children live on the streets in appalling conditions without government assistance. The London *Daily Telegraph* reported on September 26, 1990, that their Rio de Janeiro correspondent had evidence that Brazilian children are being sold abroad for organ transplants. Many countries have a very long waiting list for organ transplants. Tragically, some rich people who are unwilling to wait their turn have made unholy arrangements to buy the needed organs from unscrupulous "Frankenstein" doctors. Two Italian judges, Signor Angelo Gargani and Signor Cesare Matellino, said many Brazilian babies, who were given up for adoption, are being sent to special clinics in Mexico and Thailand where their organs are being removed and sold for transplant operations in Europe at prices up to $80 thousand per organ.

Recent reports from China show another example of the breakdown of human values. The Associated Press report from Beijing on May 21, 1990, said that more than fifty-five hundred mentally retarded people were sterilized against their will in the previous year in the small province of Gansu. Officials admit they will sterilize another 260 thousand mentally retarded people within the next year. Government officials are instructed to "reduce the births of inferior and abnormal children to a minimum," according to the *China Daily* newspaper. Officials admit that there are over 50 million physically or mentally handicapped people in the nation who will ultimately be sterilized under these laws.

These draconian laws complete the population plan for China which also includes the one-child policy I reported in my book *Armageddon—Appointment with Destiny*. This policy from 1978 on prevents any Chinese couple from having more than one child. Most couples prefer a boy to maintain the family name and to support the parents in their old age. With new sex determination techniques, these couples abort female fetuses until the wife becomes pregnant with a male fetus, which she then carries to term. Each year for the last ten years, as a result of female fetus abortions, nine boys have been born for every girl baby. This situation has caused a population time bomb for China and the world. The book of Revelation says that a 200 million-man army will come from the east to participate at Armageddon. Until this decade it was impossible to conceive how any group of nations could create such a massive army. In 1986 Chinese officials told me that China will have over 125 million single young men of military age by the late 1990s. With no women for them to marry it is possible to see how the Chinese government will send them out to conquer the world in the greatest army in human history. The combination of China's manpower and Japan's military-industrial capacity will fulfill Revelation's prophecy that "the number of the army of the horseman was two hundred million" (Revelation 9:16).

A Return to Sanhedrin Laws

Jesus' words about the "abomination of desolation" and the reference to fleeing in winter or the Sabbath seems strange to us. Some may not know about the ancient Sanhedrin laws—rabbinical interpretations of the laws which God gave to Moses—concerning a Sabbath day's journey.

The Sanhedrin, the Jewish high court, considered a Sabbath day's journey to be the distance from the Temple Mount to the Mount of Olives—one thousand paces. This was their interpretation of the Commandment, "The seventh day is the Sabbath [rest] day of the Lord your God. In it you shall do no work" (Exodus 20:10). Distances farther than a thousand paces would constitute work. Righteous Jews have often been killed in battle when they were attacked by their enemies on the Sabbath. They would not retreat more than a thousand paces, even to save their lives. Their enemies sometimes would attack on the Sabbath for that very reason.

These words of Christ concerning the last days indicate that Israel will return to the religious (or Sanhedrin) law as the law of their land. In this regard it is fascinating to observe that Israel is passing more and more religious laws, especially regarding the Sabbath regulations. In the political maneuvering for power in Israel, the government of Prime Minister Yitzhak Shamir passed strict new religious laws on November 19, 1990, after obtaining the support of another religious party, the ultra-orthodox Agudat Israel. According to the *Jerusalem Post*, the new laws forbid buses to operate on the Sabbath day from sundown Friday to sundown Saturday and on major Jewish festivals. There are a number of areas in Israel now where you cannot drive your car on the Sabbath; even taxi drivers cannot operate in these areas. In addition, laws have been enacted to ban pork sales and indecent advertising, and limit the possibility of obtaining an abortion.

These Sabbath laws and customs, together with the renewed calls to reconvene the ancient Sanhedrin, suggest strongly that we are entering the time when all of Christ's prophecy will be fulfilled.

The Gospel of the Kingdom Preached to the World

Included in Matthew's account of the signs of the times and the end of the age are Jesus' words about revival: "And this gospel of the kingdom will be preached in all the world as a witness to all the nations, and then the end will come" (Matthew 24:14).

Many in North America are concerned that while there is an exciting surge of evangelism throughout the world and the gospel truly is being preached "in all the world," there is little evidence of revival in our own country. Despite years of prayer, tremendous numbers of ministries, untold millions of dollars invested in innovative evangelism programs, and heartfelt efforts of many churches and para-church ministries, the results in our own nations have been far less than we expected. For decades we have anticipated the coming revival in North America. We must continue to pray that the Lord will move upon our nations in a sovereign move of grace before the Rapture. Time is running out!

It is true that revival is taking place in unprecedented proportions throughout many countries outside of Europe and North America. Countries that have resisted the gospel for centuries are now responding in a tremendous way to the message of Christ. A hundred years of sacrificial missionary labors within China had created one million Chinese believers. These Western missionary workers were expelled in 1949 by the communist government of Mao Tse-Tung. However, this expulsion and the subsequent persecution of the Church in China, rather than lead to extinction, resulted in the most explosive increase in believers in history. In 1990, after forty-one years of murderous persecution, there were over 80 million born-again believers in the underground church in China. This same evangelism explosion is also evident throughout Africa, Russia, Eastern Europe, and Latin America. It is estimated that, at the present rate, over 50 percent of the population of Africa will have accepted Christ by the year 1995. Therefore, we rejoice that in much of the planet the world's greatest revival in two thousand years is underway. But that still does not answer the question many North Americans ask: When will revival come to North America?

During many years of evangelistic work in both Canada and the United States I have discussed this problem with a number of ministers and evangelists. For a time I thought the main problem was that our citizens had become complacent and familiar with Christ. Many who have grown up with the message of the gospel no longer listen to the claims of Christ. However, today we have a generation of youth who has not grown up in Sunday school. Most North Americans know almost nothing about the Bible other than generalities. Yet their lack of familiarity with the Bible has not made them especially open to evangelism since they eagerly turn to cults for spiritual guidance.

Part of the reason why North America is not in revival may stem from a "rich young ruler" complex. Soldiers, priests, fishermen, the poor, the sick and the needy all willingly followed Jesus. One of the few who walked away was the "rich young ruler." He was impressed by Jesus and wanted to know how he could achieve eternal life. However, he rejected what Jesus told him because it meant he would have to "sell all that you have and distribute to the poor, and you will have treasure in heaven; and come, follow Me" (Luke 18:22). Of course, it was not the riches in and of themselves that were evil, but Jesus knew that this particular rich young man would choose riches over Christ as Lord of his life.

Relatively few wealthy people throughout history have truly followed Jesus. The tragic fact is that most men will not repent of their sin and turn to follow Christ when they are at the top of the mountain. Most of us find God in the valleys of our lives, not on the mountain tops. It is when we are confronted by our limitations, sickness, or tragedy, that we turn to God and confess our need of Him.

Wealth—A Sign of the Last Days

For the first time in history many in North America and Western Europe live in an economy that allows us to live like the rich young ruler of the Gospel. Except for those, such as the homeless, who have fallen between the cracks of our society's safety nets, the average person in our culture lives better than most kings of Europe did in the twelfth century. Consider the quality of our food, shelter, sanitation, medicine, labor laws, wages, and our freedom of speech. Most of us live better today than King Henry II of England. During much of history, even monarchs and nobility lived in unhealthy, damp, stone castles. They ate rotting food liberally sprinkled with spices to disguise the smell. Imagine living during a time when there was no aspirin or other reliable medicines and sewage ran down the open streets. Those who were not among the nobility lived in even worse squaller with little hope for themselves or their children. Even today the vast majority of the world's people still live in conditions such as those in Europe of the twelfth century. With so little hope or joy in this life, these people are open to their need for God and a better tomorrow in the next life.

Tragically, North American men and women respond to the gospel as Christ described the Church at Laodicea: "You say, 'I am rich, have become wealthy, and have need of nothing'—and do not know that you are wretched, poor blind, and naked" (Revelation 3:17).

James, in his epistle, gives a warning for the last days: "Come now, you rich, weep and howl for your miseries that are coming upon you! Your riches are corrupted, and your garments are moth-eaten. Your gold and silver are corroded, and their corrosion will be a witness against you and will eat your flesh like fire. You have heaped up treasure in the last days."

Then James contrasts the obscene wealth of the rich with the bleak poverty of the poor. "Indeed the wages of the laborers who mowed your fields, which you kept back by fraud, cry out; and the cries of the reapers have reached the ears of the Lord of Sabaoth" (James 5:1-4). The outrageous greed manifested in this last decade is unparalleled in Western history. North America was founded on the premise of opportunity for all, and the promise of a vital democracy of equals. Yet the American dream is today corrupted by a frantic accumulation of wealth by the rich, privileged few, so that a growing number of people are shut out of the system entirely. I am a strong supporter of free enterprise, business growth, and individual initiative; however, I think there is something fundamentally wrong with the situation that is developing today.

The rich are becoming richer while the average worker is slipping farther behind every year. During the last decade the incomes of the richest 1 percent of Americans rose 87 percent while the incomes of the poorest households dropped 5 percent. The average income of this top 1 percent is now $400,000 a year. Changes in the tax structure have aggravated this trend to the point where "the combined incomes of the richest 2.5 million Americans now nearly equals the combined incomes of the 100 million Americans with the lowest incomes," according to the report from the Center on Budget and Policy Priorities (*Los Angeles Times*, July 25, 1990).

This frantic search for wealth has by and large produced the most unhappy group of citizens in our history. While more and more people are becoming workaholics in a vain attempt to find meaning in their work and the things money will buy, the accumulation of wealth and status will not produce the personal happiness they seek.

In this chapter we have examined the fulfillment of many of the signs that will precede the coming King. Even though Jesus warns us that "of that day and hour no one knows, no, not even the angels of heaven," He also cautions us to "watch therefore,...be ready, for the Son of Man is coming" (Matthew 24:36,44). He warned about another time when people were unaware that their lives were threatened: "As it was in the days of Noah, so it will be also in the days of the Son of Man: They ate, they drank, they married wives, they were given in marriage, until the day that Noah entered the ark, and the flood came and destroyed them all. Likewise as it was also in the days of Lot: They ate, they drank, they bought, they sold, they planted, they built; but on the day that Lot went out of Sodom it rained fire and brimstone from heaven and destroyed them all. Even so will it be in the day when the Son of Man is revealed" (Luke 17:26-30).

The promise of the coming of the Messiah is the only hope for a world facing destruction. The Messiah is coming! "He who testifies to these things says, 'Surely I am coming quickly.' Amen. Even so, come, Lord Jesus!" (Revelation 22:20).

How do the various religions of the world see the coming Christ? In Part II of this book we will discuss the expectations of the Messiah by the Jews, Muslims, and Christians. The search for the Messiah will lead us into a fascinating area of research.

PART II

The Search for the Messiah

"Then I saw heaven opened, and behold, a white horse. And He who sat on him was called Faithful and True, and in righteousness He judges and makes war. His eyes were like a flame of fire, and on His head were many crowns. He had a name written that no one knew except Himself. He was clothed with a robe dipped in blood, and His name is called The Word of God" (Revelation. 19:11-13).

CHAPTER 8

Israel's Search for the Messiah

Judaism, Christianity, and Islam, the world's three major religions, all focus their hopes and dreams on a future Messiah. All of their writings include prophecies about the coming of a Messiah—"God's Anointed"—to redeem mankind. Exodus 30 tells how Moses was to blend a mixture of spices and oils, "compounded according to the art of the perfumer" (Exodus 30:25), into a "holy anointing oil" to be used only for very special anointing. Samuel used this holy oil to anoint both Saul and David as kings of Israel. The act of anointing confirmed the coronation of the king. Hence, the name "Messiah" was applied to the great future King of Israel.

The hope for a Messiah was born in the hearts of Adam and Eve in God's first prophecy about a "Seed" of "the woman" (Genesis 3:15). The revelation continued throughout the Old Testament until the last prophet predicted that "He is coming," the "Sun of Righteousnes shall arise with healing in His wings" (Malachi 3:1; 4:2). Israel's institutions of worship, the Tabernacle, priesthood, sacrifices, and the Law also anticipated as well as revealed the promise of the Messiah. Moses, the great Lawgiver, promised Israel a future redeemer: "The Lord your God will raise up for you a Prophet like me from your midst, from your brethren. Him you shall hear" (Deuteronomy 18:15).

Hope for the Messiah in the Old Testament

In the Old Testament, when referring to an anointed person, "Messiah" is used only twice (Daniel 9:25-26) and is a description of that One who will come from God to save

His people. This special One is also described as:

A Seed	Genesis 3:15; 12:1-3
A Priest	Psalm 10:4
A King	Jeremiah 23:5
A Prince	Daniel 9:25
Son of God	Psalm 2:7-8
Son of Man	Daniel 7:13
Immanuel-God with us	Isaiah 7:14
A Branch	Jeremiah 23:5; Zecheriah 3:8
A Servant	Isaiah 42:1-4

The Messiah's mission will be to:

Introduce the new covenant	Jeremiah 31:31-34
Preach the gospel	Isaiah 61:1-3
Bring peace	Isaiah 9:6
Die for man's sin	Isaiah 53:4-6
Unite God's people	Isaiah 19:23-25
Call the Gentiles	Isaiah 11:10
Be a priest	Zechariah 6:12-13)
Rule from David's throne	Psalm 45:5-7
Bring everlasting righteousness	Daniel 9:24).

The Greek word for Messiah is *Christos*. This word is the source of the word "Christ" and "Christian." Christians are "ones who follow the Anointed One."

The Jews did not focus strong hope for a deliverer, their Messiah, until that historic period "between the Testaments." Then both Jews and Samaritans began to hope fervently that God would send the Messiah to deliver them from their constant bondage to conquering kingdoms. By the time Jesus began His ministry, hope for the Messiah was strong and increasing. All devout Jews were looking for that One who would conquer Rome and once again make Israel a powerful nation.

When John the Baptist began preaching his message of repentance, the oppressed Jews were ready to listen to a Prophet who could give them hope. They asked John if he was the Christ. He replied that he was not but there was One among them who was the "Lamb of God." Andrew, Simon Peter's brother and one of John's disciples, understood who John was referring to and began to follow Jesus. Then, "He first found his own brother Simon, and said to him, 'We have found the Messiah' (which is translated, the Christ)" (John 1:41).

The Samaritan woman at the well of Sychar told Jesus, "'I know that Messiah is coming' (who is called Christ). 'When He comes, He will tell us all things'" (John 4:25). These two incidents indicate that worshipers of the God of Abraham in the first century were looking for the Messiah.

Old Testament prophecies contains many promises for a Savior who will come to "preach good tidings to the poor;...to heal the brokenhearted, to proclaim liberty to the captives, and the opening of the prison to those who are bound; to proclaim the acceptable day of the Lord, and the day of vengeance of our God; to comfort all who mourn; to console those who mourn in Zion" (Isaiah 61:1-3).

When God told Abraham that "in you all the families of the earth shall be blessed" (Genesis 12:3), and, "Your wife shall bear you a son, and you shall call his name Isaac; I will establish My covenant with him for an everlasting covenant, and with his descendants after him" (Genesis 17:19), He was referring to the coming Messiah.

Messiah will descend from the tribe of Judah:

> The scepter shall not depart from Judah, nor a lawgiver from between his feet, until Shiloh comes; and to Him shall be the obedience of the people (Genesis 49:10).

He will be the heir to David's throne:

> Of the increase of His government and peace there will be no end, upon the throne of David and over His kingdom, to order it and establish it with judgment and justice from that time forward, even forever. The zeal of the Lord of hosts will accomplish this (Isaiah 9:7).

He will reign forever:

> Your throne, O God, is forever and ever; a scepter of righteousness is the scepter of Your kingdom. You love righteousness and hate wickedness; therefore God, Your God, has anointed You with

the oil of gladness more than Your companion (Psalm 45:6-7).

He will be born in Bethlehem to a virgin:

But you, Bethlehem Ephrathah, though you are little among the thousands of Judah, yet out of you shall come forth to Me the One to be ruler in Israel, whose goings forth have been from of old (Micah 5:2).

Therefore the Lord Himself will give you a sign: Behold the virgin shall conceive and bear a Son, and shall call His name Immanuel (Isaiah 7:14).

Even though He is the Son of God, the Anointed One: He would be rejected by His own people:

I will declare the decree: The Lord has said to Me, You are My Son, today I have begotten You (Psalm 2:7).

He is despised and rejected by men, a man of sorrows and acquainted with grief. And we hid, as it were, our faces from Him; He was despised, and we did not esteem Him (Isaiah 53:3).

Who has believed our report? And to whom has the arm of the Lord been revealed? (Isaiah 53: 1).

He would be betrayed by a close friend:

Even my own familiar friend in whom I trusted, who ate my bread, has lifted up his heel against me (Psalm 41:9)

He would be sold out for thirty pieces of silver:

Then I said to them, "If it is agreeable to you, give me my wages; and if not, refrain." So they weighed out for my wages thirty pieces of silver (Zechariah 11:12)

He would be crucified as a criminal:

He poured out His soul unto death, and was numbered with the transgressors, and He bore the sin of many, and made intercession for the transgressors" (Isaiah 53:12).

He would then be forsaken by God:

> My God, My God, why have You forsaken Me? Why are you so far from helping Me, and from the words of My groaning?" (Psalm 22:1).

He would die and be buried with the rich:

> And they made His grave with the wicked—But with the rich at His death, because He had done no violence, nor was any deceit in His mouth (Isaiah 53:9).

But Messiah would be the victor:

> For you will not leave my soul in Sheol, nor will you allow your Holy One to see corruption (Psalm 16:10).

> But God will redeem my soul from the power of the grave, for He shall receive me (Psalm 49:15).

He would arise from the dead, ascend into heaven and reign with God His Father:

> You have ascended on high, you have led captivity captive; You have received gifts among men, even among the rebellious, that the Lord God might dwell there (Psalm 68:18).

> The prophets of God had much to say about this One who would come to redeem God's people from their sins and their enemies. But when Jesus came and proclaimed that He was the promised Messiah, the Jews did not believe Him. They were unable to connect the prophecies of God's Word with this rabbi from Nazareth.

The Third Book of Sybil predicted that the Jews and all other nations would finally find peace under the reign of the Messiah. God would use the Messiah to end all wars and establish universal righteousness under His protection. Then all nations will turn to God's Law and the Lord will dwell in Zion.

An examination of these and other prophecies in the books of Sybil will convince anyone that they are a simple restating of the biblical prophecies in a non-Jewish format.

They were well known throughout the empire at that time. The distribution of these writings created a situation where the gentile Roman world was prepared for the claims of Jesus Christ and His disciples. People who would never have been interested in the prophecies of the small nation of Israel became very fascinated by the predictions when they were presented under this format.

Additional Apocalyptic-Messianic Writings

There were many other extra-biblical books written during this period that predicted a Messiah coming and establishing His kingdom. The writings prepared the Jews for the birth of Jesus when the angels proclaimed Him to be the "Savior, who is Christ the Lord" (Luke 2:11). The following are brief descriptions of some of these references.

The Apocalypse of the Twelve Patriarchs was written in Hebrew and promised that Messiah would come and judge the entire world. It claimed that when He came He would remove the curse from the earth that had continued since Adam and Eve sinned in the Garden. The Messiah would remove the flaming sword of the cherubim that guarded the Garden, open the gates of Paradise to mankind, and finally allow mankind to enjoy the fruit of the tree of life so that they could live forever with God.

The Ethiopic Book of Enoch outlined the concept of the Messiah in a new light that was very close to the position expounded by the New Testament writers. It presented the Messiah as a person with supernatural powers, including raising people from the dead, understanding all spiritual things, and possessing an identity almost akin to God Himself. His titles include "the anointed," "the elect one," "the righteous," and most interesting of all, "the son of man."

The Psalms of Solomon (different from the psalms of Solomon in the biblical book of Psalms) tell about the Messiah cleansing Jerusalem and Israel from its sins, judging the tribes, dividing the land of Palestine. He was presented as living without sin and being in the special presence of the Holy Spirit; but He would not live forever.

Rabbinical Teachings on the Messiah

Many of the teachings of the rabbis included truths from the Old Testament. They taught that just before the Messiah comes there will be a time of unparalleled troubles throughout the world. One of the great themes told of the Messiah and of Israel's war with Gog and Magog. The writing known as *Eduyoth* II, 10 suggests that the Russian armies would be devastated by God at the end of a terrible war that would last for twelve months.

The *Sanhedrin* 110B documents stated that the Ten Tribes would finally return to Israel when the Messiah returned.

Yalkut (vol. I, 159), taught that the magnificent Temple would be rebuilt by the Messiah as foretold by the Prophet Zechariah: "The Branch will build the Temple."

Yoma 5b contains an account describing how the lost treasures of the Temple will finally be returned to the Holy City of Zion by the Messiah while Aaron and the Kohanin (the priests descended from Aaron) will once more lead in worship on the Temple Mount.

Yalkut, a commentary on Isaiah 9, says that during the reign of the Messiah He will introduce a new law. While the prophets often talked about God introducing a New Covenant with Israel when the Messiah comes, most Jewish authorities have resisted this notion because Christians claim that this is precisely what Jesus of Nazareth did.

Pesahim 118b teaches about the messianic hope of achieving peace in a politically independent and secure state. Some teachers looked to the Old Testament prophecies of Isaiah and others and believed that Israel will be the foremost nation in the world during the Messianic age. Egypt, Ethiopia, and even Ishmael (the Arabs) will carry tribute and gifts to the Messiah in Jerusalem.

The Messianic Hope in Extra-Biblical Writings

After the book of Malachi was completed in 396 B.C., the canon of the Old Testament was finalized by the Great

Synagogue. However, the religious hopes and yearnings of the Jewish people inspired a number of books during the period from 400 B.C. to the birth of Jesus Christ that are not accepted as God-inspired Scripture. Books written during this "silent period" between the Old and New Testaments have sometimes been studied diligently over the past two thousand years, and other times ignored. Students of "apocalyptic literature" will discern a great difference between the writings in Scripture and these non-canonical books. They will also discover, however, much valuable Middle East history of that time and an understanding of how Jews in this intertestamental period anticipated the fulfillment of Messianic prophecies and their coming redemption.

In this section we will examine some of these extra-biblical writings and their references to the Messiah.

The Apocryphal Books of Tobit and Maccabees

The first example of this non-biblical history is the book of Tobit. Tobit was written during the second century before Christ. In this story the protagonist, Tobit, talks about a coming King whose "light will shine brightly to all the ends of the earth. Many nations shall come to you from afar, from all the corners of the earth to your holy name; they shall bring gifts in their hands for the King of heaven. In you endless generations shall utter their joy; the name of the chosen city shall endure for ever and ever" (13:11).

The Apocryphal books of 1 and 2 Maccabees is probably the most historically reliable account in the Apocryphal writings. It is from these books that we find what happened in Israel after Alexander the Great died. One of Alexander's evil successors, Antiochus, tried to destroy Judaism but was conquered by an army led by Judas Maccabaeus and his sons. Yet, despite this heroic conquest of the evil Antiochus Epiphanes, no one thought of Judas Maccabaeus as the promised Messiah. The people knew that the Messiah must come from the royal line of David and be born in Bethlehem. Since Judas did not meet these qualifications, neither he nor anyone else claimed that he was more than a warrior sent by God to deliver his people.

The Books of Sybil

Another interesting book from this "silent" period that expresses the Jews' hope for the Messiah, was the Third Book of Sybil. These prophetic books were written by the Jews of Alexander, Egypt, and widely distributed throughout the Mediterranean world during the Roman Empire period. The Roman Senate and Emperors often used these sealed prophecies, which were kept under guard in the archives, to gain wisdom as to proposed courses of action.

Among these prophecies, which are derived from the prophetic portions of the Old Testament, are many Messianic predictions. One included the prediction that "a king would arise from the East who would rule the entire world." This prophecy was so widely known that it played a significant role in the rise to power of Emperor Vespasian. Vespasian defeated the Jewish rebellion against Rome from A.D. 66 to 70. Vespasian and his supporters used this prophecy to convince many of his right to rule the empire. Even the historian Flavius Josephus referred to this prediction when he foretold that General Vespasian, a commoner at the time who was not in the Julian family that produced all the Caesars, would ultimately become emperor of Rome (The Wars of the Jews 3:9).

The Zohar contains a great deal of mystical speculation about the future messianic kingdom. One of the major features of its study is the Suffering Messiah, that He in some way entered "the palace of diseases" and bore our sufferings. They also taught that the Messiah will actually become the sin offering that must be offered to God. Since the Temple is destroyed at this time, making the offering physically impossible, they believed that the Messiah would fulfill this function in Himself. This is fascinating in its close connection with the Christian concept of Jesus the Messiah becoming the atoning Sin-Offering for all who believe in Him.

The Zohar sees the Messiah, son of Joseph, occupying a seat in the "lower heights" of heaven. It is interesting that the Zohar accept the preexistence of the Messiah and assigns him divine character. He suffers for the sins of the people and carries the punishment for sin upon Himself. When the Messiah comes He will open the gates of wisdom and usher in the Kingdom of God, the seventh millennium, the thousand years of contemplation of God and rest in His presence.

The *Book of Zerubbabel* also presents two Messiahs. The first Messiah was the son of Joseph and used the name "Nehemiah ben Husheil"; the second was Messiah ben David who the Book of Zerubbabel names "Menahem ben Amierl." He also refers to the appearance of Elijah, a marble statute, and Armilus—an antichrist figure who is born from Satan. It is obvious that there was a cross-fertilization of ideas from the book of Revelation (Beth Hamidrash, vol. II, pp. 54-57, by Jellinek).

The Talmud and Mishnah Torah

Moses Maimonides, a Jewish philosopher, jurist and physician who lived in the twelfth century, believed that the key to fulfilling both the Torah (the books of Moses) and Mitzvot (the Commandments) was the reestablishment of the monarchy. In his view, "The king's [Messiah's] purpose and intent shall be to elevate the true faith and fill the world with justice, destroying the power of the wicked and waging the wars of God" (Halachah 4:10).

The coming of the Messiah not only fulfills prophecies but is also the key event that will allow Israel to complete the true aim of Torah—the sanctification of God's Holy name.

In the Mishnah Torah, Maimonides declares the centrality of the Messiah to the future of both Israel and the world: "He will build the Temple, gather the dispersed of Israel. Then, in his days, [the observance of] all the statutes will return to their previous state. We will offer sacrifices and observe the Sabbatical and Jubilee years, according to all their particulars mentioned by the Torah" (Halachah 11:1).

In an upcoming chapter we will explore additional material of Maimonides relating to Israel's longing for their

Messiah. Not only the Jews, but the Muslims as well, looked forward to a Messiah who would fulfill the predictions of the Old Testament prophets.

In the next chapter we will study some astonishing material relating to Islamic prophecies and the coming apocalypse. Additionally, we will examine from the Koran itself the tremendous historical evidence about the life, death, and resurrection of Jesus.

CHAPTER 9

Islam and
the Coming Messiah

One of the most significant players in the current crisis in the Persian Gulf has been dead for almost fourteen hundred years. His name was Abu al-Qasim Muhammad ibn 'Abd Allah ibn 'Abd al-Muttalib ibn Hashim. Fortunately, he is known to the world today by the shorter name of Muhammad. He was born in the Saudi Arabian Peninsula in A.D. 570 and launched his religion in A.D. 622. The Islam religion now has over 1.7 billion followers.

Muhammad accepted the divine authority of the Bible's Pentateuch, the Psalms and the Gospels. He often appealed to readers of his Koran to note the convergence in the doctrine between themes found in the Bible and the Koran.

One of the basic tenets of the Koran is that one day there will be a general resurrection of all men to participate in the general judgment. After dying, according to Islamic teaching, every person will be interviewed by two terrible angels, named Monker and Nakir, while sitting up in his grave. Because of this, some Muslims had their graves built in such a manner that a corpse would have sufficient room to sit up.

Islam teaches that the time of the Resurrection is known only to God. Muhammad is said to have asked the angel Gabriel about its timing and was told that no one but God Himself knew the day. Jesus also told His disciples five hundred years earlier, "Of that day and hour no one knows, no, not even the angels of heaven, but My Father only" [Matthew 24:36]). Islam also teaches that there are a series of events which will precede and forewarn men of the approaching appointment with God's judgment.

In light of the recent Middle East crisis and the rise of Muslim fundamentalism from North Africa to Indonesia, it is worthwhile to attempt to understand the beliefs that underlie the profound political, military and religious movements in this critical area of the world. The signs of the approaching apocalypse found in the Koran fall into two different groups: The lesser prophetic signs and the greater prophetic signs.

The Lesser Prophetic Signs:

1. The decay of faith and the rise of sensuality
2. Tumults and seditions everywhere
3. A great war with the Turks and great distress throughout the world
4. The rebellion of Iraq and Syria
5. The expansion of the sacred city of Medina.

The Greater Prophetic Signs:

1. There will be supernatural signs in the heaven, including the rising of the sun in the West, a special eclipse of the moon and smoke filling the whole earth.
2. There will be war with the Greeks (Europeans) and the capture of Constantinople by seventy thousand Jews; during the victory the Antichrist will arise.
3. The Antichrist, called al Masih al Dajjal (the false or lying Christ) will come; he will have one eye and be marked on the forehead with the letters CFR, which stands for Cafer or infidel; he will be the last in a series of antichrists; the Jews will initially accept him as Messiah ben David, believing he will be the one who will restore the kingdom to them; the Antichrist will appear near Iraq and Syria, will ride on a colt, will be followed by seventy thousand Jews, will lay waste many places, and finally be killed by Jesus who is to encounter him at the gate [the sealed Eastern Gate].
4. A terrible war will be fought with the Jews involving the Muslims and barbarians from Magog (Yajuj and Majuj); they will drain the Sea of Tiberias for water and attack

Jerusalem; Jesus and God will together destroy the army and a great sacrifice will be provided for the animals and birds; it will take seven years to burn the weapons until God cleanses the Earth with rain.

5. Jesus will descend to Earth somewhere near Damascus, defeat the armies of the Antichrist and kill him; after that, Jesus will provide great security, prosperity and peace; all hatred and malice will be destroyed and nature will be tamed, with lions and lambs at peace.

6. The Arabs will return to pagan worship.

7. A tremendous heap of gold and silver is discovered under the Euphrates River which will lead to the destruction of many.

8. The Caaba, or Temple of Mecca, will be destroyed by the Ethiopian army.

9. Fire will break out in Yemen.

10. The Mohdi or Director will come, believed to be a direct descendent of Muhammad the Prophet (Muhammad Abu'Ikasem), the last of the twelve Imams (spiritual leaders) born in year 255 of Hejra (the Arab calendar).

11. Three great blasts of a trumpet will sound: blast of consternation; blast of examination; blast of resurrection.

The Koran teaches that there will be a period of judgment of the kingdom which will last one thousand years following the great crisis which ends this age.

A Similarity to Biblical Prophecy

Although there are a number of unusual features to this Islamic eschatology, many of the prophecies were borrowed directly from the Old or New Testaments. Prominent places are given to Jesus, the Antichrist, the Millennium, and the war of Gog and Magog. Since Muhammad quoted from the prophets Ezekiel, Daniel, Joel, Isaiah, and Jesus, it is not surprising that so many features of Jewish and Christian apocalyptic are found in his writings.

The book of Revelation says that during the terrible period known as the Great Tribulation, 144 thousand Jewish witnesses from the twelve tribes will witness to the whole world about the approaching Kingdom of Christ and the coming King. The prophet John said that the response to the teaching of these witnesses and the supernatural proclamation of the angelic messengers will lead to the greatest spiritual revival in history. John describes "a great multitude which no one could number, of all nations, tribes, peoples, and tongues, standing before the Lamb" (Revelation 7:9). Later, the angel identifies this immense group as "the ones who come out of the great tribulation" (v. 14). I believe a major response to the outpouring of the message of God will come from the great unreached and unevangelized peoples of the world. Some of those in North America who have heard the name of Jesus will obviously respond to the supernatural events and message of the tribulation, because the angel says that they will come from "all nations, tribes, peoples, and tongues." However, it is unlikely that an enormous number of those who have rejected the gentle claims of Christ during the Age of Grace will suddenly accept Jesus when believing will lead either to martyrdom under the Antichrist or to exile. It is probable that the greatest response will come from among the millions of unreached peoples, including Muslim and Hindu countries where over half of all humanity live.

It seems likely that the teachings about Jesus and the Antichrist in the Koran could be used by the Lord to prepare the Muslim people to accept the truth of the gospel message preached by the witnesses during the Tribulation period.

The Koran's Teachings About Jesus the Messiah

Years ago I read that the Muslims and their Koran accepted a great deal of the truths about Jesus as revealed in the gospels of the New Testament. I felt, initially, that the author must have overstated the case. However, after talking with Muslim Arabs in Jerusalem and doing further research, I am convinced that the Koran does attest to the historicity of Jesus of Nazareth. Muhammad not only mentions Jesus but actually discusses His birth, life, teachings, death, and resurrection in detail. There are twenty-eight specific and detailed references to the life of Jesus in the Koran. Also, the Koran repeats many New Testament prophecies about the return of Jesus to save the Jewish people from the invasion of the Antichrist's army. All of these writings will prepare Muslims to finally understand who Jesus truly is during the Great Tribulation period.

Some of these quotes from the Koran will show what Muhammad taught about Jesus. (References such as "6:86" refer to section and line numbers). Jesus is acknowledged as a legitimate prophet of God: "Zecharias and John, Jesus and Elias (all were upright men)" (6:86). Although the Koran denies that Jesus is the only begotten Son of God, it does declare that He was the son of Mary and delivered the true gospel. "'I am the messenger of your Lord...and have come to give you a holy son.' 'How shall I bear a child,' [Mary] answered, 'when I am a virgin, untouched by man?'" (19:19-20). "We [God] sent forth Jesus, the son of Mary, confirming the Torah already revealed, and gave him the Gospel, in which there is guidance and light, corroborating what was revealed before it in the Torah, a guide and an admonition to the righteous" (5:46). Jesus is declared as the promised Messiah: "The angels said to Mary: 'God bids you rejoice in a word from Him. His name is the Messiah, Jesus the son of Mary'" (3:45). The Koran affirms the authority of Jesus' teaching: God said, "I am sending one to you. But whoever of you disbelieves hereafter shall be punished as no man will ever be punished" (5:115). It tells of His resurrection: "'I was blessed on the day I was born, and blessed I shall be on the day of my death and may peace be upon me on the day when I shall be raised to life.' Such was Jesus, the son of Mary. That is the whole truth, which they still doubt" (19:32-34).

In a book published in 1979, *Jesus a Prophet of Islam*, author Muhammad 'Ataur-Rahim presents the position that Jesus was sent by God as a prophet to bring men to the truth. As a Muslim, 'Ataur-Rahim rejects the Bible's claim that Jesus is the Son of God because he believes this would contradict his belief in monotheism. However, quoting extensively from the Koran and other Islamic sources, he states that Muslims accept the miracles, the escape to Egypt, the visit to the Temple when Jesus was twelve, the seventy disciples and the twelve close disciples, and the forty days of temptation. Obviously these and many other details in the Koran are derived from the gospels and the wide-spread knowledge of the life of Jesus. While the Koran accepts that there was a crucifixion, there is a disagreement over who was actually crucified. However, it does accept the resurrection of Jesus.

Islam and the Temple Mount

The Temple Mount is also sacred for more than one billion Muslim peoples of the world. The whole Temple Mount area is called the Haram ash-Sharif, which means "noble sanctuary." The area is the third most holy site for Muslims after Mecca and Medina in Saudi Arabia. Mecca and Medina are much more closely associated with the life and actions of Muhammad and his disciples than Jerusalem. However, the Muslims believe that Muhammad visited the Noble Sanctuary and, according to the tradition, he departed to the seventh heaven on his white horse, Burak, from the very rock which is now located under the Dome of the Rock. The Al-Aqsa Mosque, at the far edge of the Temple Mount, is believed by Muslims to be referred to in the Koran as the "far place" associated with this journey of Muhammad from Jerusalem.

There are a number of Islamic buildings and structures on the surface of the Temple Mount today, the most prominent and beautiful being the Golden Dome of the Rock. Many people mistakenly refer to the Dome of the Rock as the Mosque of Omar. While the Dome is a shrine that is used for prayer, the only proper mosque is the Al-Aqsa Mosque located several hundred yards to the south on the edge of the southern wall. A mosque is used for both preaching, prayers, and other religious services, while a shrine is used only for contemplation and prayers.

From the year 691, when the area was captured from the Persians, until the opening of the Dome of the Rock in 1856, the death penalty was in effect for any infidel or non-believer who entered the Dome of the Noble Sanctuary. While several brave explorers and worshipers risked their lives to provide first-hand research about the Temple Mount during earlier centuries, serious explorations could only take place after the decree in 1856 that allowed people of all faiths to enter under controlled conditions.

The Muslims agree with the Jews that this was the place of the binding of Isaac and that God used the foundation stone of Mount Moriah as the foundation upon which He fashioned the entire world. The Koran quotes parts of the Old Testament and accepts the historicity of King David and Solomon. It also contains a distinct prophecy that Jesus the Prophet will finally come to the Temple Mount through the sealed Eastern Gate.

The Al-Aqsa Mosque is known as "the furthest one," in comparison to the central mosque of Islam in Mecca. The very large Al-Aqsa Mosque was built two years after the completion of the Dome of the Rock. The major entrance is located in its northern wall where you must remove your shoes to enter into its huge open central sanctuary. The roof is supported by enormous and beautiful white marble pillars, some over five feet in diameter. Several pillars near the main door still bear the scars of bullets that were fired during the assassination of the king of Saudi Arabia while he was worshiping there.

The entire mosque is built on top of an ancient underground building that dates back to the second Temple. This hall structure is called the ancient Aqsa-al-kadeem and leads toward the south wall of the Temple and the Hulda Gates, which were used by Jesus and the disciples as the major entrance to the Temple. These double and triple gates, though sealed at the south end, still lead diagonally up stairways through the wall, under the Al-Aqsa Mosque and through to the surface of the Temple Mount just outside the doors of the mosque. The Midrash Raba declares that these gates were never destroyed.

The Eastern Gate and Muslim Belief

Another structure on the Temple Mount that is important to the Muslims is the beautiful Eastern or Golden Gate, which was sealed almost a thousand years ago. The Arab name for the gate is Bab-ad-Daharia, "the occasional gate," because in ancient times it was to be opened only on rare occasions. (The northern gate is called Bab-as-Thouba, "gate of repentance," and the southern is called Bab-ar-Rachma, the "gate of mercy.")

The sealed Golden Gate has two doors like most of the ancient gates of the Temple. It is located 1,035 feet north of the southeast corner of the mount and extends sixty-two inches out from the present wall. This gate is really a gate-building structure measuring fifty-seven feet wide and ninety feet deep. While the foundation stones of the Golden Gate clearly date back to the reign of King Solomon, the gate itself was repeatedly destroyed and rebuilt like so many other structures on the Temple Mount. The gate we now see was rebuilt by Emperor Hadrian of Rome. He destroyed Jerusalem in the year 135 during the unsuccessful Jewish Bar Kochba Rebellion, an uprising that attempted to overthrow Roman domination. Hadrian rebuilt and renamed the city as Aelia Capitolina. He also built a small pagan temple through which this gate passed. When you approach the gate from inside the Temple Mount you can see the elaborate remains of the early Roman pagan structure, including friezes and stone carvings that date back to Hadrian. Later, after Emperor Constantine's conversion, the Byzantine rulers transformed the small pagan temple into a Christian church. Persian historical records state that their Emperor Heraclius chose to triumphantly enter Jerusalem through this very gate in A.D. 629.

When the Muslim Caliph Omar captured Jerusalem and began to build the Dome of the Rock in A.D. 691, the gate had already been sealed. From time to time the gate would be opened but then a new regime would seal it again. The Crusader Kingdom of Jerusalem once again opened the gate briefly in 1183 but did not allow it to be used for normal everyday purposes. Its wooden doors were opened only on special religious feast days to allow royal or religious dignitaries to enter into the Temple precincts.

Ezekiel recorded the prophecy about the closing of this gate. He told how the Lord brought him to the Eastern Gate. "And the Lord said to me, 'This gate shall be shut; it shall not be opened, and no man shall enter by it'" (Ezekiel 44:2-3).

Suleiman the Magnificent rebuilt the walls of Jerusalem in the 1600's and his Turkish workmen rebuilt the top portion of the Golden Gate building with the much smaller stones you can see today on the topmost levels. Why has so much attention been paid to this particular gate? Ezekiel gives us the answer: "Then He brought me back to the outer gate of the sanctuary which faces toward the east, but it was shut. And the Lord said to me, 'This gate shall be shut; it shall not be opened, and no man shall enter by it, because the Lord God of Israel has entered by it; therefore it shall be shut. As for the prince, because he is the prince, he may sit in it to eat bread before the Lord; he shall enter by way of the vestibule of the gateway, and go out the same way" (Ezekiel 44:1-3). In other words, this gate is reserved for the entrance of the coming Messiah.

If you approach the sealed Eastern Gate from outside the walls you must walk through an old cemetery. Centuries ago the Arabs built a Muslim cemetery in front of the sealed gate. This cemetery now extends a great distance along the Eastern Wall. The reason for choosing that particular place to build a graveyard was an attempt to hinder the fulfillment of the prophecy that the Messiah will someday enter through the Eastern Gate and set up His eternal Kingdom. Their own priests or Imams will not defile themselves by passing through a graveyard. Arab rulers reasoned that the graveyard and sealed gate would prevent the coming of the Messiah to save His people and set up His kingdom. The gate will be opened when the Messiah finally appears.

After twelve centuries of being sealed, attempts have been made twice in this century to open the Eastern Gate. The first was in 1917 and the second fifty years later in 1967. Muslim leaders in control of Jerusalem tried and failed to break the prophecy and open the gate. Each time, on the exact day the workmen were preparing to demolish the ancient stone, the hand of God intervened and the city of Jerusalem passed out of Muslim control into the hands of the British in 1917 and the Israelis in 1967. Each time, the Eastern Gate remained sealed as the prophet declared it would. Habakkuk explains that prophecy must be fulfilled: "Write the vision and make it plain on tablets, that he may run who reads it. For the vision is yet for an appointed time; but at the end it will speak, and it will not lie. Though it tarries, wait for it; because it will surely come. It will not tarry" (Habbakuk 2:2-3).

The Third Temple and the Dome of the Rock?

The Bible clearly promises that Israel will build the Third Temple. Yet the Muslim Dome of the Rock is on the Temple Mount. During a recent exploration of the area Kaye and I spent several hours with one of the most experienced of the Muslim guides at the Temple site. I asked our guide to tell us everything he knew about the Arab buildings and their history.

As we stood on the mount and examined the walls of the Eastern Gate, our Muslim guide Muhammad, said that the gate was sealed centuries ago to make sure that no one other than the Prophet Jesus could ever enter. He claimed that the Muslims knew about the prophecy of Jesus entering the gate in the last days to begin the judgment of mankind. He then turned from the gate and pointed directly opposite us across to the small Arabic Dome of the Tablets (also called the Dome of the Spirits) and said, "This is the place where Jesus will judge the nations at the end of the age."

When I asked Muhammad to elaborate, he pointed to a huge gateway of pillars, just a few feet behind the Dome of the Tablets, joined at the top by a massive lintel stone called the Balance of the Day of Judgment, or Al-Mizaan. He explained that "this was the site of the Holy of Holies in the original Temple of King Solomon." I expressed surprise at his statement because virtually all Arabic sources claim that the Dome of the Rock stands on the site of Solomon's Temple. He then told me that he and several others had explored the cisterns and tunnels beneath the Dome of the Tablets and that "those who knew" were convinced that this was the place of the original Temple.

This revelation is quite extraordinary because it opens up the possibility that Israel could rebuild their Temple on the site of Solomon's Temple without disturbing the Muslim's sacred Dome of the Rock, which lies almost a hundred yards south.

Many question the plausibility of the Jewish Temple being rebuilt virtually side-by-side with the Muslim Dome of the Rock. While it certainly seems odd for us to contemplate this outcome, it would not be that unusual in the crowded, complicated religious architecture of Israel.

The Tomb of Abraham in Hebron, for example, includes worship sites for both Muslims and Jews in the same building because both value the site. The Church of the Holy Sepulchre in Jerusalem has been shared by five antagonistic religious groups of Armenians, Ethiopians, Coptics, Catholics and Greek Orthodox priests and their competing services for almost seventeen hundred years. In addition, Jews now worship at the Western Wall while Muslims worship above them on the Temple Mount, less than a hundred yards away.

The prophet John was given a vision of the rebuilt Temple during the Tribulation. After he was told by the angel: "Rise and measure the temple of God, the altar, and those who worship there. But leave out the court which is outside the temple, and do not measure it, for it has been given to the Gentiles. And they will tread the holy city under foot for forty-two months" (Revelation 11:1-2). The "court" that has "been given to the Gentiles" is not to be measured. The Dome of the Rock was built in the area that was once the Court of the Gentiles. Perhaps the reason the angel tells John not to measure that area is because the Dome of the Rock will still occupy this place, twenty-six yards from the outside wall of the rebuilt Temple.

When the Messiah comes, Jesus will descend to the Mount of Olives. From there He will cross the Kidron Valley and enter the Temple Mount through the Eastern Gate: "Afterward he brought me to the gate, the gate that faces toward the east. And behold, the glory of the God of Israel came from the way of the east. His voice was like the sound of many waters; and the earth shone with His glory....And the glory of the Lord came into the temple by way of the gate which faces toward the east. The Spirit lifted me up and brought me into the inner court; and behold, the glory of the Lord filled the temple" (Ezekiel 43:1-5).

The Eastern Gate will remain sealed until the day appointed by God in His prophecies to usher in the long promised Millennial Kingdom of Christ.

In the next chapter we will explore the tremendous historical evidence from Jewish and Roman sources concerning the life, death, and resurrection of Jesus the Messiah.

CHAPTER 10

The Church and Its Messianic Expectations

In previous chapters we have seen how Israel awaits her Messiah's coming and also how Islam understands the coming of the Messiah. In this chapter we will investigate historical evidence in early writings by both Gentiles and Jews that confirm the claim that Jesus was the promised Messiah.

Accounts from Eyewitnesses

Early in this century, liberal writers rejected the Gospel narratives on the grounds that they were written almost a hundred years after the events described. They felt they could not be counted on as reliable historical evidence. This opinion was commonly accepted at the time and led a whole generation of scholars to reject the Gospels as eyewitness history.

Christians who believed the Bible to be the Word of God argued that, since the writers of the Gospels and the Epistles claimed to be eyewitnesses of Jesus Christ and His ministry, it qualified their information as verifiable historical fact. For example, Luke said in his Gospel: "Inasmuch as many have taken in hand to set in order a narrative of those things which are most surely believed among us, just as those who from the beginning were eyewitnesses and ministers of the word delivered them to us, it seemed good to me also, having had perfect understanding of all things from the very first, to write to you an orderly account... that you may know the certainty of those things in which you were instructed" (1:1-4). Then in his book about the Acts of the Apostles, Luke says that his "account" shows that Jesus "presented Himself alive after His suffering by many infallible proofs, being seen by [the apostles] during forty days and speaking of the things pertaining to the kingdom of God" (1:3).

Some of these same liberal scholars have also suggested that apart from the Gospels there is little historical evidence for the life of Jesus. For example, Solomon Zeitlin claimed:

> The main witnesses to the historicity of Jesus are the Gospels. The statements of Josephus concerning him are not taken seriously by the most conservative scholars; the Talmudic statements are also rejected by many scholars as not having any historical bearing. The data of pagan historians, Suetonius and Tacitus, regarded as proofs of the historicity of Jesus are considered doubtful. Even Paul's epistles have awakened the question, Does he speak of a real historical personage or of an ideal? The main sources for the historicity of Jesus, therefore, are the Gospels.

Zeitlin then dismisses the Gospel accounts and concludes, "So we are right to assume that even the Gospels have no value as witnesses of the historicity of Jesus. The question therefore remains: Are there any historical proofs that Jesus of Nazareth ever existed?" Thus, in an unequaled display of prejudicial assumptions, a scholar has dismissed the multitude of strong historical evidence that does indeed prove the Gospel accounts about Jesus. This cavalier rejection of historical sources that contradict his assumptions is a totally useless approach to discovering the truth. If we were to apply this same arbitrary rejection of historical evidence to other persons in history we would be forced to reject also Julius Caesar or Alexander the Great.

The accumulated evidence that Jesus of Nazareth not only existed but that He is the promised Messiah is truly overwhelming to anyone who is willing to evaluate it without prejudice. The respected scholar Otto Betz in *What Do We Know About Jesus?* said that "no serious scholar has ventured to postulate the non-historicity of Jesus." F.F. Bruce, author of *The New Testament Documents: Are They Reliable*, agrees: "The historicity of Christ is as axiomatic for an unbiased historian as the historicity of Julius Caesar."

But we do not have to rely solely on "eyewitness accounts." Continuing advances in the study of archeology as well as recent archaeological findings reveal that the Gospels and Epistles were written within thirty-five years of the events they describe. The late W.F. Albright, the greatest biblical archaeologist of his day, declared: "We can already say emphatically that there is no longer any solid basis for dating any book of the New Testament after about A.D. 80."

Historical Evidence from Early Gentile and Church Writers

First-century Romans were educated, literate, and politically aware. Roman government records were carefully guarded. The people openly discussed current events throughout the Empire, which explains why we continue to find references to Jesus in their writings. Probably 99 percent of all historical evidence of any one life from that period has been lost forever. Yet, amazingly, a lot of historical evidence about Jesus continues to exist.

Tacitus—Historian of Rome

Cornelius Tacitus, a Roman historian who also served as governor of the Province of Asia (Turkey) in A.D. 112, wrote letters about Emperor Nero. In them he alluded to the persecution of the Christians after Nero falsely accused them of burning Rome. Of Jesus he says, "Christus, the founder of the name, was put to death by Pontius Pilate, procurator of Judea in the reign of Tiberius; but the pernicious superstition, repressed for a time, broke out again, not only through Judea, where the mischief originated, but through the city of Rome also" (Annals XV:44).

While he obviously hated the new religion, Tacitus was a careful historian with complete access to the government archives of Rome. These records were inviolate, with the death penalty proscribed for anyone who would tamper with government papers. It is interesting to observe that he admits in his passage that Jesus Christ was the founder of the new religion and that he was executed under the command of Pontius Pilate during the reign of Tiberius Caesar. Additionally, Tacitus declares that the new faith was so vibrant that, despite cruel persecution, it continued to break out again in Judea and Rome. This information from an enemy of Christianity confirms many details in the Gospel records and the books of Acts and Romans.

Pliney—Governor of Bithynia

Pliney was governor of the Roman province of Bithynia, in present day Turkey, during the reign of Emperor Trajan (A.D. 112). In a letter to the emperor he requested detailed instruction on how he should interrogate Christians whom he was persecuting. In his *Epistles (X:96) he states that these believers would not worship Trajan and could not be induced with torture to curse Christ. Additionally he said that these Christians were "in the habit of meeting on a certain fixed day before it was light, when they sang in alternate verse a hymn to Christ as to a god, and bound themselves to a solemn oath, not to any wicked deeds, but never to commit any fraud, theft, adultery, never to falsify their word, not to deny a truth when they should be called upon to deliver it up." In addition to supplying evidence that a large number of believers followed Christ at the cost of being tortured and killed, Pliney described a group of people who loved the truth at any cost.*

Suetonius was Rome's official historian during the reign of Emperor Hadrian (A.D. 125). In his Life of Claudius he refers to the Christians causing disturbances in Rome that led to their being banished from "the instigation of Chrestus," which was his spelling of the name of Christ.

Another early writer, Lucian, lived in Samosata during the second century after Christ. He referred to Jesus in his book *The Passing Peregrinus.* He says that Jesus was worshiped by His followers and was "the man who was crucified in Palestine because he introduced this new cult into the world."

Tertullian and Tiberius Caesar

There is fascinating evidence from early writings that the Emperor Tiberius knew about the life of Jesus. Judge and theologian Tertullian who lived in North Africa at the end of the second century wrote a number of books in defense of the Christian faith. In one passage he says, "Tiberius accordingly, in those days the Christian name made its entry into the world, having himself received intelligence from the truth of Christ's divinity, brought the matter before the senate, with his own decision in favour of Christ. The senate, because it had not given the approval itself, rejected his proposal. Caesar held to his opinion, threatening wrath against all the accusers of the Christians" (Apology 5:2). This statement is incredible because Tertullian made it to people who had ready access to official government records and could prove he was lying unless it were true.

Tiberius requesting the senate to declare Jesus to be a god is not as unbelievable as it might seem at first glance. Tertullian did not suggest that Tiberius became a Christian in any sense. However, in first-century Rome there were a multitude of gods, including deceased emperors like Caesar. When Emperor Tiberius received the annual report, the "Acts of Pontius Pilate," regarding the astonishing life, death, and resurrection of Jesus, it is possible that he was moved to add Jesus to the long list of "approved" gods in the Roman pantheon. However, due to the political implications of appointing deceased emperors as gods, the Roman senate jealously guarded its sole prerogative as the chooser of such new gods. Therefore, it would be logical that the senate would resist the dangerous precedent of allowing a living emperor, like Tiberius, to choose who would be a god.

Justin Martyr

Justin Martyr, another Christian writer, also refers to this incident concerning Emperor Tiberius in his Apology (1:35). In another book The Defense of Christianity (A.D. 148), this able writer wrote to the current emperor, Antoninus Pius, in an attempt to convince him of the truthfulness of the faith of Christianity. As part of his argument he directed the emperor to examine the existing imperial governmental archives in Rome that contain all reports from procurators and governors of provinces. Under Roman law each governor must submit an annual report of all exceptional events in their jurisdiction with an explanation of their actions in keeping the peace and good government. Justin Martyr referred the emperor to the "Acts of Pontius Pilate," specifically to a report for the year of Christ's death. Justin Martyr said: "'They pierced my hands and my feet' are a description of the nails that were fixed in His hands and His feet on the cross; and after He was crucified, those who crucified Him cast lots for his garments, and divided them among themselves; and that these things were so, you may learn from the 'Acts' which were recorded under Pontius Pilate" (Apology).

In another passage (Apology 2:48) he backs up his claims for these miraculous works of Jesus by again referring to government records: "That He performed these miracles you may easily be satisfied from the 'Acts' of Pontius Pilate." It would be suicidal to offer Emperor Antoninus Pius this evidence about Tiberius and Jesus unless it were both true and provable from government archives.

There is no evidence that, during this age of intense debate between Christians and non-Christians, any pagan writer disputed the claims of Justin Martyr, Tertullian, and others about the evidence from Roman archives.

Africanus and Thallus

Africanus was a Christian writer who lived in North Africa and wrote around A.D. 215. In one of his defenses of the faith he mentions the writing of another historian, Thallus (A.D. 52) who recorded the miraculous darkness on the face of the Earth in his history. Julius Africanus records, "Thallus, in the third book of his histories, explains away this darkness [on the day that Christ died] as an eclipse of the sun—unreasonably, as it seems to me." It was unreasonable, of course, because a solar eclipse could not take place at the time of the full moon. It was at the season of the Paschal full moon that Christ died.

This reference by Thallus, a pagan historian confirms the Gospel account that "there was darkness over the whole land until the ninth hour" (Mark 15:33) while Jesus was on the cross. There are other ancient historical references to this supernatural darkness at the death of Christ. Additionally, astronomers confirm Africanus's conclusion that a normal eclipse was astronomically impossible at the time of a full moon, which was always the case during Passover. The high priests of Israel carefully calculated the position of the moon to the smallest degree for the required feast days.

The foregoing are only a few examples of Gentile and early Church writers who speak of Jesus, His life, death and resurrection.

Evidence from Flavius Josephus

Flavius Josephus (A.D. 37), authored one of the most significant extra-biblical writings of the first century. From his earliest years Josephus was trained as a Pharisee and priest. He was descended from an old priestly family and had excellent access to Jewish historical records. Josephus witnessed events leading up to the terrible war of the Jews that ended in the destruction of Jerusalem and the Temple. He was appointed as a general by Jewish rebel forces in the region of Galilee in the ill-fated war of independence against the legions of Rome. After the fall of the city of Jotapata, he was captured by the Romans under General Vespasian. He became a friend to his son Titus, a future emperor, serving as his interpreter. During the remainder of the war he was in the Roman camp and was able to record the military campaign in great detail.

From his privileged position as a historian with unlimited access to both Roman and Jewish governmental records, he was certainly well able to describe the turbulent decades of that historic century. Considering these qualifications, if Josephus had never said anything about the life, death, and resurrection of Jesus it would indeed cast doubt on the historicity of Christ. However, such was not the case. Josephus recorded several historical events that are supported by New Testament Scripture.

About Jesus, Josephus said the following: "Now, there was about this time Jesus, a wise man, if it be lawful to call him a man, for he was a doer of wonderful works—a teacher of such men as receive the truth with pleasure. He drew over to him both many of the Jews, and many of the Gentiles. He was [the] Christ; and when Pilate, at the suggestion of the principal men amongst us, had condemned him to the cross, those that loved him at the first did not forsake him, for he appeared to them alive again the third day, as the divine prophets had foretold these and ten thousand other wonderful things concerning him; and the tribe of Christians, so named from him, are not extinct at this day" (Josephus, *Antiquities of the Jews*, Book 18, 3:3).

In another section of *Antiquities of the Jews* (Book 20, 9:1), Josephus also mentions the death of James, the brother of Jesus: "When, therefore, Ananus [the High Priest] was of this disposition, he thought he had now a proper opportunity [to exercise his authority]. Festus [the Roman Procurator] was now dead, and Albinus [the new Procurator] was but upon the road; so he assembled the Sanhedrin of judges, and brought before them the brother of Jesus, who was called Christ, whose name was James, and some others; and when he had formed an accusation against them as breakers of the law, he delivered them to be stoned."

In another place Josephus describes the death of John the Baptist: "Now some of the Jews thought that the destruction of Herod's army came from God, and that very justly, as a punishment of what he did against John, that was called the Baptist; for Herod slew him, who was a good man, and commanded the Jews to exercise virtue, both as a righteousness towards one another, and piety towards God, and so to come to baptism; for that the washing [with water] would be acceptable to him, if they made use of it, not in order to the putting away [or the remission] of some sins, but for the purification of the body; supposing still that the soul was thoroughly purified beforehand by righteousness. Now, when [many] others moved [or pleased] by hearing his words, Herod, who feared lest the great influence John had over the people might put it into his power and inclination to raise a rebellion (for they seemed ready to do anything he should advise), thought it best, by putting him to death, to prevent any mischief he might cause, and not bring himself into difficulties, when it should be too late. Accordingly he was sent a prisoner, out of Herod's suspicious temper, to Macherus [Masada], the castle I before mentioned, and was there put to death" (*Antiquities of the Jews*, Book 18, 5:1).

Evidence from the Talmud About Jesus

The Talmud, the authoritative works of Jewish tradition, has two notable groups of writings. The Babylonian Talmud (*Babli* or *Baritha*) was a comprehensive commentary on Jewish Law that was written in Babylon (Iraq) over a period of six hundred years (from 100 B.C. to A.D. 499). The second group is the Jerusalem Talmud (*Yerushalmi*) or Palestinian Talmud, written by Jewish scholars who remained in Tiberias, Israel, after the Roman destruction of the Temple.

The Talmud contains two layers of rabbinic tradition, the Mishnah which was completed in A.D. 220, and the Gemara, finished in A.D. 425 when the Tiberius Talmud school at the Sea of Galilee finally closed. The teachers and rabbis of the Mishnah were known as Tannaim and this period of scholarship was known as the Tannaitic Period. Within this group of writings we find several divisions, including the Baraitha and Tosefta (a compilation of sayings), the Midrashim and Halachic (religious legislation), and Haggadic (inspirational) writings that include elaborations on the Passover.

Despite the religious and historic importance of the Talmud to Jews, the entire collection of Talmudic material contains very little information on events that took place during the Second Temple Period—from the Captivity until the burning of the Temple in A.D. 70. For example, the hero of the tremendously important Maccabbean rebellion against the Syrians from 168 to 165 B.C., Judas Maccabeus, is not referred to in the Talmud. Also, despite the admitted historical evidence for the life of the Apostle Paul and his aggressive missionary journeys to preach in Jewish synagogues, the Talmud does not mention him. Another surprising omission was discovered by the great Jewish scholar Ginzberg: not one single quotation from the great number of Jewish "Apocalyptic writings" was included in the Talmud. If the Talmud, despite its huge volume of writings over a six-hundred-year period, does not mention Judas Maccabeus, the Apostle Paul, or Jewish Apocalyptic writings, we should not really be surprised that little is said about the life of Jesus. But there is a very good "secret" reason for this lack of reference to Jesus.

Censored Material About Jesus

There is significant evidence that much of the original material about Jesus Christ, which was initially in the Talmud, was removed and censored during the Middle Ages. This was done in an attempt to eliminate inflammatory passages that were misused by bigots as an excuse to assault Jewish ghettos in Europe. As you would expect, this censored material included both positive and negative comments about Jesus. Even negative comments are very helpful, in terms of establishing the historical truth of the life of Christ. Fortunately for us, some of this material about Jesus did miraculously escape the censors and remains available in existing copies of the Talmud. It is essential that we closely examine whatever precious material escaped the censors and remains to this day.

The Babylonian Talmud

The Babylonian Talmud, Baraitha, says: "It has been taught [in a Baraitha]: On the eve of Passover they hanged Yeshu, the Nazarene. And an announcer went out, in front of him, for forty days [saying]: 'Yeshu, the Nazarene, is going to be stoned, because he practised sorcery and enticed and led Israel astray. Anyone who knows anything in his favour, let him come and plead in his behalf.' But, not having found anything in his favour, they hanged him on the eve of Passover" (Sanhedrin Text 43a; this translation is from the Munich manuscript of the Babylonian Talmud which was completed in A.D. 1343).

This account from the second century period of the trial and death of "Yeshu," Hebrew for Jesus, confirms the Gospel history in a number of important points: (1) it identifies Yeshu, which is a short form for *Yehoshua*— Joshua, which is used throughout the Tannaitic period of the Talmud to refer to Jesus Christ; (2) it identifies the method of execution and time of year He was put to death, "hanged" on a cross on the eve of the Passover Feast; (3) it proves that there was a trial before His execution, as all the Gospels record, when it proclaims that an "announcer" sought anyone who could produce evidence "in his favour"; (4) it says that Jesus "practised sorcery and enticed and led Israel astray"; and (5) it confirms the Jewish Sanhedrin law of stoning one who was condemned to die.

First, regarding the use of *Yeshu*, because the Gospel accounts were written and distributed in the Greek language, the Greek form, "Jesus" was commonly used rather than the Hebrew Joshua. He is called the "yeshu, the Nazarene" (the Hanotzri in the original Hebrew), which identifies Jesus specifically as the Nazarene: "And he [Joseph, Jesus' legal father] came and dwelt in a city called Nazareth, that it might be fulfilled which was spoken by the prophets, 'He shall be called a Nazarene'" (Matthew 2:23).

Second, as to the time when Jesus was crucified, a manuscript copy of this Talmudic text from Florence, Italy, written in A.D. 1176, mentions that Jesus was hanged "on the eve of the Sabbath," which agrees with the Gospel of Mark: "Now when evening had come, because it was the Preparation Day, that is, the day before the Sabbath, Joseph of Arimathea, a prominent council member, who was himself waiting for the kingdom of God, coming and taking courage, went in to Pilate and asked for the body of Jesus" (15:42-43).

Third, the statement that "an announcer went out...for forty days" looking for someone who "knows anything in his favour" refers to the Mishnah law regarding the responsibility to search for evidence of both guilt and innocence prior to the execution of a death sentence following a trial verdict. The reference to "forty days" is intriguing in light of the Gospel accounts of three "forty-day" periods in Christ's life: (1) the days of His mother's purification before presenting Jesus in the Temple; (2) the forty days of Jesus' temptation in the wilderness; (3) the forty days from His resurrection to His ascension.

Fourth, the statement, "Because he practised sorcery," is consistent with the account in Matthew 12:22-29 where Jesus was accused of sorcery by the Pharisees when He cast the demon out of the man who was blind and dumb. The accusation that He "enticed and led Israel astray" was a fear the chief priests and Pharisees voiced in John 11:47-48: "What shall we do? For this Man works many signs. If we let Him alone like this, everyone will believe in Him, and the Romans will come and take away both our place and nation" (John 12:47-48).

Fifth, is the seeming contradiction between the statement that Yeshu "is going to be stoned," and that He was "hanged" on the eve of Passover. The Jewish Sanhedrin law required that a death penalty be carried out by stoning. However, the Roman government had removed the Jews' right to carry out capital punishment during this period, so Jewish authorities could not execute Jesus for violating their religious laws. Pilate told the priests that he saw no crime worthy of death and told them to "take Him and judge Him according to your law." But the Jews replied, "It is not lawful for us to put anyone to death." Then John adds, "that the saying of Jesus might be fulfilled which He spoke, signifying by what death He would die" (John 18:31-32), which was by crucifixion. The situation was resolved by switching the accusation against Jesus from a religious point of view to a political one. That way Roman law could be invoked— which leaned toward instant crucifixion for anyone attempting political revolt against the empire. The accusations against Jesus then centered on the claim that He said He was the King of the Jews—a political accusation. Finally Pontius Pilate, for fear of reprisals from Rome, used the ultimate Roman authority to order His death by crucifixion.

The Sanhedrin Text

Another reference to Yeshu in the Sanhedrin Text of the Babylonian Talmud reads: "Our rabbis taught [in a

Baraitha]: Yeshu had five disciples—Mattai, Nakkai, Netzer, Buni, and Todah." We cannot determine at this time why the Talmud concentrated on only these five followers, but we can surmise which ones were referred to in this short list. Mattai is almost certainly Matthew; Todah is likely Thaddeus; Nakkai may be Luke; Netzer could be Andrew; Buni is possibly John or Nicodemus. The fact that only five disciples are listed does not contradict the Gospel accounts of twelve major disciples and a further seventy who were later sent out by Jesus. It is possible that the rabbis were only aware of the names of a few of the more prominent ones.

There is a reference also in the Talmud to a Rabbi Elazare ben Damah who was offered healing "in the name of Yeshu." This was recorded by a man named Jacob (Baraitha-B. Abodah Zarah 16b, 17a, and Tosefta-Hullin II:24). This indicates that healing in the name of Jesus was a practice that was recognized in the Talmud in the early years of the Church.

Another Talmudic reference to Jesus concerned an encounter Rabbi Eliezer, a famous Jewish scholar of the day, had with a disciple of Jesus who was named Jacob. Rabbi Eliezar admitted that he was impressed by some of Jesus' teaching. The writer, Joseph Klausner, makes an interesting case in his "Jesus of Nazareth" that this Jacob was none other than James, the brother of Jesus, and that the event occurred approximately in A.D. 60. Regardless who this disciple of Jesus was, this Talmudic passage confirms that some Jewish rabbis indicated interest in Jesus' teachings at a very early date.

Talmudic References to the Birth of Jesus

The Talmud, of course, also has some very negative comments about Jesus, particularly His virgin birth. In one of these accounts, Jesus is referred to as "Yeshu, son of Panthera." This comment falsely suggested that Mary had a relationship with a Roman legionnaire named Panthera. Hugh Schonfield, in his book about Jesus, claimed that the "Rabbi Shimeon ben Azzai said: '...found a genealogical scroll in Jerusalem and therein was written, "so-and-so, bastard son of an adulteress."'" A fascinating aspect of these comments is that they serve to prove only that there was something so unusual about the birth of the child Jesus that it demanded an explanation. If Jesus had been born to Joseph and Mary in a normal fashion, there would have been no need to create such stories. Anyone who rejects the biblical truth of the miracle of the virgin birth would need to come up with another more natural explanation, such as the above. Along this same line, it is interesting that the Islamic Koran refers to Jesus as "the son of Mary." This is quite unusual in that, normally, both Arabs and Jews identify people by their father, such as "Ishmael, the son of Abraham." The reference to Jesus as "the son of Mary" acknowledges that Joseph, while the legal father of Jesus, was not the biological father. In other passages the Koran acknowledges specifically that Jesus was miraculously born of a virgin.

The Mishnah Torah's Reference to Jesus

These are only a few references to Christianity in the Talmud that escaped censorship. Within the past few years, the Jews of Yemen have brought back to Israel the "uncensored" copies of the Mishnah Torah. This manuscript includes some wonderful material about Jesus of Nazareth that had been censored for more than seven hundred years. Some of this material was quoted in my book *Heaven – The Last Frontier*. In a later chapter we will explore Maimonides' "censored" material on Jesus. The Mishnah Torah is a fourteen volume set of books by Moses Maimonides which compiled all of the laws of Judaism on the Temple, the Messiah, etc. Perhaps future research will reveal copies of the Talmud that have not had material about Jesus censored out. Such a revelation will be of great interest to all Christians and Jews.

The King of Edessa

One of the most interesting of the ancient writings that has come from the first centuries of the Christian era is a letter from the king of Edessa, near the Euphrates River, to Jesus requesting healing and the reply which Jesus purportedly made. While many scholars doubt the authenticity of the actual text contained in the writings of the early Church fathers, it is more than probable that the original story is based on reality. Various Christian writers, including Eusebius, Julius Africanus, and Tertullian, declare that the government archives at Edessa contained these letters which had been examined by numerous people. These archives were kept at Edessa until A.D. 550. The writer Eusebius quotes the letters, which he translated from the original Syriac.

King Abgar to Jesus:

> Abgar Uchomo, sovereign of the country, to Jesus the good Savior, who has appeared in the country of Jerusalem: Peace. I have heard about Thee and about the healing which is wrought by Thy hands without drugs and roots. For, as it is reported, Thou makest the blind to see, and the lame to walk; and Thou cleansest the lepers, and Thou castest out unclean spirits and demons, and Thou healest those who are tormented with lingering diseases, and Thou raisest the dead. And when I heard all these things about Thee, I settled in my mind one of two things: either that Thou art God, who has come down from heaven, and doest these things; or that Thou art the Son of God, and doest these things. On this account, therefore, I have written to beg of Thee that Thou wouldest weary Thyself to come to me, and heal this disease which I have. For I have also heard that the Jews murmur against Thee, and wish to do Thee harm. But I have a city, small and beautiful, which is sufficient for two.

From Jesus by the hand of Hananaia, the scribe, to Abgar, sovereign of Edessa:

> Blessed is he that hath believed in me, not having seen me. For it is written concerning me, that those who see me will not believe in me, and that those will believe who have not seen me, and will be saved. But touching that which thou has written to me, that I should come to thee—it is meet that I should finish here all that for the sake of which I have been sent; and, after I have

finished it, then I shall be taken up to Him that sent me; and, when I have been taken up, I will send to thee one of my disciples, that he may heal thy disease, and give salvation to thee and to those who are with thee.

A report in the Aramaic language declares that Thaddeus, the Apostle (Jude), one of the twelve, went to visit King Abgar at Edessa after Christ's resurrection, King Agbar was healed and led to a personal faith in Christ. There is strong evidence of missionary work by Thaddeus in the city of Edessa.

The question is, Are these letters genuine? Due to the length of time and without the original documents it is impossible to declare dogmatically whether the letters are authentic. However, there is nothing in the letters that contradicts either the history of the period or the truthfulness of the Gospel accounts. We know that King Agbar Uchomo was fourteenth king of Edessa and ruled there during the life of Jesus. Eusebius, an accurate historian (A.D. 325), said that he went to Edessa and examined the original letters himself. His report must be taken at face value. Matthew tells us that Jesus' "fame went throughout all Syria; and they brought to Him all sick people who were afflicted with various diseases and torments...and He healed them" (4:24). Edessa became a major center of Christian activity during the first century, and this tradition of the letters is alluded to by almost all early Christian writers. Numerous accounts of this incident are in the Ante-Nicene Library (a collection of early Christian writings from the time of Christ until the Council of Nicea in A.D. 325).

Miscellaneous Evidence of Jesus' Existence

Millar Burrows made an intriguing discovery of an ossuary, a funeral jar, in Jerusalem that contained a reference to the name "Jesus, son of Joseph," as reported in *What Mean These Stones?* (New Haven: American School of Oriental Research, 1941, pp. 9, 65, 193). Initially, many were very excited about the possibility that this ossuary was archaeological proof of the Gospel account of Jesus. However, the name "Jesus" was not unusual at that time (nor is it today in many countries). Josephus says that of the twenty-eight High Priests in a period of one hundred and seven years leading up to the burning of the Temple, three men used the name: Jesus, son of Phabet; Jesus, son of Damneus; Jesus, son of Gamaliel. We have to acknowledge that there is no conclusive proof of a relationship between the ossuary's reference to the name Jesus and the Jesus of the Gospels.

The oldest known painting of Jesus, dated approximately A.D. 150, was located in the Catacomb of Priscilla at Rome. It is possible that the artist reconstructed the painting from accounts people gave of what their parents or others who knew Jesus told them of the way Jesus looked. This discovery was documented in *Light from the Ancient Past*, by Jack Finegan (Princeton University Press, 1946, pp. 371-408). The next oldest representation of Christ was discovered in a church in Dura-Europas, Syria, dated approximately A.D. 225.

In the next section we will consider some fascinating research material on Jerusalem, the building of Solomon's Temple and the mysterious Copper Scroll. We will explore the lost treasures of the Temple, and the secrets of Jersusalem's underground city.

PART III

Jerusalem and the Temple

"Now Solomon began to build the house of the Lord at Jerusalem on Mount Moriah, where the Lord had appeared to his father David, at the place that David had prepared on the threshing floor of Ornan the Jebusite" (2 Chronicles 3:1).

"Now Solomon assembled the elders of Israel and all the heads of the tribes, the chief fathers of the children of Israel, in Jerusalem that they might bring the ark of the covenant of the Lord up from the City of David, which is Zion" (2 Chronicles 5:2). "But I have chosen Jerusalem, that My name may be there; and I have chosen David to be over My people Israel" (2 Chronicles 6:6).

CHAPTER 11

Jerusalem and
the Temple of Gold

"For the Lord has chosen Zion; He has desired it for His habitation: this is My resting place forever; here I will dwell, for I have desired it" (Psalm 132:13-14).

Zion, the city of Jerusalem, is the setting for the coming of the Messiah. This "city which cannot be moved, but abides forever" (Psalm 125:1) has stood at the crossroads of human history for thousands of years—politically, militarily, and spiritually. The city of Jerusalem occupies a central place in the unfolding drama of God's redemptive plan for Earth. The prophets of Jerusalem promised the world that a "Son of David" would someday rule the planet from Jerusalem, the capital of His eternal kingdom. Many of the most important events in Bible history occurred here. The streets and stones of Jerusalem witnessed the awesome events surrounding the death and resurrection of Jesus the Messiah some two thousand years ago. Now the city awaits the most important of all prophecies, the coming of its promised King, Jesus the Prince of Peace.

Jerusalem sits on the most strategic trade routes and military lines of march in the Middle East. Because it is revered by Jews, Christians and Muslims, Jerusalem has attracted an endless list of merchants, warriors, travelers, scholars, archaeologists, and clergy.

The name—Jerusalem—means "foundations of peace" (*salem, shalom*—Hebrew; *salaam*—Arabic) yet it has known more anguish of war than any other place on this planet. From its humble beginnings (Salem, Genesis 14:18) this place has attracted attention. It became the capital city of the land of Israel when David was king, and remained the capital when Solomon finally obtained all the land which

God had promised Abraham. While he was king, Solomon built the Temple of God on Mount Moriah, the place where God tested Abraham. Even after the kingdom divided, Jerusalem remained the capital of the Southern kingdom of Judah. Jerusalem was the place where God's people offered sacrifices for their sins on the sacred altar of the Temple; it was the city God chose to give the ultimate sacrifice—His Son. Someday it will be the focus for the greatest battle the Earth has ever known. Finally, as Isaiah saw in a vision, it will be made new, a city whose "righteousness goes forth as brightness" (Isaiah 62:1).

Mount Moriah—City of Zion

In the earliest record we have of the city, Jerusalem—then called Salem—was inhabited by the Jebusites. This tribe remained in the area for over a thousand years, from the time of Abraham (2000 B.C.) until the conquest of the city by King David (approximately 1000 B.C.). When the Jebusites first settled in this fertile area of Canaan they found an excellent water supply, the Pool of Siloam, at the foot of a low hump-backed mountain. The Jebusites built defensive stone walls around their village-city that followed the oblong outline of the small mountain ridge which ran to the north of this pool of water. The adjacent valleys on either side of the mountain city made it exceedingly difficult for invaders to attack successfully. Over the years they built stronger and stronger walls to repel all invaders.

Archaeological evidence indicates that the lower part of the city was inhabited by the poor, while the nobility and kings built their palaces and government buildings on the higher reaches known as the Upper City. This Upper City was the place King David chose for his magnificent palace when he finally conquered the city.

Melchizedek—King of Salem

The writer of the book of Hebrews talks about "Melchizedek, king of Salem, priest of the Most High God, who met Abraham returning from the slaughter of the kings, and blessed him" (Hebrews 7:1). Abraham and his small army had gone to the aid of Abraham's nephew, Lot, when the armies of five kings attacked Sodom and Gomorrah. They carried away all the goods from the towns and also Lot and his family. Abraham's small army of three hundred and eighteen miraculously defeated the armies of the kings and rescued Lot.

On his way back to his own camp, as he drew near Mount Moriah (according to the Talmud), Abraham was met by the king of Salem, Melchizedek. The king brought out bread and wine and blessed Abraham. The Bible records that Abraham responded by giving the priest-king one-tenth of all the plunder he had regained from the five kings, the first tithe ever mentioned in Scriptures.

The account in Hebrews goes on to say that Melchizedek is a type of Jesus Christ, the Messiah, "Without father, without mother, without genealogy, having neither beginning of days nor end of life, but made like the Son of God, [who] remains a priest continually" (Hebrews 7:3). The description goes on to describe "another priest who has come, not according to the law of a fleshly commandment, but according to the power of an endless life....But He, because He continues forever, has an unchangeable priesthood. Therefore He is also able to save to the uttermost those who come to God through Him, since He ever lives to make intercession for them. For such a High Priest was fitting for us, who is holy, harmless, undefiled, separate from sinners, and has become higher than the heavens" (Hebrews 7:15-16, 24-26).

The Sacrifice of Isaac—A Prophecy of Messiah

Several years after this first encounter near Salem, Abraham had another occasion to visit Mount Moriah. God spoke to him one day and told him: "Take now your only son Isaac, whom you love, and go to the land of Moriah, and offer him there as a burnt offering on one of the mountains of which I shall tell you" (Genesis 22:2). Abraham had learned by now to trust God and obey His commands. So he rose early the next morning, saddled his donkey, and with Isaac his son and two other young men, went to Moriah. "On the third day Abraham lifted his eyes and saw the place afar off" (v.4). This "third day" has so much significance in God's Word. Jesus' body lay in the tomb for three days; Jonah stayed in the belly of the fish for three days; Esther fasted before seeing the king for three days; and Abraham traveled for three days before he stopped to sacrifice his only son. Three days was the amount of time which God often set aside for preparation and spiritual testing.

"The place afar off," the specific site God chose as the place of ultimate sacrifice was Mount Moriah. This hilltop later became known as the *Even Sheteyeh*, the Foundation Stone, where the Levites carefully set the holy Ark of the Covenant in Solomon's Temple. This was the second of the two hilltops on Mount Moriah, north of the city of the Jebusites which ultimately became known as Jerusalem, the City of David.

The reason God gave Abraham this strange order was to test His servant's obedience. Abraham was asked to sacrifice the most important thing in his life, his son Isaac. God waited until Abraham was a hundred years old before granting him the promise of a son who would father a great and mighty nation. However, God now asked Abraham to sacrifice his promised son. Isaac was a strong young man at this point in his life, capable of resisting his father. One of the most touching incidents of trust in the whole Bible was that of Isaac's question to his father: "My father!... Look, the fire and the wood. But where is the lamb for a burnt offering?" (Genesis 22:7). Abraham replied: "'My son, God will provide for Himself the lamb for a burnt offering.' And the two of them went together" (v. 8). Isaac's total trust in his father and in God are just as awesome as the trust Abraham displayed in the Lord. Can you imagine Abraham's thoughts as he silently pondered the Lord's strange command during their three-day journey?

Two thousand years later another Father prepared to sacrifice His only Son near Mount Moriah. This Son also trusted His Father and willingly obeyed.

Abraham proceeded to build the altar of sacrifice on the Foundation Stone, which ultimately became the floor of the Holy of Holies. Isaac let his father bind him and lay him upon the wood of the altar. As Abraham raised the knife to kill his son, the "Angel of the Lord called to him from heaven and said, 'Abraham, Abraham! ...Do not lay your hand on the lad, or do anything to him; for now I know that you fear God, seeing you have not withheld your son, your only son, from Me'" (Genesis 22:11-12).

When God the Father of the Lord Jesus Christ prepared to offer His Son as a sacrifice, no voice came from heaven to stop Him. There is no voice greater than God's. But when Abraham was willing to kill his son in obedience to God, the "Angel of the Lord," Jesus Christ the Son of God Himself, stopped him. We know this because Abraham called the name of the place *Jehovah Jireh,* "The-Lord-Will-Provide; as it is said to this day, 'In the Mount of The Lord it shall be provided'" (Genesis 22:14).

A hundred yards away a ram was entangled in a thicket of thorns—on the very spot, according to the rabbis, where today stands the Muslim Dome of the Rock. Abraham went and got the ram and offered it up for a sacrifice instead of his son. But the free decision of both Abraham and Isaac to sacrifice the seed of promise was the ultimate test of whether they were truly willing to trust in God to accomplish the stupendous promises He had made to Abraham: "By Myself I have sworn, says the Lord, because you have done this thing, and have not withheld your son, your only son, in blessing I will bless you, and in multiplying I will multiply your descendants as the stars of the heaven and as the sand which is on the seashore; and your descendants shall possess the gates of their enemies. In your seed all the nations of the earth shall be blessed, because you have obeyed My voice" (Genesis 22:16-18). This successful test of Abraham's love and obedience to God literally changed the course of human history for eternity. Abraham's seed, the children of Israel, will multiply to infinity throughout eternity in an immeasurable universe and will bless all the nations perpetually because Abraham obeyed God's voice on Mount Moriah.

From this point in history Mount Moriah became the most sacred spot on Earth. In fact, it would not be an exaggeration to say that for the next several thousand years a majority of the spiritually significant events recorded in the Bible occurred either on Mount Moriah or within a mile of it.

The Altar of Sacrifice

Human sacrifice was not unknown in the area where Abraham lived, but God prohibited it (see Leviticus 20 regarding human sacrifice to Molech, a god that required the sacrifice of children). The first animal sacrifice was made by God when He shed the blood of an animal to make tunics for Adam and Eve after they sinned and "the eyes of both of them were opened, and they knew that they were naked" (Genesis 3:7,21). Mankind's first sin resulted in the death of an innocent animal. In this way the Lord began to teach Adam and Eve that their sin would have awesome and terrible consequences. In the end the only sacrifice that could atone for all man's sin, and reconcile mankind with God, would require the ultimate, effective sacrifice of His own Son, who was "slain from the foundations of the world" (Revelation 13:8). God Himself sacrificed the first animal in the Garden of Eden to cover the sin of Adam and Eve. He later offered His Son at Calvary to cover the sins of all mankind, the ultimate sacrifice.

The first sacrifice by man recorded in the Bible, unfortunately, ended in violence. Cain and Abel, two sons of Adam and Eve, brought an offering to the Lord. Cain made a vegetarian offering, which was unacceptable to the Lord. However, Abel showed his understanding of the sacrificial offering when he freely killed a firstling lamb from his own flock as his offering. God would surely have told Adam and Eve the details of a proper acceptable sacrifice; therefore, Cain and Abel would also have been aware of God's command on this subject. When Cain's offering was not accepted but Abel's was, Cain, in a violent jealous rage, killed his brother. Abel, the first believer in God died, but he had "offered to God a more excellent sacrifice than Cain." Abel was the first man to enter heaven; thus, through his sacrifice "he being dead still speaks" (Hebrews 11:4). In 1 John 3:12 we are told that this murder was not a spontaneous act but that Cain was "of the wicked one." His motive for killing his brother was "because his works were evil and his brother's righteous."

The next time the Bible mentions a sacrifice it is offered by Noah, "a just man, perfect in his generations" (Genesis 6:9). After the devastating flood that destroyed all life, Noah "built an altar to the Lord" to thank God for delivering him and his family. He "took of every clean animal and of every clean bird, and offered burnt offerings on the altar. And the Lord smelled a soothing aroma. Then the Lord said in His heart, 'I will never again curse the ground for man's sake, although the imagination of man's heart is evil from his youth; nor will I again destroy every living thing as I have done. While the earth remains, seedtime and harvest, and cold and heat, and winter and summer, and day and night shall not cease'" (Genesis 9:20-22).

God renewed His covenant with mankind through Noah by accepting Noah's sacrifice of "clean" animals. These clean animals were those that were acceptable for sacrifice. Rather than only one each of male and female animals, such as were the instructions for "unclean" animals, Noah was told to take seven males and seven females of clean animals to assure that there would be available a larger genetic pool of sacrificial animals without blemish.

As a result of Noah's acceptable sacrifice, God covenanted with Noah that He would never again destroy all life on our planet regardless of the provocation of our sinfulness. This is important to consider, because God has prophesied that, at the end of the Millennium after living in a veritable Paradise for a thousand years, man will still fail in a final test of obedience. During this test, Satan will be released to lead the nations in a last rebellion against God. God will destroy Satan's armies and burn up the surface of planet Earth. The Bible does not explain how God will preserve the animals, plant life, and the righteous Jews and Gentiles who are alive on Earth during the Millennium. But Isaiah 65 clearly tells us that in the New Earth, which will come out of the old, cleansed Earth, there will be animals, vineyards, houses, and people who will have seed and offspring forever without sin or death. Since God promised Noah that He would never again destroy "every living thing," we can be assured that He will somehow preserve all living things so they can continue in the New Earth forever, without sin or death. The Lord also promises that His Church will reign and rule over all these in the New Earth.

During the Millennium and in this New Earth, according to the prophet Zechariah, nations will send representatives to Jerusalem: "And it shall come to pass that everyone who is left of all the nations which came against Jerusalem shall go up from year to year to worship the King, the Lord of hosts, and to keep the Feast of Tabernacles." He goes on to describe the Millennial Temple: "In that day 'HOLINESS TO THE LORD' shall be engraved on the bells of the horses. The pots in the Lord's house shall be like the bowls before the altar" (Zechariah 14:20-21). These verses, and Isaiah 66:20-23, tell us that not only will the Millennial Temple continue after the thousand years, but that the New Earth will also have horses.

God confirmed His covenant with Noah through the introduction of the rainbow: "I set My rainbow in the cloud, and it shall be for the sign of the covenant between Me and the earth. It shall be, when I bring a cloud over the earth, that the rainbow shall be seen in the cloud" (Genesis 9:13-14). According to scientists who have studied the Greenhouse Effect, which would have existed before the Flood, no one would have been able to see a rainbow until after the deluge opened up the firmament to allow regular rainfall and unobstructed sunlight. Prior to the flood "a mist went up from the earth and watered the whole face of the ground" (Genesis 2:6). It is fascinating to read in Ezekiel that when he was granted a vision of God he saw Him in "brightness all around. Like the appearance of a rainbow in a cloud on a rainy day, so was the appearance of the brightness all around it. This was the appearance of the likeness of the glory of the Lord" (Ezekiel 1:27-28). When John was lifted up to heaven he saw "a throne set in heaven, and One sat on the throne. And He who sat there was like a jasper and a sardius stone in appearance; and there was a rainbow around the throne, in appearance like an emerald" (Revelation 4:2-3). God's covenant to mankind, confirmed by His acceptance of Noah's sacrifice of thanksgiving, is a covenant of life. Each of these sacrifices ultimately pointed forward in time to the coming Messiah and His redemptive sacrifice for our sins.

The Tabernacle Sanctuary

When Moses led the Israelites out of the spiritual and physical bondage of Egypt, God delivered them from the Egyptian army. When they traveled into the spiritual proving ground of the Sinai wilderness, Moses sang a song of worship to God: "The Lord is my strength and song, and He has become my salvation; He is my God, and I will praise Him; my father's God, and I will exalt Him....You will bring [the people whom You have purchased] in and plant them in the mountain of Your inheritance, in the place, O Lord, which You have made for Your own dwelling" (Exodus 15:2,16- 17).

Then God commanded Moses to build a Tabernacle, a movable sanctuary which would contain the Holy of Holies that would house the Ark of God's presence during their travels. Moses talked about the "mountain of Your inheritance" where God has made His "own dwelling." This mountain of inheritance had been chosen by God and identified to Abraham about four hundred years before the Exodus. It would be another five hundred years before the Tabernacle would finally be moved up to Mount Moriah by order of King Solomon in preparation for transferring the Ark of the Covenant to the new Temple.

Within this Tabernacle, which was built precisely according to God's instructions, Moses was to "put the mercy seat on top of the ark, and in the ark you shall put the Testimony that I will give you. And there I will meet with you, and I will speak with you from above the mercy seat, from between the two cherubim which are on the ark of the Testimony, of all things which I will give you in commandment to the children of Israel" (Exodus 25:21-22).

This magnificent sanctuary is unique in the history of the world. No other people had ever created an enormous center of worship that was movable. It was constructed in the wilderness out of materials at hand along with the treasures they had brought from Egypt. The Jews "had asked from the Egyptians articles of silver, articles of gold, and clothing. And the Lord had given the people favor in the sight of the Egyptians, so that they granted them what they requested. Thus they plundered the Egyptians" (Exodus

12:35-36). Whether out of fear of what was happening to them or because they were grateful for the years of service the Jews had given them, the Egyptians gave gifts to those departing Egypt. So when Moses asked for donations to build the Tabernacle the people gave so much that Moses finally had to put a limit on the gifts. "Then the Lord spoke to Moses, saying: 'Speak to the children of Israel, that they bring Me an offering. From everyone who gives it willingly with his heart you shall take My offering. And this is the offering which you shall take from them: gold, silver, and bronze; blue and purple and scarlet yarn, fine linen thread, and goats' hair; rams' skins died red, badger skins, and acacia wood; oil for the light, and spices for the anointing oil and for the sweet incense; onyx stones, and stones to be set in the ephod and in the breastplate'" (Exodus 25:1-7).

This amazing Tabernacle was carried for forty years by the Israelites until they entered their promised land. It was Joshua, not Moses, who finally led them across the Jordan River and into the land of Canaan. God had told Moses that when He brought them into the Promised land He would "cast out many nations before you, the Hittites and the Girgashites and the Amorites and the Canaanites and the Perizzites and the Hivites and the Jebusites, seven nations greater and mightier than you" (Deuteronomy 7:1). Later, in Joshua 24:11, we are told that God delivered all these people into their hands, including the city of the Jebusites, Jerusalem. In the years following, many of these places were lost to their enemies, primarily because they did not "utterly destroy them" as God had told them to do (Deuteronomy 7:2).

The Conquest of Jerusalem

It was not until some four hundred years later after Joshua's partial conquest that King David, who had ruled Israel for seven years from the city of Hebron, was instructed by God to reconquer Jerusalem and make it his capital. After the conquest, King David ruled for another thirty-three years from Jerusalem. "And the king and his men went to Jerusalem against the Jebusites, the inhabitants of the land, who spoke to David, saying, 'You shall not come in here; but the blind and the lame will repel you,' thinking, 'David cannot come in here.' Nevertheless David took the stronghold of Zion (that is, the City of David)" (2 Samuel 5:6-7).

The unique defensive qualities of Jerusalem are illustrated by these strange taunts the Jebusites hurled at King David and his army. With great contempt they said their defensive wall was so strong that only the lame, deformed, and old women would be needed to man the walls and effectively defeat David's siege. But it was time for God to judge the sins of the pagan, idol-worshiping, child-sacrificing Jebusites. The one-thousand year kingdom of the Jebusites came to an end quickly under David's mighty army of Israel. Upon conquering the city, David began to rebuild its mighty walls to create a truly impregnable city for his son Solomon's reign. He assembled an enormous quantity of building materials and built his palace and government structures.

One day as he contemplated the beautiful palace he had built on the heights of his city, he said to Nathan, the prophet: "See now, I dwell in a house of cedar, but the ark of God dwells inside tent curtains" (2 Samuel 7:2). At first Nathan told the king to go ahead and fulfill his heart's desire to build a Temple for God. But God had other plans. He told Nathan to go back to David and say that he could not build the Temple. But, "When your days are fulfilled and you rest with your fathers, I will set up your seed after you, who will come from your body, and I will establish his kingdom. He shall build a house for My name, and I will establish the throne of his kingdom forever" (vv. 12-13).

Solomon Builds the Temple

To his great sadness, David was not permitted to build the Temple, but God would provide him with detailed blueprints for its ultimate construction by Solomon, and would allow him to collect the materials that would be needed for the building. King David used his overwhelming military and strong alliances with neighboring states to accumulate the most imposing array of construction materials ever seen. Various kings, including King Hiram of Tyre (Lebanon), sent workman, craftsmen, and enormous quantities of cedar, gold and silver to be used in this glorious undertaking. "Indeed, said David, "I have taken much trouble to prepare for the house of the Lord one hundred thousand talents of gold and one million talents of silver, and bronze and iron beyond measure, for it is so abundant. I have prepared timber and stone also, and you may add to them. Moreover there are workmen with you in abundance; hewers and workers of stone and timber, and all types of skillful men for every kind of work" (1 Chronicles 22:14- 15). According to one calculation, one hundred thousand talents of gold would today amount to approximately 2.6 billion dollars; a million talents of silver would be another two billion. Without even considering the cost of labor and other material, you can see that this was the most costly construction project in human history.

One unusual detail in the building of the sanctuary in Jerusalem was the command that "no hammer or chisel or any iron tool was heard in the temple while it was being built" (1 Kings 6:7). Some rabbis have interpreted this command to mean that no iron was to be used during the preparation of the stones; others believe that the injunction against the use of iron tools applied only to the final assembly of the quarried stones on Mount Moriah. The Lord established the sanctity of the Holy Mount from the first day of its construction.

One curious rabbinical story concerning the building of Solomon's Temple is that none of the many thousands of skilled workers died during the seven years of Temple construction. This tradition says that after dedicating the sanctuary God caused all the workers to die and immediately enter Paradise as their eternal reward for participating in the completion of the sacred project. This prevented any other profane king from employing these skilled craftsmen on their own temples or palaces and later boasting that the same workers who built the house of God also built their profane palaces. This is only a Jewish tradition, it is not scriptural. However, it illustrates how the Jews felt about the magnificent Temple of Solomon.

The Sanctuary Blueprint

The Bible says that both the Tabernacle and the Temple of Solomon were patterned after the master Sanctuary of God in heaven. David says that the instructions from God were actually in writing: "All this,...the Lord made me understand in writing, by His hand upon me, all the works of these plans" (1 Chronicles 28:19). The book of Hebrews quotes God as saying, "See that you make all things according to the pattern shown you on the mountain" (Hebrews 8:5). The writer continues to describe the relationship between the earthly sanctuaries and the heavenly Temple: "Therefore it was necessary that the copies of the things in the heavens should be purified with these [the blood of the sacrifice], but the heavenly things themselves with better sacrifices than these. For Christ has not entered the holy places made with hands, which are copies of the true, but into heaven itself, now to appear in the presence of God for us" (Hebrews 9:23-24).

John, in his vision of heaven, is shown the temple of God "in heaven, and the ark of His covenant was seen in His Temple" (Revelation 11:19). Some wonder if this vision of John means that God took the earthly Ark of the Covenant to heaven after it disappeared from Solomon's Temple. However, when we realize from Exodus 25, verses 8 to 10 and verse 40 that there has always been a heavenly Ark of the Covenant, even during the time the earthly Ark was in Solomon's Temple, then we see that there is no contradiction. As I revealed in my book, Armageddon – Appointment With Destiny, God has preserved the Ark of the Covenant in Ethiopia and it will be returned and placed in the rebuilt Temple before the return of Messiah.

According to the Mishnah Torah, the volume on Hilchos Bais HaBechirah—the Laws of God's Chosen House—there are six Mitzvot or commandments for Israel concerning the Temple:
1. They are to build a sanctuary.
2. They are to build the altar with stone that is not hewn.
3. They are not to ascend to the altar on steps but on a ramp.
4. They must fear and reverence the Temple.
5. They must guard the Temple completely.
6. They must never cease watching over the Temple.

Moses Maimonides comments that the Temple had two distinct purposes for Israel. First, the Temple's fundamental goal was to reveal the divine Presence and the Shechinah Glory of God to mankind. The second purpose was to provide a place for sacrifices: "Speak to the children of Israel, and say to them: 'When any one of you brings an offering to the Lord, you shall bring your offering of the livestock—of the herd and of the flock....And the priest shall bring it all and burn it on the altar; it is a burnt sacrifice, an offering made by fire, a sweet aroma to the Lord'" (Leviticus 1:2,13).

Insufficient Sacrifices

One aspect of the earthly sanctuary which is not found in the heavenly sanctuary is that God commanded the offering of animal sacrifices in the earthly sanctuary so that men would be reminded of the sinfulness of their unredeemed nature. Only the sacrifice of innocent blood could atone for their sin. However, these Temple sacrifices covered the sin only temporarily. Ultimately, sin had to be atoned through "one sacrifice for sins forever" (Hebrews 10:12), the innocent Lamb of God. From the time when God sacrificed an animal to make clothes of skin to cover the sin of Adam and Eve, until He sacrificed His Son on the cross, all the sacrifices in between which men offered to God were not enough to "make those who approach perfect. For then would they not have ceased to be offered? For the worshipers, once purged, would have had no more consciousness. But in those sacrifices there is a reminder of sins every year. For it is not possible that the blood of bulls and goats could take away sins" (Hebrews 10:1-4).

There are amazing parallels between the sacrifice of Jesus and the Temple sacrifice of animals including the details of the Passover sacrifice of the lamb. According to the Mishnah and Sanhedrin documents, when the priest took his knife and cut the throat of the Passover lamb he would cry out, "It is finished." He would open up the lamb with a knife and roast it upon a vertical spit with a horizontal cross piece holding the front legs wide apart. Then he would wrap the lamb's intestines around its head while it was being roasted. This was called "the crown of the Passover lamb."

Even the smallest detail of the sacrifice system pointed prophetically and typically to the ultimate sacrifice by Jesus of Nazareth, as Paul declared: "For indeed Christ, our Passover, was sacrificed for us" (1 Corinthians 5:7).

All the thousands upon thousands of animals and birds that were offered to God on the altars in the Tabernacle and in the Temple in Jerusalem never accomplished man's redemption: to take away sin. There was only one sacrifice that was perfect enough to do that—the Lamb of God, the Messiah.

Jesus lay down His own life voluntarily, for no man could take it from Him. Only then could "this Man, after He had offered one sacrifice for sins forever" sit "down at the right hand of God, from that time waiting till His enemies are made His footstool" (Hebrews 10:12-13). In the past only the High Priest could enter the Holy of Holies, all those who accept the great sacrifice of the Son can have "boldness to enter the Holiest by the blood of Jesus." Therefore, "Let us draw near with a true heart in full assurance of faith...Let us hold fast the confession of our hope without wavering...let us consider one another in order to stir up love and good works" (vv. 19-24).

Now He is sitting at the right hand of God waiting for the fullness of time when "this same Jesus, who was taken up into heaven, will so come in like manner" (Acts 1:11).

Rebuilding the Third Temple—The Sign of the Coming Messiah

For two thousand years Jews have longed to return to the Promised Land and rebuild their beloved Temple on the Temple Mount. During these centuries of exile, three times a day, righteous Jews turned toward Jerusalem, the Holy City, and prayed to God that He would return the divine Shekinah Presence to their rebuilt Temple: "May the Temple be rebuilt speedily in our day!" All this time it was impossible for most Jews even to visit the ruins of the Temple, so their longing had to be limited to studying its features and to prayer. Since 1948, however, a growing number of Israelites have begun to transform this longing into a practical plan of action that will lead to the rebuilding of the Temple in our generation.

A fascinating brochure from the "Jerusalem Temple Foundation" tells of their commitment to the practical steps required to fulfill the unchanging commandment of God, "Let them make Me a sanctuary, that I may dwell among them" (Exodus 25:8). This organization is headquartered in Jerusalem and is involved in sponsoring study groups and archaeological investigations in connection with the Temple Mount. For many years people have wondered if the idea of rebuilding the Temple was simply a curious topic of interest to students of prophecy. Today an astonishing array of serious-minded groups in Israel and in the Diaspora are completing studies into rebuilding the Temple and resuming the ancient worship.

As one example, the following items are the official "Aims of the Jerusalem Temple Foundation":

A. To undertake research into the history of the Holy Places in Israel

B. To provide scientific means and equipment for the efficient investigation of such places and of archaeological sites

C. To study the religious, political, economic, social, cultural, and ethnic aspects and implications of those investigations and explorations

D. To advance the learning and application of the Scriptures

E. To work for the safeguarding and preservation of the integrity of Holy Places in Israel, and their restoration, with special emphasis on the Temple Mount

H. To launch worldwide competitions for the design and construction of suitable edifices and similar projects in Israel

I. To raise funds for the promotion and development of these and allied activities.

The brochure summarizes the history of Israel with the following:

The First Temple	Location: Mount Moriah - The Temple Mount
The Second Temple	Location: Mount Moriah - The Temple Mount
The Third Temple	Location: Mount Moriah - The Temple Mount

"You want the Temple to be rebuilt, but how can you really want it if you are not prepared?" —the Hafeta Haim

Gentile Participation in Rebuilding the Temple

The question is often asked, "Can a gentile participate in the rebuilding of the Temple?" This interesting question has actually been debated over the centuries by various rabbinical authorities. Today, many evangelical Christians are the strongest supporters for the rebuilding of the Temple. Based on the biblical account of gentile participation in providing materials, craftsmen, and labor in the building of Solomon's Temple, it would seem that no fundamental problem would stand in the way of gentiles contributing to the Third Temple. When I asked several Levites and Orthodox Jews in Jerusalem why they were so helpful to me and others in discussing research questions on the Temple project, a few replied that they had an ancient tradition that gentiles would assist Israel in the last days to rebuild their ancient sanctuary.

Remember, there was a Court of the Gentiles in both Solomon's and the Second Temple. Also the prophet Zechariah predicted that in the Millennial Kingdom, "It shall come to pass that everyone who is left of all the nations which come against Jerusalem shall go up from year to year to worship the King, the Lord of hosts, and to keep the Feast of Tabernacles" (Zechariah 14:16).

"For the Lord has chosen Zion; He has desired it for His habitation: this is My resting place forever; here I will dwell, for I have desired it" (Psalm 132:13-14). Zion, the city of New Jerusalem, is the place from which Messiah will rule—both Jew and Gentile—forever.

What happened to the great treasures from the Temple when first the Babylonians and then the Romans destroyed the sanctuary? Did the priests succeed in hiding any of these precious treasures? Will they be found before the Temple is rebuilt in our days? In the next chapter we will examine the mystery of these lost treasures.

CHAPTER 12

Search for the Treasures of the Temple

What happened to the treasures of the Temple when it was destroyed first by the Babylonians, and later by the Romans? Many of the gold artifacts, as well as the gold that was stripped from the walls—were carried off by the Romans. There is silence in Scripture regarding these precious objects. They were never mentioned again. Were they secretly hidden away?

In this chapter we will examine what is being done either to locate or to duplicate these ancient treasures. The recovery of these sacred objects in our generation is the key to the rebuilding of the Temple and the fulfillment of messianic prophecy.

The Dead Sea Scrolls

In 1947 the world was startled to hear of the discovery of a group of ancient biblical manuscripts at Qumran, near the Dead Sea. These priceless documents had been hidden by the religious community known as the Essenes. Although a portion of the scrolls which has been published has proven of tremendous interest, over half of the scrolls from the cave have been secretly guarded for forty years by the original scholars. There is great controversy over this withholding, causing some to speculate that the unreleased manuscripts may contain controversial material about Jesus. Hopefully, due to some recent decisions by the custodians and the Israeli government, the balance of these scrolls will be released within the next year.

Some scholars believe that there are additional scrolls in the Dead Sea area that were not recovered in the original dig forty years ago. Dr. Gary Collett and Dr. Aubry L. Richardson are two archaeologists who have completed some fascinating research that indicates there are still some unexplored caves at Qumran. Sophisticated finding equipment indicate that these caves contain undamaged clay jars of the type that were used to protect manuscripts. Initial readings on their equipment indicated that up to forty jars are in one cave. If the research team is successful in recovering more manuscripts, they have a commitment from the Israeli government that the manuscripts will be released to the larger scholarly community for evaluation and publication.

The National Aeronautics and Space Administration (NASA) team has developed some fascinating new technical instruments that enable scientists to do a molecular frequency analysis of subsurface (underground) features of a given area. During the Apollo moon landings an earlier variation of this system enabled the astronauts to know which areas would be most likely to prove worthwhile to dig core samples. This element-frequency analysis reads non-visible elements of the electromagnetic spectrum which provide readings of the type of molecules found in the material located beneath the surface. Test sites confirm that this technology provides a reliable indication of underground caves, tunnels, and the objects within them. This device has been used on caves at Qumran by Dr. Collett and Dr. Richardson. It indicates that there is an unexplored artificial cave that contains forty clay jars. Further, the readings indicate that the jars are intact and contain parchments. Over thirty readings picked up evidence of a second copper scroll, pottery, artificial cement, wood, various metals and leather. Based on these readings and additional explorations with a government archaeologist, the Israeli government has given written permission for the group to commence a dig for these objects. The Israelis are well aware of the potential for this technology due to their own research efforts regarding its obvious defense and intelligence applications.

It will take at least eighteen months and possibly several years for the group to dig down to the largest artificial cave (forty feet deep) because they must follow exacting archaeological requirements, recording each layer, and using only spades and picks. Their progress will, naturally, depend on the financial and volunteer support they receive.

The team is looking for volunteers who are athletic and can work for months at a time in a hot dusty climate. If you would like to get involved either in supporting this important archaeological dig, or joining them by volunteering your time to dig, contact Dr. Gary Collett, Jerusalem Ministries International, P.O. Box 1667, Everett, WA 98201 for more information. They need a standard job application, a photo, and a pastor's referral. As this project continues, Kaye and I will keep our readers informed in future books. We will also film important discoveries as they occur and share them on our "Appointment with Destiny" television program.

The Mysterious Copper Scroll

In March of 1952, in cave number 3-Q-15 near Qumran, a strange document was discovered. The thousands of manuscripts discovered thus far at the Dead Sea site had been of parchment or leather. This one was composed of three copper sheets, riveted together, and was rolled up like a scroll. It became known as the Copper Scroll. It was eight feet long, one foot wide, and its Hebrew letters had been engraved into the copper with several carved chisels. Composed during the siege of the Temple by a member of the Essenes in A.D. 68, it was buried in Cave 3. There it lay undisturbed for almost two thousand years until its discovery in 1952.

If any of the Essene group had survived, the Copper Scroll would have been removed from its hiding place. This fact suggests that, if the list is genuine, some of the objects may have escaped chance discovery over the centuries, awaiting this moment in history to be revealed.

When they finally unraveled and translated the scroll, scientists discovered that it was a list of sixty-four secret locations where treasures of gold and silver from the Temple were hidden. The amount of treasure listed was awesome in value and included a number of sacred Temple vessels, including manuscripts and the Breastplate of the High Priest.

A number of archaeologists, led by J.T. Milik, concluded that this list must be a mythological tale of buried treasure. Their reason for believing that it was fiction was primarily the enormous size of the treasure, which amounts to some forty-five hundred talents of gold and silver (each talent is equal to almost a hundred pounds of precious metal). However, there are reasons for concluding that this list could be genuine. While this is a great amount of gold and silver, Josephus states that when General Pompey captured Jerusalem in 63 B.C. he received a tribute within "a little time" of "above ten thousand talents" of gold (*Antiquities*, XIV, 4:5 [78]). The Temple was the central bank and depository for the nation in those days. It held enormous wealth.

The list is a very basic bookkeeping accounting of objects with no embellishment of the contents as you would expect in a fictional story. Many of the hiding places were caves and cisterns surrounding Wadi Ha Keppah. This ancient valley has been identified, based on ancient maps and exact references to a series of toponyms, as the valley of Qumran. One-third of the sites are located around Jerusalem. These geographically detailed descriptions may enable an investigator to determine the precise location of the sixty-four detailed sites. For example, one listing for site 54, as translated by Dr. Bargil Pixner, reads: "Close by (BTKN ' SLM on the treading place (BHBSH) at the top of the rock facing west against the garden of Sadok, under the great stone slab of the water outlet: untouchable (anathema!) (HRM)." This particular item, because of the special warning against disturbing its resting place, is definitely of a sacred nature, probably from the Temple in Jerusalem.

The question is, could this list contain the location of gold and silver Temple objects that were buried for safekeeping? The sanctuary was the most strongly guarded storehouse in Israel and was used both as the national central bank and religious treasury. In addition to Temple treasures, the list could include the huge accumulated treasure of the Essenes themselves, a two-hundred- year-old religious community at Qumran.

Many of the details of the geographical descriptions are subject to interpretation. Over the centuries a great deal of wind and occasional water erosion has transformed smaller, once easily identifiable features of this Qumran area. In the next few years a special group of archaeologists will systematically examine the clues to locations of this hidden treasure revealed in the Copper Scroll.

What are some of the Temple treasures that could be unearthed by the discovery of this scroll? In the chapter "The Coming Messiah" we will examine the incredible discovery of the "oil of anointing" for messianic kings that was found at Qumran just as the Copper Scroll indicated. In my next book we will explore the tremendous secrets of Qumran and the Copper Scroll.

The Importance of the Temple Treasures

Besides the great wealth represented in the gold, silver and brass vessels associated with the worship services, the Temple vessels and other ornaments are important religiously. Moses was instructed by God Himself on Mount

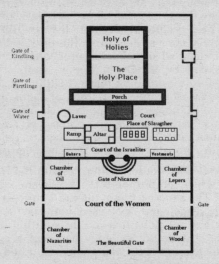

The Second Temple

Sinai about the construction and particular furnishings of the Tabernacle. (See Exodus 25:9 to 28:43.) When Solomon began the building of the great Temple he created a new group of vessels for the expanded Temple worship services according to specific instructions which King David had received from the Lord. (See 1 Chronicles. 28:11-18.) God gave the instructions for these vessels and objects of worship because they prophetically taught Israel about the Messiah and illustrated the atonement He would accomplish in His life and death on the cross. These objects also point to the final reality when Christ will reign and rule from His Messianic throne during the Millennial Kingdom.

The Need for New Temple Vessels and Robes

More than one-third of the 613 biblical commandments that are itemized in the Talmud concern laws relating to the Temple in Jerusalem. Since the destruction of the sanctuary in A.D. 70, many generations of Jews have longed for the time when they could return to Zion and commence the rebuilding of the Temple. However, the rebuilt Temple will require a trained priesthood of Levites and kohanin. In addition, a great number of special Temple vessels will need to be duplicated if the prophecy of a Third Temple is to be fulfilled. This activity has already begun in Jerusalem with the forming of the Temple Institute, a group of dedicated religious scholars and Levites.

The Temple Institute has been doing research on ninety-three of the sacred vessels and garments described in the Bible. This group of dedicated Jewish students, who possess a great love for the Temple and the Messiah, are determined to do everything in their power to obey the Lord's command to "prepare Me a sanctuary." They do not want to act presumptiously, but they want to be prepared to build the Temple once the Lord gives the sign.

The Holy Garments

Let us begin with descriptions of the "holy garments" for the priests serving in the Temple as given to Moses by God: "And you shall make holy garments for Aaron your brother, for glory and for beauty....And these are the garments which they shall make: a breastplate, and ephod, a robe, a skillfully woven tunic, a turban, and a sash" (Exodus 28:2,4). These robes were burnt or looted by the Romans in A.D. 70. Hundreds of new robes will have to be woven for the priests and Levites for future Temple services.

The High Priest's Breastplate

One of the most unusual objects in the Temple worship of ancient Israel was the breastplate of gold and precious stones that was worn on the chest of the High Priest. "You shall make the breastplate of judgment.... It shall be doubled into a square; a span shall be its length, and a span shall be its width. And you shall put settings of stones in it, four rows of stones. The first row shall be a sardius, a topaz, and an emerald;... And the stones shall have the names of the sons of Israel, twelve according to their names, like the engravings of a signet, each one with its own name...You shall make chains for the breastplate" (Exodus 28:15-22).

This breastplate was one of the treasures that was lost when the Temple was burnt in A.D. 70, and is one of the hidden objects mentioned in the Copper Scroll.

A group of Levites and Jewish craftsmen are now studying the Talmud and Torah references to the breastplate with a view of reconstructing the precious treasure to be worn by a future High Priest. This is the first attempt, since the time of Christ, to duplicate this special object. By the time you read this, the Breastplate of the High Priest of Israel will be finished.

The High Priest's Robe

God's description for the High Priest's robes, and the robes of the other Temple priests were very elaborate: "You shall make the robe of the ephod all of blue. There shall be an opening for his head in the middle of it; it shall have a woven binding all around its opening, like the opening in a coat of mail, so that it does not tear. And upon its hem you shall make pomegranates of blue and purple and scarlet yarn, all around its hem, and bells of gold between them all around; a golden bell and a pomegranate, a golden bell and pomegranate, upon the hem of the robe all around. And it shall be upon Aaron when he ministers, and its sound will be heard when he goes into the holy place before the Lord and when he comes out" (28:31-35); "They made tunics, artistically woven of fine linen, for Aaron and his sons, a turban of fine linen, exquisite hats of fine linen, short trousers of fine linen, and a sash of fine linen and blue and purple and scarlet thread, woven as the Lord had commanded Moses" (39:27-29).

The Lord commanded Moses to have craftsmen create the necessary robes for the ancient priesthood. Today in Jerusalem various Levites, including a young Levite woman named Yehudah Avrasham, are weaving the garments that hundreds of priests will require for their service in the revived Temple. These robes are constructed from a special six-ply linen thread. The sash is fifty-five feet long. The trousers are worn to insure modesty at all times. On special feast days more than three hundred kohanin (Levites who also perform Temple duties) now gather to offer the Blessings of the kohanin while wearing their special linen garments. In October, 1990, some elderly Orthodox Jews attempted to bring a cornerstone to the Temple Mount. Arabs used the incident to provoke a riot that led to the deaths of eighteen Palestinians. One of the Levites was wearing the robe which was woven for the High Priest (see the photo section in this book). Many of the special garments—including the robe of the ephod and the sash—were to be "all of blue"; the ingredients for this special blue dye, known as *tchelet*, was lost after the Second Temple period. Several manuscripts, including one by Rabbi Yaacov Herzog, father of Chaim Herzog, president of Israel, mentioned the lost dye. However, the source of this blue pigment was discovered a few years ago. The Israelis found a deep water snail which they thought was extinct. This creature, when crushed and dried, makes the deepest dark blue pigment imaginable. The Temple Institute has a display showing the snail dye. This blue dye is also used to color the *tsitsit* fringes worn by religious Jewish males in the Temple.

The High Priest's Gold Crown

"You shall also make a plate of pure gold and engrave on it, like the engraving of a signet: HOLINESS TO THE LORD. And you shall put it on a blue cord, that it may be on the turban; it shall be on the front of the turban. So it shall be on Aaron's forehead, that Aaron may bear the iniquity of the holy things which the children of Israel allow in all their holy gifts; and it shall always be on his forehead, that they may be accepted before the Lord" (Exodus 28:36-38).

The crown, known as *tsitz azahv tahor*, was worn across the brow of the High Priest and was fastened by the blue *tchelet* thread. During my last trip to Israel, I held in my hands the new High Priest's Crown. It is crafted of solid gold. Like the other objects, the crown will have to be purified before it is used in the Temple.

Temple Vessels and Furnishings

The book of Exodus gives the details for many of the vessels and furnishings that were used in the Tabernacle, and later the Temple. Among these are (1) the Ark of the Covenant; (2) the table for the showbread; (3) the gold lampstand; (4) the altar of incense; (5) the altar of burnt offering; (6) the bronze laver. When Solomon built the Temple he had the craftsmen make the bronze altar; ten lavers for the priests to wash in; ten lampstands of gold; ten tables; pots, shovels, bowls, and forks of gold and bronze.

The Ark of the Covenant

The most important religious object in history is the golden Ark of the Covenant. The Ark of the Covenant was described as the place where God "will meet with you, and...speak with you......of all things which I will give you in commandment to the children of Israel" (Exodus 25:22). God told Moses that the High Priest was to sprinkle the blood of the sacrifice upon the mercy seat of the Ark of the Covenant to typify the future sacrifice of the blood of the only begotten Son of God. At the Last Supper Jesus "took the cup and gave thanks, and gave it to them, saying, 'Drink from it, all of you. For this is My blood of the new covenant, which is shed for many for the remission of sins" (Matthew 26:27-28).

For Solomon's Temple, "Bezaleel made the ark of acacia wood; two and half cubits was its length, a cubit and a half was its width, and a cubit and a half its height. He overlaid it with pure gold inside and outside, and made a molding of gold all around it. And he cast for it four rings of gold to set in its four corners: two rings on one side and two rings on the other side of it. He made poles of acacia wood, and overlaid them with gold. And he put the poles into the rings at the sides of the ark, to bear the ark" (Exodus 37:1-5).

The Ark was forty-five inches by twenty-seven inches by twenty-seven inches and completely covered inside and out with pure gold. The Ark of the Covenant was never to be transported in any way except on the shoulders of four priests, by the poles inserted into the rings at each corner. One time King David and the Levites disregarded this strict command of God regarding the procedure for carrying the Ark. Their intention was to bring it from the place where it had been stored to Jerusalem. Instead of having the Levites carry it on foot by means of the poles, they put the Ark on a new cart, pulled by oxen. "Uzzah put out his hand to the ark of God and took hold of it, for the oxen stumbled" (2 Samuel 6:6). The result of this act of disobedience was that "God struck [Uzzah] for his error; and he died there by the ark of God" (v. 7). King David was so distressed at the consequences that he ordered the Ark stored in the house of Obed-Edom instead of taking it on to Jerusalem. During the three months the Ark was in Obed-Edom's home, "the Lord blessed Obed-Edom and all his household" (v. 11). Finally, after being told how Obed-Edom was being blessed, David once again prepared to bring the Ark to Jerusalem. This time he did it the way God had commanded, and the Ark arrived safely and triumphantly at Jerusalem. The Ark was placed in the Tabernacle in the Holy of Holies.

When the Ark was in the Holy of Holies it was placed so that the poles pressed against the veil that separated the Holy of Holies from the Holy Place. This way, the priests could see that the Ark was in its place behind the veil without entering the Holy of Holies, for only the High Priest could go behind the curtain.

Covering the top of the Ark of the Covenant was the pure gold Mercy Seat. Affixed to the Mercy Seat were two cherubim of hammered gold. Inside the Ark were the Tablets of Testimony (the Ten Commandments), Aaron's rod, and a pot of manna. However, by the time of King Solomon "there was nothing in the Ark except the two tablets of stone which Moses put there at Horeb, when the Lord made a covenant with the children of Israel" (1 Kings 8:9). The Ark of the Covenant was the central focus of worship for Israel from the time it was made in 1490 B.C. and placed in the Tabernacle when "the glory of the Lord filled the tabernacle" (Exodus 40:34) through the reign of Solomon. All the time the Israelites wandered the Sinai Peninsula the Spirit of God rested in the Ark of the Covenant. God led them by day with a huge cloud, and by night with a cloud of fire. Wherever the cloud went, the people followed.

The Ark of the Lord would sometimes be taken out of the Holy of Holies and carried into battle ahead of the Israelite army. This terrified the surrounding nations as well as the enemy. After forty years in the wilderness, Joshua led the people into their Promised Land. As the Levites carried the Ark of the Covenant before them, the river stopped its flow as soon as the Levites stepped into the water, so that the people crossed a dry river bottom.

The Ark of the Covenant disappeared from Bible history more than three thousand years ago, while Solomon was still king. In my books *Armageddon — Appointment With Destiny* and *Heaven — The Last Frontier* I recount the historical and biblical research indicating that the Ark has been hidden in an underground Temple in Aksum, Ethiopia, for these past many centuries. There are a number of intriguing prophecies (see Isaiah 18; Zephaniah 3:9-10; Jeremiah 3:15-16) which suggest that the ancient Ark of the Covenant will be returned to Israel and the rebuilt Temple in the last days before the coming of Messiah.

The avid search for the lost Temple vessels continues while many new vessels are being remade in Jerusalem at this time. However, the rabbis and Levites I interviewed unanimously concurred that the Ark of the Covenant could never be replaced with anything except the original. They all believe that the Ark still exists somewhere, either in Ethiopia or hidden beneath the Temple Mount, waiting to be revealed at the moment of God's choosing.

The Mizdrot and the Lottery Box

Once every year, on the sacred Day of Atonement, Yom Kippur, the High Priest entered the Holy of Holies, and only on that day. God had told Moses: "Tell Aaron your brother not to come at simply any time into the Holy Place inside the veil, before the mercy seat which is on the ark, lest he die" (Leviticus 16:2). The High priest first washed his entire body and put on special clothing. When he was properly cleansed and prepared he would (1) kill a bull as a sin offering for himself; (2) kill a young goat offering for the sins of the people; (3) lay his hands on the head of a young live goat. He confessed the sins of the people and placed all their sins on this scapegoat. The scapegoat would then be turned out to wander in the wilderness, bearing on itself all the iniquities of the people.

The two goats were chosen for their roles by means of a lottery. The priest would draw from an oval shaped box, decorated with gold handles, the two lots: one for the Lord— the goat that was sacrificed, the other for the wilderness— the scapegoat. The lottery box has been duplicated in Jerusalem (see the photo section).

At the completion of the ceremony the slain bull and goat would be carried outside the camp and burned. In between each of these actions the High Priest would use the laver and go through a ritual of washing his clothing and bathing his body. Yom Kippur is still a high holy day for dedicated Jews.

The mizdrot is a silver vessel weighing eighteen pounds. The priests used the mizdrot to catch the blood from the sacrificed animal. He then poured the blood on the horns of the altar.

The Table of Showbread

Each week the priests serving the Temple would place bread on the Table of Showbread to acknowledge that God was the Lord of the harvest and their source for all the sustenance of life. God instructed Moses to "make a table of acacia wood; two cubits shall be its length, a cubit its width, and a cubit and a half its height. And you shall overlay it with pure gold, and make a molding of gold all around" (Exodus 25:23-24). Its dimensions were three feet by eighteen inches by twenty-seven inches. It had a five-inch-high golden crown bordering the top, and a golden ring at each of the four corners to enable the priests to carry it on wooden poles that were also overlaid with pure gold.

The Hebrew sages say that one of the miracles of the Temple was the fact that, because of God's Divine Presence, the bread remained supernaturally fresh all week until the next bread offering was placed on the Table of Showbread. This bread typifies the ultimate offering of the Body of Christ. Jesus said, "If anyone eats of this bread, he will live forever; and the bread that I shall give is My flesh, which I shall give for the life of the world" (John 6:50-51). On the night of the Last Supper, Jesus "took bread, gave thanks and broke it, and gave it to them, saying, 'This is My body which is given for you; do this in remembrance of Me'" (Luke 22:19).

The Gold Lampstand

"You shall also make a lampstand of pure gold; the lampstand shall be of hammered work. Its shaft, its branches, its bowls, its ornamental knobs, and flowers shall be of one piece. And six branches shall come out of its sides; three branches of the lampstand out of one side, and three branches of the lampstand out of the other side...All of it shall be one hammered piece of gold ....You shall make seven lamps [oil holders] for it....And see to it that you make them according to the pattern which was shown you on the mountain" (Exodus 25:31-32, 37, 39-40).

The Lampstand represented to Israel the divine light of God that manifested its Presence in the Tabernacle and the

Temple through the "seven lamps" showing God's perfection. The Lampstand provided the light for the sanctuary. Throughout the Bible God has used images of light and darkness to illustrate the light of His truth against the darkness of sin. The Lampstand is a symbol of Jesus Christ who was "the true Light which gives light to every man who comes into the world" (John 1:9), and "Jesus spoke to them again, saying, 'I am the light of the world. He who follows Me shall not walk in darkness, but have the light of life'" (John 8:12).

This gold lampstand, or Menorah, was lost from the Temple when the Roman armies captured the Temple in A.D. 70. They took it along with captives in chains to Rome, an event recorded in the bas relief sculpture on the Arch of Titus which commemorates the Roman victory. The Levites of the Temple Institute have now cast a pure bronze Menorah that is seven feet high and weighs hundreds of pounds. A gold Menorah, costing over two million dollars will be cast this year.

The Altar of Incense

Just outside the veil that hid the Ark of the Covenant stood the Altar of Incense. Every morning and evening the High Priest burned sweet incense to God when he came into the Holy Place to light the oil in the Golden Lampstand that gave the sanctuary light in the evening services. "You shall make an altar to burn incense on; you shall make it of acacia wood" (Exodus 30:1); this altar was also overlaid with gold and had rings by which it could be carried when it was moved. Eleven special incenses were made from various spices following God's instructions to Moses. A copper tray, called the *kaf*, and a silver chalice, the *bazikh*, that held two hundred grams of incense, were used to carry the precious incense into the sacred precincts of the Temple. A *makhtah*, a copper vessel with a long handle, carried coals from the outer altar to the inner Altar of incense. Additionally, a silver ring, known as the *mitultelet*, and a cloth covering were used in the daily service.

God commanded that incense should be burnt as "a perpetual incense before the Lord throughout your generations" (Exodus 30:8). The incense was sweet smelling and created a most wonderful fragrance that filled the whole of Jerusalem with the aroma of God's divine worship. According to the rabbis, the cloud of perfume was so fragrant that the women of the city of Jerusalem never needed to wear perfume.

Today, in Jerusalem, the Levites have gathered the necessary ingredients to provide a continual supply of the incense which they will use in their daily worship.

The Temple incense typifies the sweet smelling savour of Christ's Holy Spirit whose presence fills our surrendered life and makes us acceptable to our Father in heaven. In the book of Revelation, John tells about the four living creatures and twenty- four elders that surround the Throne of the Lamb, "each having a harp, and golden bowls full of incense, which are the prayers of the saints" (5:8). Our prayers are a sweet fragrant incense as they arise to heaven's throne.

After studying the Torah and Talmudic references to the Altar of Incense, Jewish craftsmen are now reconstructing a replica of it for future Temple worship services.

The Altar of Burnt Offering

This beautiful altar stood in the courtyard before the sanctuary and the place of sacrifice. The priest would offer a clean animal, without blemish, to be sacrificed for the sins of the people for the year. By participating in the offering of sacrifice, the people were acknowledging their sin and asking God to cover their sins, as demanded by the law of Moses. This sacrifice typified Jesus in His role as Messiah-Redeemer. John the Baptist, when Jesus approached him at the River Jordan, prophetically declared: "Behold! The Lamb of God who takes away the sins of the world!" (John 1:29).

The first Altar of Burnt Offering in the Tabernacle was cast by artisans led by "Bezaleel the son of Uri, the son of

Hur, of the tribe of Judah." God also appointed "Aholiab, the son of Ahisamach of the tribe of Dan." Bezaleel and Aholiab and the other artisans were filled with "the Spirit of God, in wisdom, in understanding, in knowledge, and in all manner of workmanship, to design artistic works, to work in gold, in silver, in bronze, in cutting jewels for setting, in carving wood, and to work in all manner of workmanship" (Exodus 31:2-6).

The second Altar of Burnt Offering for Solomon's Temple was cast by a craftsman supplied by Hiram, "In the plain of Jordan... between Succoth and Zaretan" where they were "cast in clay molds" (1 Kings 7:46).

When the Levites are ready to resume the sacrifice system in modern Jerusalem, this Altar of Burnt Offering will have to be built from scratch prior to the actual Temple construction.

The Bronze Laver

The laws of purification for priests on the Temple Mount were strictly enforced. Part of the Temple service rituals included the washing of the priests' hands and feet, before they sacrificed the animals and washing up after. It was essential that the priests clean their hands and feet continually so they would remain sanctified for their Temple service. For this they needed special washing vessels. "You shall also make a laver of bronze, with its base also of bronze, for washing. You shall put it between the tabernacle of meeting and the altar. And you shall put water in it, for Aaron and his sons...shall wash with water, lest they die" (Exodus 30:18-20).

Christians today need to continually be washed and purified by the everlasting water of Him who "saved us, through the washing of regeneration and renewing of the Holy Spirit" (Titus 3:5). In Paul's words, those who believe in Christ are "washed,... sanctified,...justified in the name of the Lord Jesus and by the Spirit of our God" (1 Corinthians 5:11).

It is not tribulation or experience that sanctifies and purifies the Bride of Christ, the Church. It is the washing and sanctifying process of the daily cleansing of the Word that purifies us "that He might sanctify and cleanse [the Church] with the washing of water by the word, that He might present it to Himself a glorious church, not having spot or wrinkle or any such thing, but that it should be holy and without blemish" (Ephesians 5:26-27). Just as the priests in the Old Testament were purified continually by the waters of the Laver, we are purified by submitting ourselves and our conduct to the cleansing action of the Word of God. A fundamental truth of our spiritual life is that the Word of God and sin are mutually antagonistic. A Christian who gets involved in sin will often neglect the reading of the Bible. However, if he turns to the cleansing truth of the Scriptures when he is being tempted, sin and temptation will flee from him.

In the photo section of this book you will see a picture of the reconstructed bronze and copper Laver, with six faucets.

Other Temple Furnishings

When Solomon built the Temple he added to the furnishings that had been in the tabernacle. He had the artisans make ten lavers (1 Kings 7:43), ten lampstands (v.49), ten carts (v.27), and miscellaneous pots, shovels, bowls, and forks of gold and bronze, which "Solomon did not weigh...because there were so many; the weight of the bronze was not determined" (v. 47).

The Mishnah records that up to two hundred silver trumpets were used during Temple festivals. God commanded Moses to make two silver trumpets for "calling the assembly and for directing the movement of the camps" (Numbers 10:2). When the Temple Institute of Jerusalem began to reconstruct the silver trumpets they sent technicians to the Arch of Titus in Rome to obtain the exact dimensions of the sculpture that shows Jewish captives carrying a table with crossed silver trumpets on it. These beautiful 36-inch- long sterling silver trumpets, inlaid with pure gold, have now been made, and are ready to use for future festival days.

The Ashes of the Red Heifer

One peculiar sacrifice commanded by God was not performed in the Tabernacle or Temple but "outside the camp." In this ordinance the Israelites were to choose "a red heifer without blemish, in which there is no defect and on which a yoke has never come" (Numbers 19:2). The young female cow was to be killed outside the camp on the Mount of Olives. The priest would then take some of the blood from the red heifer and sprinkle it seven times in front of the Tabernacle. Then the heifer was burned in the sight of the priest. While it was being burned, the priest would toss cedar, hyssop, and a scarlet thread into the fire burning the heifer. The scarlet thread, called *lashon zehurit*, spoke of the great sin sacrifice and the need for atonement. When the heifer, cedar, hyssop, and scarlet thread were completely consumed by fire, the ashes were stored for future use outside the camp in a clean place. These ashes were used to prepare the water of purification, "for purifying from sin" (vv. 7-9).

After the ceremony the priest would wash his clothes and bathe, then re-enter the camp. But he remained unclean until evening. He would put ashes in a water cistern. This water was sprinkled on those who had become defiled.

In my book *Heaven — the Last Frontier* I cover the subject of the ashes of the red heifer more fully than I will here. However, the importance of these ashes of the red heifer cannot be overestimated. When it is time to rebuild the Temple in Jerusalem the ashes of the red heifer will be needed to produce the water of purification that will purify the Temple Mount before the new Temple can be built. Centuries of defilement and desecration have left the Temple area defiled. Because a red heifer is very rare, the chief rabbi of Israel sent a team of scientists to Europe in October 16, 1989, to obtain frozen embryos of a breed of red heifers descended from an ancient Egyptian breed that will be used to raise a pure red heifer on an Israeli cattle ranch. This pure red heifer will then be prepared in the prescribed manner so that the ashes can be put in the purifying water to cleanse the Temple Mount. Each of the priests and the Levites must be cleansed before they would dare rebuild the Temple.

The Divine Presence

"The Lord is in His holy temple" (Psalm 11:4). The greatest glory and treasure of the Temple was the Divine Presence who dwelt in the Holy of Holies in the Temple. When Solomon dedicated the Temple he prayed that God's blessing and presence would always dwell at the Temple site, even though he knew that "heaven and the heaven of heavens cannot contain You; how much less this temple which I have built!" (2 Chronicles 6:18). Solomon also prayed that, even if Israel went into captivity because of sin, they would "return and confess God's name and pray and make supplication before You in this temple" (v. 25) that God would listen to the prayers of His people.

God's response to Solomon's prayer was, "I have heard your prayer, and have chosen this place for Myself as a house of sacrifice...if My people who are called by My name will humble themselves, and pray and seek My face, and turn from their wicked ways, then I will hear from heaven, and will forgive their sin and heal their land...For now I have chosen and sanctified this house, that My name may be there forever; and My eyes and My heart will be there perpetually" (7:12,14,16).

In Solomon's song of songs he prophesied, "Behold, he stands behind our wall" (Song of Solomon 2:9). These prophecies and traditions have caused the Jews throughout their past and into their present to place a special reverence on the last remaining wall of Herod's enlarged and rebuilt Temple, the Western Wall. The Midrash says, "Behold, there He stands behind our wall—behind the Western Wall of the Holy Temple; why? —because the Holy One, blessed is He, vowed to it that it would never be destroyed" (Shir hoShirim, Rabbah 2:9 4).

The rabbis have an interesting tradition from the Talmud which suggests that the Holy Place on the Temple Mount is directly opposite the Holy Temple above in the heavenly realm. Their sages believe that whenever anyone regards the holy site he is immediately enveloped in the aura of purity and holiness. In a sense, the ancient sages believed that the holy place was a point of spiritual contact to enable them to sense the sovereign King of heaven in all His glory.

Some of the Levites and rabbis I have interviewed believe that the Temple priests must have utilized the vast subterranean tunnel system beneath the Temple Mount to hide some of the precious treasures from their enemies.

In the next chapter we will explore the mysterious hidden city beneath Jerusalem. Thousands of years ago, workmen labored in deep underground caverns and tunnels under the Holy City and Temple to create a complex system of secret passageways. These tunnels and chambers have played a crucial role in the history of Israel. They may lead us someday to the discovery of some of the treasures of the Temple.

CHAPTER 13

The Hidden City, Underground Jerusalem

Hidden deep beneath the streets and buildings of Jerusalem lies an underground city, carved out of rock thousands of years ago. This vast subterranean complex of tunnels, cisterns, storage chambers, and treasuries is unknown to most of the millions of visitors and inhabitants of the city. Although, over the past century and a half, individual researchers and archaeologists have come across the remains of tunnels and cisterns in many areas of the Old City, few have guessed that the entire city of Jerusalem sits on a honeycomb of secret underground passageways, cavernous rooms, and wonderful mysteries.

This enormous infrastructure has served the needs of kings and rebels, priests and citizens during several millennia of peace and warfare. As they have in the past, these underground complexes could today enable part of the city to enjoy a measure of protection in times of war, even against chemical or nuclear attack.

The colonnades and arches underneath the El Aqsa Mosque and the southeast corner of the Temple Mount were explored in the 1800s by a competent English architect named Catherwood. As he walked about Jerusalem he recorded his observations and made diagrams of the construction. During the explorations of Major C. W. Wilson, during the 1860s, beneath the present Wilson's Arch and the Gate of the Chain on the Western Wall, an amazing complex of passages, tunnels, storage rooms, and secret entrances to the Temple was discovered. My own explorations have been aided immeasurably by studying the obscure original research notes of adventurous explorers from the last century such as Wilson, Warren, Barclay, and Robinson.

The Talmud, the Mishnah Torah and many other writings of Jewish sages throughout the history of Jerusalem refer to the construction and usage of this underground complex. According to the Mishnah, King David was the first to dig deeply into the bedrock of Mount Moriah, north of the City of David. This allowed him to lay out the exact foundation lines for the Temple which God had revealed to him and which were to be followed by King Solomon's architects (see Meilah 3.3; Succah 53a; 1 Chronicles 28:11-12).

This tunnel system has played a pivotal role in the life of Jerusalem and its Temple throughout history. Josephus refers to the fact that many Jews, including the Zealot leader Simon, attempted to hid in the tunnels when the Romans burned Jerusalem in A.D. 70. He was captured by the Roman Soldiers of the Tenth Legion when he came out of the underground hideout a week after the battle. Later, in the sixth century, when Julian the Apostate tried to rebuild the Temple, fire burst forth from the tunnels under the Temple, forcing his workmen to abandon their efforts.

Caverns were built to support a vast and sophisticated water storage and tunnel system. Storage chambers were dug out of the earth to secure the treasures of the Temple and the royal household. The underground city also included an elaborate interconnected system of guard rooms, holding chambers for sacrificial animals, and prison cells.

In this chapter I will attempt to share with you some of the things I have discovered during many years of study and discussion with fascinating and little known men who have devoted their lives to unlocking the secrets of this mysterious city. I trust it will help you to understand the marvelous structure of the Temple and how these tunnels played a role in Bible history. Additionally, in this last generation these tunnels are being carefully explored to discover the secrets of Jerusalem and its Temple.

A Sophisticated Water System

Perhaps the best known of the labyrinth beneath Jerusalem is what is called Hezekiah's water system. In the eighth century before Christ, King Hezekiah, one of Judah's good kings, designed a water system that would assure the city of fresh water in the event of a siege. The tunnel began at Gihon Spring and extended for one-third of a mile—1,749 feet of solid bedrock—and emptied into the Pool of Siloam.

During the invasion of King Sennacherib, King Hezekiah "took counsel with his leaders and commanders to stop the water from the springs which were outside the city; and they helped him. Thus many people gathered together who stopped all the springs and the brook that ran through the land, saying, 'Why should the kings of Assyria come and find much water'" (2 Chronicles 32:3-4).

A plaque in classical Hebrew was found in the tunnel leading to the pool and now hangs in a museum in Istanbul. It reads:

"Behold the tunnel. This is the story of its cutting. While the miners swung their picks, one towards the other, and when there remained only three cubits to cut, the voice of one calling his fellow was heard—for there was resonance in the rock coming from both north and south....and the water flowed from the spring towards the pool, 1200 cubits. The height of the rock above the head of the miners was 100 cubits."

As Kaye and I climbed through tunnels along the Western Wall we saw traces of the many ancient pipe systems that carried vast amounts of water, in and out of the courtyards, that were needed for Temple ceremonies. Thirty-nine huge cisterns, carved out of rock under the Temple Mount, have been identified to date; the largest would hold more than twelve million gallons of water. Near Golgotha they have found one of the cisterns where Jeremiah was let "down with ropes. And in the dungeon there was no water, but mire. So Jeremiah sank in the mire" (Jeremiah 38:6).

This cistern is today known as the Grotto of Jeremiah. It can be seen several hundred feet east of Golgotha.

A Treasure Storehouse Carved Out of Mount Moriah

Large chambers were quarried out to provide secure guard rooms for Temple treasures as God had instructed King David. (See 1 Chronicles 28:11.) Almost four hundred years later, his descendent King Hezekiah violated the rules of caution and boastfully revealed the enormous riches of the treasury to the ambassadors of the rising Babylonian Empire, six hundred miles to the east: "And Hezekiah was pleased with them, and showed them the house of his treasures—the silver and gold, the spices and precious ointment, and all his armory—all that was found among his treasures. There was nothing in his house or in all his dominion that Hezekiah did not show them." When Isaiah the prophet asked what the king had shown the Babylonians, Hezekiah replied: "They have seen all that is in my house; there is nothing among my treasures that I have not shown them" (Isaiah 39:2,4).

Isaiah prophesied that Hezekiah's pride in foolishly revealing Israel's stupendous wealth beneath the Temple would attract the unwelcome interest of the Babylonian Empire. True to Isaiah's prediction, in 606 B.C., 598 B.C., and finally in 587 B.C., the armies of King Nebuchadnezzar of Babylon attacked and finally destroyed the Temple and captured the wealth which God had allowed Israel to accumulate.

But Scripture seems to indicate that some of it was hidden so deeply that the Babylonians could not find it. Daniel says that Nebuchadnezzar was able to take "some of the articles of the house of God, which he carried into the land of Shinar to the house of his god; and he brought the articles into the treasure house of his god" (Daniel 1:2, italics added). When Cyrus of Persia decreed that the Jews could go back to Jerusalem and build their temple, he gave them back "the articles of the house of the Lord...thirty gold platters, one thousand silver platters, twenty-nine knives, thirty gold basins, four hundred and ten silver basins of a similar kind, and one thousand other articles" (Ezra 1:8-10); but no mention is made of the most precious of Temple furnishings, except for the "carts and bronze Sea" that were broken in pieces and carried to Babylon (2 Kings 25:13).

Royal Escape Routes

When King Herod rebuilt and enlarged the Temple, which Zerubbabel had built after the Jews were allowed to return from captivity, he was very concerned with the possibility of revolt against his rule because he was an Idumean (an Arab) and not an Israelite. He got his position as a favor from Rome. He built a number of fortresses for refuge in case of revolution, among them the mountain fortresses of Masada and Herodium. In addition, King Herod had his engineers build a secret escape tunnel that led diagonally from his Tower of Antonia palace to a special defense tower near the Eastern Gate.

One of the most fascinating of recent discoveries under the Temple Mount is one of these escape tunnels that was used by the ancient kings of Judah, including King Zedekiah. On our final evening in Jerusalem during one of our trips, Kaye and I received a most unusual invitation. A telephone call asked if we were interested in exploring even deeper under the Temple Mount than we had been allowed on previous trips. Naturally, we said yes. From my earliest years I have loved exploring tunnels and caverns. Many times as a teenager I would explore for hours the huge cavern systems that lay under Frontier Ranch, our family's resort camp in Canada. However, this midnight trip through tunnels beneath Jerusalem and the Temple Mount was the highlight of my exploring adventures.

We met our Israeli friend at the Western Wall at 2:00 A.M. as agreed. To our surprise, despite a rainy night, about two dozen yeshiva students were dancing and worshiping at the Western Wall with their rabbi. My friend told me that the wall is never without worshipers, even through the long nights of winter. For the next two-and-a-half hours Kaye and I were thrilled to walk where few people in history have ever explored. As we began our exciting trip we were able, without pressure or interference, to photograph many of the gates, tunnels and rooms that we had not previously photographed. Tunnel after tunnel opened into guard rooms, ancient synagogues, and storage chambers. After walking along the entire length (over eleven hundred feet) of the Western Wall tunnel excavation, we arrived at a point under the foundations of the ancient Tower of Antonio where the kings of Israel used to build their palaces.

The King's Gate

In the north end of the tunnel, that parallels the Western Wall, under a hundred and fifty feet of rubble and the basements of Arab buildings, we came upon an unusual stone gate cut through the enormous foundation stones that led up into the kings' palaces immediately north of the Temple. This huge gate, known as the King's Gate, has been sealed by large stones carefully fitted into the opening. This was the secret escape tunnel entrance built beneath the huge fortified palace for protection of the king. Since the Temple Mount itself was the most strongly defended part of Jerusalem, it is natural that the kings would use this area for their last retreat.

King Zedekiah's Escape Tunnel

When King Nebuchadnezzar besieged Jerusalem, King Zedekiah of Judah decided to flee the city with his soldiers and family. "Then the city wall was broken through, and all the men of war fled at night *by way of the gate between two walls*, which was by the king's garden, even though the Chaldeans were still encamped all around against the city. And the king went by way of the plain. But the army of the Chaldeans pursued the king, and they overtook him in the plains of Jericho. All his army was scattered from him" (2 Kings 25:4-5, italics added). The king, after a two-year siege, had to flee at night. Of course he could not have fled with his army and his family by any means other than a tunnel. Now, after twenty-five centuries, the proof of the accuracy of this biblical history has been revealed by the spade of archaeologists. For security reasons I cannot reveal the exact location of the exit from this tunnel system.

The prophet Ezekiel had predicted the precise course of these events: "And the prince who is among them shall bear his belongings on his shoulder at twilight and go out. They shall dig through the wall to carry them out through it. He shall cover his face, so that he cannot see the ground with his eyes. I will also spread My net over him, and he shall be caught in My snare. I will bring him to Babylon, to the land of Chaldeans; yet he shall not see it, though he shall die there" (Ezekiel 12:12-13). King Zedekiah was captured by the Babylonians and blinded and his children were killed, exactly as Ezekiel had foretold, because he would not obey the command of God to submit to Babylon. He passed by within a few hundred yards of the cistern prison in which he had condemned the prophet Jeremiah. King Nebuchadnezzar freed the prophet Jeremiah, but he took the blind King Zedekiah back to Babylon in chains. As the photographs in the center section of this book show, this tunnel is most unusual in that the roof is more than sixty feet high for much of its length. Yet its width is only four feet. The description in 2 Kings that the escapees went "between two walls" is the most accurate I could find to describe this narrow escape tunnel which led more than eight thousand feet north to emerge outside the ancient walls of the city.

Throughout the book of Jeremiah there are repeated references to moving Jeremiah from prison cisterns to the Temple and the king's house by means of tunnels, including this especially long one.

Just opposite the gate, were the remains of a large and elaborate mikveh, ritual baths, which the kings used to ritually purify themselves prior to entering the Temple itself. Passing this historic mikveh we entered a newly opened tunnel that led under the Temple Mount. Only a year earlier I had been told that archaeologists had just discovered this elaborate tunnel complex. When I asked for more information I was told that there was a mystery connected with it.

Rooms for Temple Guards

While the area near the sanctuary itself was holy, those areas farther away from the Sanctuary on the thirty-five-acre Temple Mount were used for fortifications, espionage, and communication systems. Special tunnels connected strategic points of the enormous Temple Mount for fortification and military defense. The royal intelligence forces and Temple guards both made use of these secret passages. Large guardrooms have been located under the Temple area for those whose duty it was to guard the nation's treasury as well as keep out trespassers.

Enormous arched basement rooms, built by King Solomon, were used during the Crusades to hold the soldiers' horses. The area was called Solomon's Stables by the Crusaders, but it is doubtful that Solomon kept his cavalry and chariot horses in these caverns.

There is a curious story recorded in Yoma 35a about a magician named Parvah who dug a secret tunnel through the limestone under the Temple to come up inside the inner courtyard. He wanted to clandestinely witness the High Priest during secret Temple worship service. The story says that Parvah was killed for defiling the sacred precincts, and the area from where he watched the ceremony was named the "Chamber of Parvah" to remind others of the sanctity of the Lord's house.

Access to these tunnels was described as being through "winding underground passageways" (Mishnah Torah 8.7), which is a good description of several of the tunnels we explored. These unconsecrated tunnel passages were used by priests who had defiled themselves: "There he would immerse himself [in a mikveh]. He would then return and sit among his fellow priests until the gates were opened" (Halachah II.5). The purification rules were so strict that any priest who defiled himself had to immediately leave the Temple through these tunnels, without speaking to anyone. Niches in the tunnels once held candles.

Various Temple Services

These underground caverns and tunnels were used in the many worship rituals. The priests who were serving in the Temple were required to be ceremonially clean and the animals used for sacrifice also had to be kept clean. Tunnels, ramps, and chambers were used to bring the many animals up to the surface for the sacrifice.

The Ritual Cleansing of Priests

With approximately a quarter of a million people visiting the ancient Temple Mount each year during the feasts of Passover, Pentecost and Tabernacles, which God commanded all males to attend, twenty thousand priests were needed to serve. It was necessary for the priests who were participating in these Temple services to remain ritually clean throughout the service. The tunnels provided private access for those priests who had undergone the purifying ceremony. They had to protect themselves from becoming defiled by contact with the common people, which would prevent them from serving in the Temple.

Several tunnels led directly to mikvehs where the priests cleansed themselves before entering the Temple Mount to serve the Lord. I have already mentioned one of the most interesting mikvehs which was located just outside the Western Wall at the King's Gate (now sealed) where the king would exit from the Tower of Antonia (the palace) and privately prepare himself to enter the Temple.

The purification ceremony was especially necessary for anyone who had touched a dead body. God required this cleansing after contact with a body, even for a soldier (see Numbers 31:19-21), because death is connected to the curse of sin. Touching anything dead would ritually defile a priest; it was necessary for him to go through the cleansing ceremony before participating in Temple services (see Numbers 19:11-22).

Keeping the Temple Mount Pure

Not only did the priests have to be ceremonially clean, the entire Temple Mount had to be kept from defilement. In the "Laws of God's Chosen House" (Mishnah Torah 5.1), Maimonides, referring to the Temple Courtyard, quoted eyewitnesses from the time of the second Temple: "Mount Moriah, the Temple Mount, measured five hundred cubits by 500 cubits. It was surrounded by a wall. The earth beneath it was hollowed out to prevent contracting [ritual impurity] due to Tumas Ohel. Arches above arches were built underneath [for support]. It was entirely covered, one colonnade inside another."

The "arches above arches" also supported the ramp from the Temple Mount to the Mount of Olives. Across this ramp the red heifer was led to the plateau where the priests sacrificed it in A.D. 68 for the last purification ceremony just before the destruction of the Temple by the Roman army.

Additional eyewitness accounts recorded in the writings of Maimonides state: "The underground passageways which open to the Temple Courtyard are consecrated. Those that open to the Temple Mount [outside the Courtyard] are not consecrated" (Mishnah Torah 6.9). Orthodox Jews today, and most rabbis in Jerusalem, believe that no Jew should enter any part of the Temple Mount without being ceremonially cleansed with ashes from the Red Heifer lest they inadvertently defile the site of the Holy of Holies. One of the most famous of Temple visitors, Moses Maimonides, however, personally explored the Temple Mount during a research trip to Palestine in A.D. 1165: "On Thursday, 5th Marcheshvan 4926 [A.D. 1165] I entered the great and Holy House and prayed there." This fact was recorded by Rabbi Elazar Ascari who copied it from Maimonides own book *Sepher Charedin*, written in his own hand. The only reason Maimonides would have entered the Temple Courtyard with such confidence is that he knew precisely where the true site of the Holy of Holies was and therefore did not trespass the sacred place.

The zeal for keeping the Temple Mount undefiled seems strange to Western people but was very serious to Jewish lawmakers. Rabbis taught that if a corpse was buried in the earth below the Temple it would render the sacrifices invalid. The Mishnah Parah declares that the rock underneath the city and the Temple were purposely tunneled out to create open spaces that would protect the surface area above from ritual defilement arising from contamination with the remains of dead bodies that might be buried in the ground below: "The entire earth below was hollowed out...to prevent the possibility of impurity from a grave under the Temple courtyard" (Parah 3.3).

This ritual defilement was known as tumeah and the sages believed that the creation of open space below the pavement of the Temple would effectively insulate the ground immediately under the Temple Mount and the city from the tumeah.

The Mishnah Middoth (1.6) describes another secret chamber that was hollowed out under the Chamber of Showbread as a repository for the defiled altar stones. These stones had been desecrated by Antiochus Epiphanes, the Syrian tyrant, in 168 B.C. when he sacrificed a pig on the altar. When the Hasmonean priests cleansed the Temple on Hanukkah (the twenty-fifth day of Chisleu), they did not know what to do with the defiled stones, so they carved out this secret chamber and stored the altar stones there "until the Messiah should come and instruct them in what should be done" with them.

Another fascinating story from the Mishnah says that pregnant wives of priests were sometimes housed in special chambers near the Temple Mount above hollowed out areas. They believed that a child born and raised in such a place would be protected from defilement. Such special children were trained to take their place as "clean" ones to participate in the Ashes of the Red Heifer ceremony.

An interesting parallel to this practice was revealed during a conversation I had with the Jewish-Christian Prince Stephen Mengesha of Ethiopia. We discussed the elaborate rituals the black Jews of Ethiopia use to protect their underground Temple with its Ark of the Covenant in Aksum, Ethiopia. (See chapter 8 in *Armageddon-Appointment with Destiny*.) The prince said that an innocent young boy is specially sanctified and trained by the High Priest's family. When the present guardian of the Ark dies, a seven-year-old boy replaces him. For the rest of his life he lives in the Holy of Holies in the underground temple, never leaving it until the day of his death when another takes his place. This has gone on without interruption for three thousand years.

The Gate of the Levites

One of the tunnels under the city led to a secret gate of the Levites that opened through the underground portions of the Western Wall. This special gate was described quite clearly in the Mishnah as being next to a larger gate that required six men to close. If a Levite was delayed in Temple service after the main gate was locked at night he had to use the special Gate of the Levites. Only thirty by fifty inches, the Levite who was late leaving the Temple had to stoop to exit and close the iron door. The discovery of this gate has helped present-day Levites to measure the precise location of their ancient Temple.

A Hiding Place for the Ark of the Covenant

I introduced a great deal of evidence in my previous book that the lost Ark of the Covenant is in an underground temple in northern Ethiopia. It is important to tell about another strong tradition concerning the Ark and other Temple treasures. Some believe that these Temple objects are still buried under the Temple Mount where they were placed when Judah was conquered and the Temple was first destroyed in 587 B.C. Some believe that these treasures will remain there until the rebuilding of the Temple.

Jewish sages say that, thirty-five years before the event, King Josiah was given special prophetic insight about the coming destruction of the sanctuary by the Babylonians. They believe that God led the king and the priesthood to bury the treasures of the Temple, including the oil of anointing, Aaron's rod, and the pot of manna in a special chamber that had been hewn out for this purpose five hundred years before by King Solomon (Mishnah Shekalim 6.1). Also, buried there, according to this tradition, is the Ark of the Covenant (or, more likely, its replica).

In "The Laws of God's Chosen House," Maimonides gives this account: "When Solomon built the Temple, he was aware that it would ultimately be destroyed. He constructed a chamber in which the Ark could be entombed below the Temple in deep, maze-like vaults. King Josiah commanded that the Ark be entombed in the chamber built by Solomon, as it is said (2 Chronicles 35:3), 'And he said to the Levites who were enlightened above all of Israel, Place the Holy Ark in the chamber built by Solomon, the son of

David, King of Israel. You will no longer carry it on your shoulders. Now, serve the Lord, your God.' When it was entombed, Aaron's staff, the vial of manna, and the oil used for anointing were entombed with it. All these sacred articles did not return in the Second Temple" (Hilchos Bais HaBechirah).

In Exodus 16:33, Moses commanded Aaron to "take a pot and put an omer of manna in it, and lay it up before the Lord, to be kept for your generations." An account in Numbers also mentions these treasures. The Levite Korah had led a revolt against Moses and Aaron, accusing them of behaving as if they were the exclusive leaders from God. The result was that the instigators of the revolution, along with their families, were destroyed by God. When the people objected to their deaths, God threatened to destroy the whole group with a plague. Moses commanded Aaron to take a censer of incense and make atonement for the people so that God would spare them. When the plague stopped, God devised a method whereby He would show the Israelites who was His chosen spiritual leader. Twelve rods, representing the twelve tribes, and Aaron's rod were placed before the Lord in the tabernacle. The next day when Moses went into the Tabernacle, only Aaron's rod "had sprouted and put forth buds, had produced blossoms and yielded ripe almonds" (Numbers 19:8). God commanded Moses to "bring Aaron's rod back before the Testimony, to be kept as a sign against the rebels, that you may put their murmurings away from Me, lest they die" (v. 10). So, Aaron's budding rod was also placed in the Ark of the Covenant.

When Kaye and I were in the Western Wall excavation tunnels, exactly opposite the original Temple position, we noticed a picture of a menorah hanging from a spike in the Western Wall. When I asked the Levite archaeologist why the picture was hanging in a working archaeology dig, he told me that as nearly as they could calculate, the ancient Menorah stood in the Second Temple directly behind that picture. He also said something quite curious to me that I understood only after studying Maimonides "censored" volume on the Temple. He said, "Grant, we believe that the sacred Ark of the Covenant is located in a secret chamber directly behind this Western Wall." We were standing more han a hundred feet below the level you would walk on today if you visited the Temple Mount. Now I realize that he had calculated the possible location of the Temple treasures by assuming that King Solomon and King Josiah had lowered them on a special ramp into the secret hiding chamber a hundred feet below the floor of the Temple.

I personally believe that the Ark of the Covenant disappeared from Israel long before the reign of King Josiah and is buried in Ethiopia where it was taken by Prince Menelik, the son of Solomon and the Queen of Sheba. What could be hidden behind the menorah is a perfect replica of the Ark that was created by Solomon's craftsmen. Ethiopian history claims that this replica was substituted for the real Ark in the Holy of Holies. (See *Armageddon — Appointment With Destiny*.)

A Replica of the Ark of the Covenant

The Jerusalem Talmud clearly refers to a second Ark of the Covenant: "A second Ark containing the Tablets broken by Moses accompanied the people to war at all times" (Shekalim 6). While this does not prove the case that a replica was made, it certainly adds evidence to the Ethiopian Royal Chronicle regarding a second Ark. Only the passage of time and further research will conclusively prove the true location of the lost Ark. However, biblical prophecies clearly indicate that the Ark (wherever the Lord has preserved it) will be involved in the motivation of the Jews to build the Third Temple.

An Underground Church?

After burning the Temple in A.D. 70, Roman soldiers threw the burned stones into a valley west of the Western Wall so that nothing remained of the Temple. This was just as Jesus had prophesied: "Assuredly, I say to you, not one stone shall be left here upon another, that shall not be thrown down" (Matthew 24:2). When the inhabitants of Jerusalem began to rebuild their city, they used these available stones, even though they were badly damaged from being thrown down a hundred feet into the valley.

One of the most remarkable discoveries made during the Western Wall tunnel excavation was an immense room underneath the rubble of the destroyed Temple. Kaye and I walked through the tunnels and entered this colossal room with our Israeli friend. It was larger than any we had explored, more than a hundred feet in length and, in some places, fifty feet wide. The majestic roof, which had obviously been rebuilt during the time of the crusades, arched above our heads some sixty feet. Yet the whole building was a little more than fifty feet below the present basements of Arab buildings that have been built during the last thousand years. Capitals and columns reconstructed during the Crusades led archaeologists to name it as the Hall of Capitals.

The most amazing thing about the building is that it is in the shape of a cross, with the wings of the cross extending almost eighty feet across. I asked my Israeli friend, who has studied Temple archeology for twenty years, if this could be a Jewish- Christian church located almost at the foot of the Western Wall. He slowly nodded yes. There are no Muslim or Jewish buildings anywhere in the world that are in the shape of a cross. However, many early Christian churches were built that way. The most extraordinary feature of this building is that, from the floor to about twelve feet up, it is constructed from the actual stones of the Temple which the Romans destroyed. Above that point the builders were forced to use newer and smaller stones to complete their walls. Could this be the remains of a first-century Jewish-Christian church built of stones from the destroyed Temple?

The location of this possible ancient church, for more than a thousand years, was unknown except in legend. To say that the Israeli authorities were surprised to find what appeared to be a Christian church, built from the sacred stones of the Temple, within a hundred feet of the Western Wall, is certainly an understatement. Some of the archaeologists I talked to do not believe that this structure could be a church. However, while the evidence is promising, more investigation needs to be done to make a final determination.

Even after the destruction of the Temple, Jews still remained in Jerusalem until they were expelled by Emperor

Hadrian. Does the existence of this church imply that a large number of Jews became believers in the Messiah Jesus? The archaeologist Dr. Bargil Pixner has done some fascinating research on the remains of another Jewish-Christian church found in the basement of the Upper Room building. Inscriptions about Jesus and its unusual orientation convinced him that this was the Church of the Apostles, referred to in ancient church history.

How Were These Ancient Tunnels Excavated?

Although some of the caverns under the city are natural, most were carved out by miners. Subterranean passages connect in a vast system of tunnels extending from the Pool of Siloam area in the south of the ancient City of David all the way to Golgotha— Calvary, to the north of the city walls and the Gate of Damascus. Some of the tunnel system connects westward to the upper city (now the Jewish Quarter) and parts of the Muslim and Armenian quarters. During one of the Arab-Jewish wars, soldiers explored some of these extensive tunnels and planted an enormous cache of explosives under an enemy building across the line dividing Jerusalem. Fortunately, it did not detonate and the explosives were later removed.

Seeing these vast caverns and tunnels provokes the question, How was it possible that such a great extent of tunnels could be dug underneath a city, through rock, without the aid of explosives and with the primitive tools of more than two thousand years ago? The answer is two-fold.

First, ancient engineers during the reign of King Solomon and King Herod were not nearly as primitive as some historians have assumed. The complex engineering on the Temple Mount defies explanation even today. How could they have quarried and moved forty-six-foot-long stones that weighed a thousand tons and placed them so closely together that you cannot insert a razor blade between them? We cannot move such stones today with all our modern technology.

The second part of the answer lies in the unusual nature of the limestone that forms the foundation of the whole city of Jerusalem. While I was in one cave far beneath the city, a small stone broke off from the ceiling overhead. As I reached up to touch the place where the stone had been I was surprised at how soft the rock surface felt. I was able to carve a small square in the exposed limestone with my index fingernail. The archaeologist with me said that while the limestone is very easy to work with when first exposed, a few years from now the exposed surface would be as hard as any other type of stone. Workers could carve out tunnels through newly exposed soft limestone with very basic iron chisels and picks with relative ease. Eventually, through exposure to air, the walls would become as solid and strong as any other "cured" construction.

The quarrying of the huge stones from beneath the city served a dual purpose: (1) it created large chambers for storage purposes or for use as cisterns; (2) it provided material to construct the magnificent Temple buildings, palaces, and government structures. A unique factor in the incredible beauty of the city of Jerusalem is that regardless of the government the city was under—Rome, Turkey, Britain, or modern Israel, all required that buildings be constructed of Jerusalem limestone. This has created the wonderful uniform golden limestone buildings that retain their diverse architecture from many cultures.

Further Explorations of the City of God

After almost three decades of reading musty old books from rabbis and extensively researching original reports by early explorers, including the Palestine Exploration Fund, and having the great privilege of actually exploring the tunnel system myself, I am convinced that we still know less than 10 percent of the secrets of Jerusalem and the Temple Mount. My own explorations have focused on Mount Zion, the Temple Mount, the Western Wall excavations, the Old City, and Golgotha. I fully expect that long years into the Millennium we will still be uncovering new chambers and tunnels that will open up our understanding of the fascinating history of this most remarkable of ancient and modern cities. If the Lord allows, I trust I will be among those still exploring the incredible secrets of Jerusalem, the City of God. There are many more mysteries yet to be solved.

All those who have the opportunity to explore the underground secrets of the Temple Mount will be profoundly moved by the experience. It truly puts you in touch with some of the most incredible moments and places in history. The loss of the Temple was a great tragedy for the Jewish nation. But the same prophets that predicted the Temple's destruction also promised that the Messiah would return to redeem the world.

As we approach the pivotal days for the coming of the Messiah, those mysterious tunnels under the city of Jerusalem will play a significant role in the search for the treasures of the Temple. Archaeological research in these tunnels and chambers will also help prepare for the rebuilding of the Temple. God's unchanging promise is that the Temple will once more stand in all its glory.

In the next chapter of this book we will look at the mystery of the Church which the Lord created when Israel rejected her Messiah. The promised kingdom was postponed for almost two thousand years. However, the Kingdom of the Messiah is coming.

PART IV

The Coming Messiah

"And I saw a new heaven and a new earth, for the first heaven and the first earth had passed away. Also there was no more sea. Then I, John, saw the holy city, New Jerusalem, coming down out of heaven from God, prepared as a bride adorned for her husband. And I heard a loud voice from heaven saying, 'Behold, the tabernacle of God is with men, and He will dwell with them, and they shall be His people, and God Himself will be with them and be their God. And God will wipe away every tear from their eyes; there shall be no more death, nor sorrow, nor crying; and there shall be no more pain, for the former things have passed away,'" Revelation 21:1-4.

CHAPTER 14

The Mystery of the Church—The Kingdom Postponed

The ultimate purpose of man is to manifest God's glory and to sanctify His holy name. As the "Shorter Catechism" says: "What is the chief end of men? To glorify God and to enjoy him forever." This is not simply something God commanded us to do, it is the very reason we were created in the first place. In the beginning God said: "Let Us make man in Our image; according to Our likeness;...So God created man in His own image; in the image of God He created him; male and female He created them" (Genesis 1:26-27). We were created to reflect and glorify God. Tragically, history and personal experience reveal man's continued sinful rebellion and failure to glorify God.

The first chance they had, Adam and Eve turned their backs on God and listened to Satan's voice. They failed to fulfill their purpose and cut themselves off from their Creator and Sustainer. Man's rebellion could have led to man's destruction.

But God was not willing to destroy the world, eliminate a rebellious humanity, and start over. Rather, He began a plan to redeem His fallen children and restore mankind once again to the image of His glory and into His fellowship. He set the stage for a Messiah who would reconcile us to our God and establish His kingdom.

The Kingdom of God has two aspects: (1) the future universal rule of Jesus Christ in the Millennium as Messiah; and (2) the spiritual kingdom that exists today in the transformed hearts and souls of redeemed men and women who allow Jesus to reign as Lord of their lives. It was a mystery to Old Testament saints, and is still somewhat a mystery to the Church today. The Lord is calling out a particular people, a royal priesthood of believers composed of both Jews and Gentiles, to glorify His name after Israel as a people had rejected her Messiah. When the Messiah was presented to Israel on Palm Sunday in A.D. 32, the tragic result was that the Jewish people and leaders rejected Christ. When He was crucified five days later, the promise of the Millennial Kingdom of God was postponed for both Israel and the world.

In this chapter we will talk about why the Millennial Kingdom was postponed, God's plan for the Church to reach a lost world and how Christ will bring about His ultimate redemptive purpose for mankind.

Why Did God Choose the Jews?

There are more than six billion humans living on this planet, and within that number, fewer than sixteen million are Jews. Yet today, as they have throughout history, this tiny percentage (less than one-fourth of 1 percent) of humanity has enormously contributed to the world's progress in proportions that far outweigh their numbers. What other group of people have accomplished so much?

The list of Jews who have transformed society reads like a Who's Who of man's greatest scientific, religious, philosophical, and technological accomplishments. It is hard to imagine what man's religious outlook would be if Abraham, Moses, David, and all the biblical prophets had never lived to reveal God's character and law to man. What would civilization look like if Jesus, the apostles, and Paul had not transformed our lives through the revelation of Christ's redeeming love? Others who have made a difference in our Western civilization include Moses Maimonides, Karl Marx, Albert Einstein, Niels Bohr, Sigmund Freud, Baruch Spinoza, and Henry Kissinger. Almost 12 percent of the Nobel Prizes in the sciences have been won by Jews. How have these people, who have been dispersed among the nations, persecuted, and misunderstood, been able to hang onto their Jewishness in the face of such obvious hatred? The answer is that they are special to God and the Lord has revealed His hand in history.

When the world was young, God set in motion His plan to reconcile His highest creation, mankind, to fellowship with Him. That plan included the selecting of a people who would sanctify God's name, manifest God's nature and His laws, and be a light to the nations. The Jews did not choose God. Rather, God chose them to "be a people for Himself, a special treasure above all the peoples on the face of the earth...not...because you were more in number than any other people, for you were the least of all peoples; but because the Lord loves you" (Deuteronomy 7:6-8). With them he made an "everlasting covenant," meaning one that He would not break, even if the chosen people did not fulfill their end of the agreement. Because of God's everlasting covenant with them, the Jews are committed to survive as Jews. They determined not to be assimilated into the general cultures of other people but to retain their uniqueness even though they have been dispersed (diaspora) among the nations many times in their history. They are still a distinct people who refuse to be stamped out despite many attempts to destroy them, not for their sake but because of God's covenant with them.

Judges, Kings, and a Rejection of God's Plan of Kingdom Rule

Initially, God used the Old Testament Patriarchs to reveal the promise of His final redemption—men such as Abel and Enoch and Noah. Later, He chose a whole tribe of people who, through their father Abraham, would be a special repository of the truth of the Torah, God's Law, and a witness to all nations of the nature and commands of God. He entrusted His written Word the Bible to Israel, both in writing His words and in preserving the manuscripts through the centuries.

On Mount Sinai the Jewish people clearly accepted this covenant arrangement with God and the responsibilities that accompanied it. Thus, God held Israel to a much higher standard of obedience to His revealed purpose, than the pagan nations surrounding them who did not possess the Scriptures of the Most High God. When the chosen people finally reached the land that God promised would be theirs forever, they began a series of governments that would lead toward the final Kingdom of the Messiah.

The Theocratic Kingdom Under the Judges

For a period of four hundred and fifty years the chosen people practiced a very unusual form of human government. They received their guidance from God through a series of men and women judges. This system existed from the time the Israelites settled Canaan under Joshua until Samuel's judgeship. While there were several lapses from obedience to God, which were followed by a period of punishment from God, such as their captivity by the Philistines, over three hundred and fifty years of the judge's rule were spent in peace and prosperity. This period was the most peaceful the nation of Israel had ever known and would not be enjoyed again until Solomon became king.

The Apostle Paul said that "He [God] gave them judges" (Acts 13:20), proving that this system of government was distinctly provided by God.

Even though the system was successful for many years, the people wanted to be like the nations surrounding them and have a king. The last judge, Samuel, appointed his two sons Joel and Abijah as judges in Beersheba, but they "did not walk in his ways; they turned aside after dishonest gain, took bribes, and perverted justice" (1 Samuel 8:3). So the elders approached Samuel and demanded that he appoint a king "like all the nations" (v. 5). Samuel was upset but when he prayed about the matter, God reassured him: "Heed the voice of the people in all that they say to you; for they have not rejected you, but they have rejected Me, that I should not reign over them" (v. 7).

Israel Under the Kings

Even though God had chosen the system of judges as an ideal theocratic government, He allowed Israel to choose human kings. They soon found out that it was a mistake to reject His will.

When God agreed to let the people have a king, He told Samuel to warn the nation that a king would make their sons his servants and soldiers, and their daughters "perfumers, cooks, and bakers" for him. A king would take the best of their fields, vineyards, and olive groves and a further tenth of the grain and wines they produced from the land he left to them; he would take the best of their livestock. But the people did not care. They wanted a king.

Just as God warned, from the first king, Saul, in 1096 B.C. until the last king, Zedekiah, who fell in 587 B.C., the kings of Israel heaped up treasures for themselves, built huge armies, and exacted enormous taxes and slave labor to support such efforts. The high points included King David, "a man after God's own heart," and King Solomon who "reigned over all the kings from the River [Euphrates] to the land of the Philistines, as far as the border of Egypt" and who "made silver as common in Jerusalem as stones" (2 Chronicles 9:26-27). However, Israel's path led downward through a tragic list of evil kings who caused the physical destruction of the nation and the spiritual decline of its people. Israel wanted to be like the surrounding pagan nations. They rejected their exalted role as God's chosen people who were supposed to be a light to the Gentiles.

Throughout the reign of the kings the people turned further and further away from the commands of God and plunged deeper into sin. The prophets of God continued to risk their lives to warn the nation of the consequence of their sin and the coming judgment of God. Through all the tragic litany of war, pagan assaults on their faith, and misguidance of evil kings, the prophets never stopped predicting that God would finally send His Messiah to redeem the land and the people from their sins. This Messianic hope was the only beacon of light to guide Israel during the long dark years under one evil king after another. Even the ancient sages of Israel knew that the reason Israel lost her kingdom, her Temple, and her holy city Jerusalem was due to her failure to glorify and sanctify God's holy name. Ezekiel predicted: "The Gentiles shall know that the house of Israel went into captivity for their iniquity; because they were unfaithful to Me, therefore I hid My face from them. I gave them into the hand of their enemies, and they all fell by the sword" (Ezekiel 39:23).

257

The Promise of a Deliverer

In the midst of Israel's hopelessness, God spoke to Isaiah and promised that He would send a Deliverer to Israel—and to the Gentiles: "For unto us a Child is born, unto us a Son is given; and the government will be upon His shoulder. And His name will be called Wonderful, Counselor, Mighty God, Everlasting Father, Prince of Peace. Of the increase of His government and peace there will be no end, upon the throne of David and over His kingdom, to order it and establish it with judgment and justice from that time forward, even forever" (Isaiah 9:6-7).

The King Rejected—The Kingdom Postponed

The final redemption of Israel and the world will ultimately be obtained when the Messiah-Redeemer, sent from God, sits on the throne of David in Jerusalem and establishes forever the kingdom of God on Earth. Tragically, when Jesus the Messiah-Redeemer first came, both Israel and the Gentiles rejected Him. Despite fulfilling hundreds of Old Testament prophecies, performing dozens of miracles, and teaching the deep truths of God, the majority of mankind rejected His claim that He was the Messiah sent from God. The result was His crucifixion at Calvary. Every man and woman who has ever lived was present at the Cross, because it was our sinful rebellion against God that necessitated His terrible punishment of the Son of God, a punishment deserved by us. Just as the prophet said, the Messiah suffered, was tortured and killed for our sins when we rejected Him. Yet the rejection of the Messiah opened the door to all mankind—Jew and Gentile—to enter the spiritual kingdom through the blood of the Lamb sacrificed at the altar of Calvary. It also led to the postponement of Christ's Millennial Kingdom and Israel's blessing for almost two thousand years.

A Spiritual Kingdom of God—The Mystery of the Church

One of the fundamental roles of Israel was to be "a light to the Gentiles" (Isaiah 42:6) and to manifest God's nature and teach His Law, the Torah, to the Gentile nations. That is why there was a Court of the Gentiles in the Temple. That is why the prophet Jonah was sent to the Gentile nation of Nineveh with the astonishing result that the entire city repented in a revival that has never been equalled. The tragedy is that during most of its history, Israel was usually content to withhold the Torah rather than freely share it with the Gentile nations. But God's purpose would not be changed. The light which the Jews were to shine on the nations was finally shed on the Gentiles when Jesus, the Light of the world gave His life on the cross.

When the Jews rejected Jesus it prepared the way for the Gentile nations to accept openly both Jesus as Messiah and God's plan of redemption. Billions of Gentiles who would believe in God's Son could now be counted as "Abraham's seed, and heirs according to the promise" (Galatians 3:29) when Israel failed to recognize Jesus of Nazareth as Messiah. "Through their [Israel's] fall, to provoke them to jealousy, salvation has come to the Gentiles....some of the branches were broken off, and you, being a wild olive tree, were grafted in among them, and with them became a partaker of the root and fatness of the olive tree" (Romans 11:11,17).

How else would Gentiles have come to know God? Do most Gentiles know or care about the doctrines of the Hasidic Orthodox Jews of Israel today? No! There is little reason, in the natural, for most Gentiles to care about the religious beliefs of a small group of Jews in Israel. If Israel had accepted Jesus as their Messiah, the Gentile nations would probably have been just as indifferent to their God and their Jewish Messiah. An exclusive Jewish Christianity would not have interested the nations. But when the Jews rejected Jesus, those Jews who became His followers were led by God to evangelize the Gentile nations. The new faith transformed itself into a true missionary movement in which Greek pastors evangelized Greeks and Roman converts spread the good news to those in Italy. The truths of monotheism, the Ten Commandments, the Torah, the Psalms and the warnings of the prophets spread rapidly throughout a world that had never heard of the religion of the Jews until Christians began to preach Christ as the fulfillment of God's promises in the Old Testament.

The gospel of Jesus spread like wildfire through the Roman Empire in the first few centuries of our era. Today, virtually the whole world operates with a basic understanding of these foundational truths because the followers of Jesus fulfilled the Great Commission.

How can anyone look at this remarkable result without marveling at the mysterious ways God has revealed His truths through the efforts of both Jew and Christian?

Israel's Future Mission—The Great Harvest

But God's Word will be fulfilled in another way regarding His command that the Jews would be a light to the Gentiles. During the terrible period of the Great Tribulation, Israel will finally fulfill its prophesied role as the Two Witnesses and the 144 thousand Jewish witnesses evangelize the entire world. Despite the awesome spiritual battles with the Antichrist and Satan's armies, they will prevail. The spiritual harvest of that great mission field will be the largest in human history. John saw this "great multitude which no one could number, of all nations, tribes, peoples, and tongues" in heaven who were saved out of the Great Tribulation. "Who are these arrayed in white robes, and where did they come from?" the angel asked John. The answer was, "These are the ones who come out of the great tribulation, and washed their robes and made them white in the blood of the Lamb" (Revelation 7:9,13-14).

The Lord will accomplish one of the purposes of His chosen people when the Jewish remnant witness to His name during the terrible Tribulation period and also as they become the preeminent nation during the eternal reign of the Messiah. In that glorious day a faithful Israel will truly bless the nations.

Where Does That Leave Israel?

The question, "What will God do about Israel now that they have rejected His only begotten son?" was asked by many early followers of Christ. The question is still being asked by Gentile believers. The answers have been many.

Some, including those in the Roman Catholic Church and many Reformers decided that God must be through with Israel as a nation because they rejected their Messiah. However, the Apostle Paul in Romans 11:1 and 2 clearly rejects this answer: "I say then, has God cast away His people? Certainly not! For I also am an Israelite, of the seed of Abraham, of the tribe of Benjamin. God has not cast away His people whom He foreknew."

God's people continually turned their back on Him as their Supreme Being, worshiped idols, and broke His commandments. God had to punish them. They "went into captivity for their iniquity; because they were unfaithful to Me, therefore I hid My face from them. I gave them into the hand of their enemies and they fell by the sword" (Ezekiel 39:23). However, God has not abandoned the Jews or broken His covenant with His chosen people. God does not break His word, even if we break ours. Even when the Jews were in exile God helped them to preserve the Torah and the synagogue that would remind them of their uniqueness and their obligation to worship God and glorify His name. The good news of prophecy is that "Now I will bring back the captives of Jacob, and have mercy on the whole house of Israel; and I will be jealous for My holy name....When I have brought them back from the peoples and gathered them out of their enemies' lands, and I am hallowed in them in the sight of many nations, then they shall know that I am the Lord their God.... And I will not hide My face from them anymore; for I shall have poured out My Spirit on the house of Israel" (Ezekiel 39:25-29).

Now, after thousands of years lying in the graveyard of the nations, The Jews have returned to Israel, the land of prophecy. The holy city of Jerusalem is being rebuilt as the prophets predicted. The nation of Israel now takes its appointed place in the councils of the nations. A supernatural stirring in the hearts of many Jews, both young and old, is provoking a strong desire to rebuild their ancient Temple. As Israel and the nations approach their climactic appointment with destiny, as prophesied by Isaiah, Ezekiel and Daniel, the eyes of the world increasingly turn toward the Holy Land, the focal point of human history.

Replacement Theology

"All Israel will be saved," the Apostle Paul said. He warned the church at Rome to avoid becoming proud of their new-found faith in contrast to the failure of the Jews to accept their Messiah. "For I do not desire, brethren, that you should be ignorant of this mystery, lest you should be wise in your own opinion, that hardening in part has happened to Israel until the fullness of the Gentiles has come in. And so all Israel will be saved" (Romans 11:25-26).

Despite this warning, many people in the Church have written off the nation and people of Israel because they rejected Jesus. This sin of pride has led many to ignore Israel prophetically and spiritually. Others have constructed a "replacement theology" which suggests that God has replaced Israel as His Chosen people and given that honored position to the Church so that all the promises to Israel will be fulfilled in the Church. When they do this they are very selective. They carefully avoid the transfer of the curses that Israel received from God for her sins. This replacement theology flies directly in the face of thousands of specific biblical statements that God will not break His covenant with Israel. His prophesied blessings for Israel in the coming Millennial Kingdom of the Messiah are absolute. God does not change. He is committed by His unchangeable nature to fulfill His ancient covenants with Abraham and David. He will establish the Messiah on the throne of David; He will bless the Gentile nations through a redeemed Israel restored to their Promised Land. We can thank God that His covenant with Israel will not be broken, because we can also know that He will not break His covenant of atonement with His Church.

This replacement theology has often resulted in a subtle kind of anti-semitism that seeks to deny Israel's role in God's plan. If we substitute the Church for Israel in the detailed prophecies of Daniel, Matthew 24, and Revelation 4 through 19, we will never understand how God will accomplish His prophecies that Israel will be a light to the nations during the terrible days of the Great Tribulation. This misunderstanding has already led to some confusion about the 144 thousand witnesses and the Rapture of the

Church. Also, such a misunderstanding will result in a failure to appreciate the final redemption and reconciliation of Israel to their rejected Messiah at the close of the Great Tribulation period. If we understand the specific roles which Israel, the Church, and the Gentile nations will play in prophecy, God's whole plan becomes much clearer to the believer.

The Centrality of Israel and Jerusalem

During the next few years we will witness the final struggle for the destiny of mankind conclude in the turbulent Middle East. In a profound way, Israel is the spiritual center of this world. It is no accident that the final spiritual battle will find its conclusion here.

Ultimately, Jerusalem will be the focus of God's redemptive program for mankind. Here in the future, as in the past, the central issues of man's spiritual struggle will unfold until Jesus the Messiah finally reigns, not only from the throne of David but on the throne of men's hearts everywhere.

The Power of the Gospel to the Jew and the Gentile

When God gave His disciples the commission to "go therefore and make disciples of all the nations, baptizing them in the name of the Father and of the Son and of the Holy Spirit, teaching them to observe all things that I have commanded you" (Matthew 28:19), the majority of the Jews had rejected Christ. Early in His ministry Jesus said He was sent "to the lost sheep of the house of Israel" (Matthew 10:24). But after He and His Kingdom were rejected He began to reveal the "mystery of the kingdom of God" (Mark 4:11) in the hearts and souls of all those who would accept Him as their personal Savior.

Not all the Jews rejected Christ. A great deal of new historical evidence indicates that early Jewish Christian believers were much more widespread than previously thought.

Jewish Christian Synagogues

Archaeologists in Jerusalem have discovered, in the basement of the site of the Upper Room, the remains of a first-century Judeo-Christian congregation that met in a synagogue. A fascinating article by Dr. Bargil Pixner in the *Mishkan* Magazine reveals startling archaeological evidence of the Church of the Apostles on Mount Zion (Jerusalem: Fall, 1990). He reports that when a mortar shell hit this site in the 1948 War of Independence, damage was done to the tomb of David. The Israeli archaeologist, Jacob Pinkerfield, studied the damage in 1951 and found evidence of an extremely old synagogue, with a niche to hold the ark of the Torah orientated in such a manner as to suggest Christian ownership. Further, he found some plaster in the original wall on which were written, in ancient Greek letters, the words that translated, "Conquer, Saviour, mercy," and "O Jesus, that I may live, O lord of the autocrat [the all-powerful]."

Part of the congregation of Jewish synagogues in the first century were the "Proselytes by the Gate." These were Gentiles who converted from paganism to Judaism and joined the local Jewish synagogues. While, today, Judaism is not actively involved in missionary efforts, it was quite different with early Jewish believers in the one true God. The Midrash quotes the passage in Genesis 12:5 regarding "the people whom they [Abraham's family] had acquired in Haran" and refers to them as people whom Abraham had converted from paganism while he lived in Haran. The passage declares that every proselyte should be considered as if God had created a new soul. Jethro, Moses' father in law, Rahab the harlot, and Ruth the Moabite, are given as prime examples of God's people converting the Gentiles to a belief in the Most High God. Jesus commented to the Pharisees about their first-century enthusiastic missionary efforts when he said, "You travel land and sea to win one proselyte" (Matthew 23:15). Also, throughout the wilderness journey and the settling of Canaan, many Gentiles embraced the teachings of God's laws. When the Temple was built the Gentile converts worshiped in the Court of the Gentiles. Later, in the first century, they attended the synagogues in their communities.

As the Holy Spirit convicted these Gentiles of the sinfulness of their pagan religions, they joined the Jews as fellow worshipers. Some were circumcised, others simply obeyed the basic tenets of the Torah and tried to worship God with the Jews. The New Testament refers often to these Jewish converts as being among the first of the Gentiles who immediately recognized Jesus as Messiah. Luke describes the elders of the Jews who told Jesus about a Roman centurion who "loves our nation, and has built us a synagogue" (Luke 7:5). The Lord prepared a great number of these Gentile converts in Jewish synagogues to accept Christianity by first introducing them to the prophecies of the coming Messiah and the truths of the Torah.

After Jerusalem was destroyed in A.D. 70, the members of the Jerusalem church fled to the four corners of the Roman Empire. By the end of the first century a majority of the new believers in Jesus Christ were Gentile because of the missionary zeal of the Jewish Christians. At this time the Christian Jews were still accepted as a legitimate Jewish sect in their Jewish synagogues. However, in A.D. 135, Simeon Bar Kochba, an Israeli military leader, provoked an uprising against Rome. He allowed himself to be declared as the Messiah who would lead the Jews to victory. The Jewish-Christian followers of Jesus—the true Messiah—felt they could not fight against the Roman armies in the name of a false messiah, no matter how much they hated the Roman occupying forces. This decision caused non-Christian Jews to feel as if they had been abandoned by the Jewish Christians at a critical time. This produced a final split between Jewish-Christian believers and mainstream Judaism.

The Role of the Church—The Mystery Revealed

In the near future the world will fully realize the Kingdom of God in all of its aspects, spiritual and millennial. From the time He gave the Great Commission the Lord has recruited citizens for His spiritual kingdom from both Jews and Gentiles of every nation and tongue. The physical embodiment of Christ's spiritual kingdom, the expanding "grain of mustard seed," is found in the true

Church of Jesus, the Body of Christ, in every country of the world. His kingdom has prevailed in the Church, the Body of Christ for the past two thousand years while awaiting its fullest expression in the Millennial Kingdom.

The role of the Church of Jesus Christ is to sanctify the name of Jesus the Messiah through manifesting, to a lost world, His glory, His truth, and the power of His salvation. In faithful witness to the gospel we are to fulfill this Great Commission by teaching, witnessing through our transformed lives, and sharing the truth of His salvation. Just as the early disciples were to begin their work in Jerusalem, so are we to begin by exhibiting in our own changed lives and motives the inner spiritual reality of the coming Kingdom of God.

When the Lord Jesus Christ descends to Earth to set up a kingdom that will never end, the Kingdom of God will expand from its spiritual dimension in the hearts of the believers. The Kingdom of Christ will then be revealed in the practical establishment of the government of the Messiah in all the Earth. On that day the kingdoms of the world, including Israel, shall truly become the kingdoms of our Lord and of His Christ. Jesus of Nazareth will be "anointed" with the oil of anointing in the Temple. He will also be "anointed" in the hearts of all men and women, Jew and Gentile, who will stand before Him to usher in the Millennial Kingdom. On that glorious day the prophesied mystery of the Kingdom of God will be fulfilled in the ushering in of the Age of the Messiah, the Age of Redemption. The spiritual Kingdom and the physical Kingdom of God will both be totally fulfilled at the coming of Jesus the Messiah.

CHAPTER 15

The Road to Armageddon, The Day of the Lord

The nations of the world are racing down the road toward Armageddon to keep an appointment with destiny. The time has been set by God. It will not be postponed. No effort by diplomats or statesmen can divert this final cataclysm. This meeting with God will take place at Armageddon in "the valley of decision" (Joel 3:14) in our generation, just as the ancient prophets declared.

We have rushed past all the road signs that warn "Danger Ahead." And, although God has provided a detour away from the eminent destruction, many have refused His way out. They will not escape the worldwide destruction that lies just ahead. The supreme cataclysm of Armageddon will end thousands of years of warfare on this planet with Jesus the Messiah and His heavenly army the victors.

Not since Jesus Christ transformed humanity forever by His supreme sacrifice on the Cross have we lived in such a great divide. Yet, the average person is unaware of the "Danger Ahead." He plans his days as if all is well, believing that life will continue without interruption or crises, just as it did for his father and his grandfather before him.

In this chapter we will cover the final events that lead up to the Millennial Kingdom when Jesus Christ takes His place on the Throne of David to rule during the Messianic Age: The Rise of the Antichrist; The Great Tribulation Period; The Satanic Trinity; The Armageddon Battle Plan; God's Purpose in the Battle of Armageddon and The Day of the Lord.

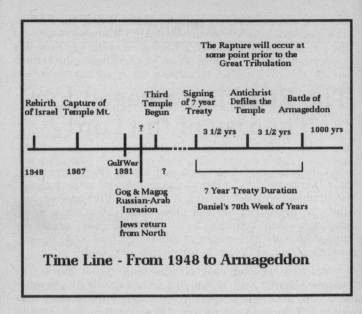

Time Line - From 1948 to Armageddon

The Rise of the Antichrist

As we explored in chapter 3 of this book, the War of Gog and Magog will completely destroy Russia's position as a military superpower. In the power vacuum that follows her destruction, the ten nations of Europe will arise to replace her. The Antichrist will take advantage of the chaos and violence to seize power in Europe.

The ten-nation confederacy will already exist when the man of sin arises. The Prophet Daniel describes a vision of "four beasts" that came up from the sea. The fourth of these beasts was "dreadful and terrible, exceedingly strong....It was different from all the beasts that were before it, and it had ten horns" (Daniel 7:7). The prophet goes on to describe how as he was watching, "considering the horns,...another horn, a little one" came up among the ten (v. 8). This "little horn" is the man of sin, not one of the initial ten leaders. The eleventh horn arises among the ten leaders to take over the ten-nation confederacy. Daniel goes on to say how this eleventh horn will subdue three of the kings--pluck them out by their roots. The remaining seven nations will bow down and accept his dictatorial rule.

This man of sin will manifest satanic intelligence and supernatural occult power. In his hatred of God he will "speak pompous words against the Most High,...persecute the saints of the Most High, and shall intend to change times and law" (Daniel 7:25). In the violence of that period he will offer what appears to be an irresistible plan for world peace and prosperity. The world's nations, believing that he has the solution to all their problems, will initially obey his rule and hegemony. However, as tyranny progresses, first Israel and then other nations, led by the kings of the East, will rebel. The last period of three-and- one-half years will be characterized by continuous warfare and God's wrath poured out on unrepentant humanity. Those Jews who become believers in the coming Messiah will flee to Petra, the wilderness, and to other nations in an attempt to escape his persecution. God will miraculously intervene to protect "the woman" Israel as she flees from Satanic destruction (see Revelation 12).

The book of Revelation outlines the roles of the coming Four Horsemen of the Apocalypse. The rider of the White Horse with his bow symbolizes the false peace during the Antichrist's first three and one half years. This short peaceful period rapidly unfolds into Satan's plan for mankind's destruction as the Red Horse of war, the Black Horse of famine, and the Pale Horse of death inevitably follow the false peace.

The Great Tribulation Period

As part of his rise to world power, the Antichrist will negotiate a seven-year treaty with Israel, guaranteeing them security. Israel will rely upon this "covenant with death" (Isaiah 28:18), the treaty with Rome, despite the fact that God has just saved them from the invading Russian and Arab armies.

Israel desires peace perhaps more than any other nation on earth. For over fifty years she has lived in a permanent state of war with enormous defense budgets and ruinous taxes. The peace treaty with the Revived Roman Empire will guarantee Israel secure borders. Israel's politicians will rely on a piece of paper rather than on their eternal covenant with Jehovah, believing that true peace has arrived at last. In the euphoria of this peace treaty with her neighbors, Israel will bask in her new-found freedom and will revive Temple worship in Jerusalem. Priests will offer daily sacrifices in the rebuilt Temple and all will seem well.

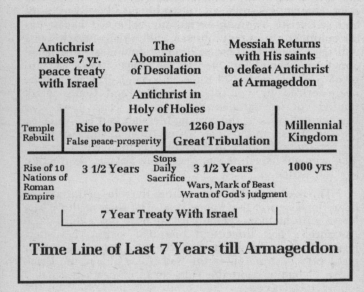

Time Line of Last 7 Years till Armageddon

However, the bible tells us that when Satan is cast out of heaven he will motivate "the prince who is to come" (Daniel 9:26) to break his treaty with the Jews. First, he will cut off the daily sacrifice in the Temple courtyard. Someone, possibly a Jewish believer, will kill him with a knife wound to the neck (Revelation 13:3,12,14). However, Satan miraculously revives the Antichrist and he will claim to be God. He will enter the Holy of Holies of the Third Temple and "bring an end to sacrifice and offering" (Daniel 9:27). The Apostle Paul, in 1 Thessalonians 2:3- 4, prophesies that the Antichrist will sit "as God in the temple of God, showing himself that he is God." After his revival the False Prophet will command all men to worship the Antichrist, the First Beast, or his miraculously speaking statue. Any who refuse to worship him will be beheaded.

As part of his satanic enforcement the False Prophet will require everyone to receive the Mark of the Beast on their foreheads or right hands. Those without the mark will not be able to buy or sell. Many will accept the mark and be eternally damned; some will refuse because they have found faith in Christ; and some, hopefully, may be able to flee into the mountains to live off the land. That may be why the Lord will say to new believers at that cruel time, "He who endures to the end will be saved" (Matthew 10:22).

The reason the Lord revealed the precise length of the Great Tribulation as 1,260 days (three and one-half years) was to encourage the tribulation believers to persevere until He returns at Armageddon rather than accept the Mark of the Beast. To human eyes there will be no way to escape the satanic power of the Antichrist. The Lord promises that the Antichrist is doomed, and believers in that day will know the specific day this will occur.

The Lord also promises that the 144 thousand Jewish Witnesses will be sealed to protect them from the great day of God's wrath that will be poured out on unrepentant, rebellious sinners. The reason only the 144 thousand are sealed is because the Christian Church, the true believers in Jesus, have already been removed to heaven in the Rapture.

As nations begin to rebel against his dictatorial rule, the Antichrist will move his military headquarters from Rome to the holy city, Jerusalem.

The Satanic Trinity

Satan, from the very beginning, has tried to set himself up as God. In his final attempt, Satan will establish a Satanic trinity in imitation of the Holy Trinity of God the Father, God the Son, and God the Holy Spirit. Satan will imitate the father, the Antichrist and the False Prophet will attempt to fill the roles of Jesus Christ and the Holy Spirit.

When Michael the Archangel casts Satan and his false angels out of heaven, Satan will descend to Earth with fury. He knows he has only a short time before Jesus Christ returns and brings about his destruction. When the Antichrist receives a fatal wound to his neck, Satan will miraculously resurrect him in imitation of Jesus Christ's resurrection.

The Antichrist and the False Prophet will both be possessed by the demonic power of Satan. While in the direct sight of the Antichrist, the False prophet will manifest miraculous satanic powers, including causing fire to come down from heaven. These satanic miracles will be used to deceive men about the true identities of Satan's partners. The False Prophet will hold himself out to be the prophet Elijah, and the Antichrist will pretend to be the Messiah.

The False Prophet will not accept worship himself; rather, he will force humanity to worship Satan who is empowering the Antichrist. Neither will the False Prophet be the leader of the worldwide false church that will still remain on Earth after the Rapture of the true believers. Revelation describes this false church as the Great Whore of Babylon. It will be composed of all religiously minded people of all denominations, including the New Age followers. Not one true Christian will be left on Earth after the Rapture. This false church will join its vast organizational power to that of the Antichrist in his amazing rise to world power. However, once he and the False Prophet have used the false church to obtain the dictatorship they seek, the ten kings of the ten-nation confederacy will turn and burn the Great Whore of Babylon. Satan will not share the world's worship with anyone. This proves that the False Prophet could not be the leader of the false church.

The Great Battle of Armageddon

The prophet John tells us that Satan will send out three demonic spirits who will inspire "the kings of the earth and of the whole world, to gather them to the battle of that great day of God Almighty" (Revelation 16:14). The place of the final conflict will be "the place called in Hebrew, Armageddon" (v. 16). The armies of the entire world will be centered on this vast plain that extends from the north of Israel, south past Jerusalem, and to ancient Bozrah. However, the Bible describes that the war will involve far more than just the huge plain of Megiddo. The Greek word translated "battle" of Armageddon is *polemos*, which implies a battle campaign or war. A careful analysis of the parallel passages in Revelation, Zechariah, Joel, etc., reveals that a final series of battles in a number of locations will be waged for several days. For the entire final three-and-one-half years of the Great Tribulation the world will be in bloody warfare, as characterized by the terrible prophetic Red Horse and its rider.

The History of Armageddon

Armageddon (Greek *harmagedon*—the "Mount of Megiddo") has become a symbol for this cataclysmic conflict. But the truth is that this particular valley has seen more climactic battles than any other place on Earth.

Originally, Megiddo was one of the capital cities of the Canaanites. The Egyptian King Thothmes III, the founder of an empire, once said, "Megiddo is worth a thousand cities." The reason is that it sits on the pass leading through Mount Carmel to the Mediterranean, one of the most strategic crossroads in Palestine. Anyone who wishes to control the Middle East must control the vital trade and military routes which connect Europe, Africa, and Asia. The city of Megiddo is southwest of Mount Carmel, just ten miles south of the ancient city of Nazareth where Jesus grew up. It is amazing that Jesus spent His childhood wandering the hills and valleys where He will someday lead the armies of Heaven in the final battle for the earth.

Megiddo was the capital of the portion of land given to Joshua (Joshua 12:21). King Solomon rebuilt and fortified it as one of his chariot cities (1 Kings 9:15). In our various trips to Israel we traveled through the valley and examined the ancient ruins. Archaeologists have uncovered some ruins of the city including a marvelous underground tunnel leading to a secret well outside the city walls. The well was dug to provide a secure source of water during the recurring sieges of the city. In 1800 the great conqueror Napoleon stood at Megiddo before the battle that thwarted his attempt to conquer the East and rebuild the Roman Empire. Contemplating the enormous plain of Armageddon, the marshal declared, "All the armies of the world could maneuver their forces on this vast plain."

A woman judge known as Debra won a great victory for Israel here (Judges 4—5). Later, Judge Gideon won a miraculous battle near Megiddo against overwhelming odds (Judges 7). King Saul was slain here after the blessing and anointing of God was removed from his kingship (1 Samuel 31:8). The evil King Ahaziah also lost his life while fighting Jehu in the Valley (2 Kings 9:27)). The righteous King Josiah was killed here by the Egyptian king Pharaoh-necho in a critical battle for control of Palestine (2 Kings 23:29). The whole nation of Israel mourned the loss of their king. This mourning at Megiddo became proverbial as Zechariah reported, "Like the mourning of Hadad Rimmon in the plain of Megiddo" (12:11). The prophet Zechariah indicated that the nations will mourn the loss of hundreds of millions killed in the final Battle of Armageddon.

The Time of the Battle of Armageddon

The most carefully guarded mystery of the Bible is the time of the end of this age. We know it will end with the Battle of Armageddon. The Messiah's victory will allow mankind to experience the full redemption the Lord planned from the beginning. The apocalyptic encounter with the Messiah will culminate two separate but parallel programs of God: the times of the Gentiles, and the times of Israel. Both will terminate during the last seven years of this age—the seven-year-treaty between the Antichrist and Israel. Both will end with Christ's victory at Armageddon and the establishing of the Kingdom of the Messiah (See Daniel 9:24-27 and Revelation 16:16).

God planned the War of Armageddon from the moment of man's first rebellion in the Garden of Eden. When the Apostle Paul addressed the Athenians he told them that God

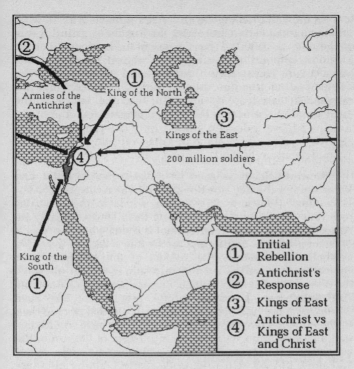

**Stages in
The Battle of Armageddon**

"has appointed a day on which He will judge the world in righteousness by the Man whom He has ordained. He has given assurance of this to all, by raising Him from the dead" (Acts 17:31). In this marvelous prophecy the Lord declares that His glorious victory and judgment of the earth is assured by the truth of Jesus' resurrection. Further, He promises that God's appointment with Earth's destiny, the "day of the Lord," was set from the beginning of time. God, through the Cross, also made an appointment for our salvation: "The hour has come that the Son of Man should be glorified" (John 12:23). God has not left believers in darkness concerning Christ's glorious victory over Satan.

In my book *Armageddon – Appointment With Destiny* I show that the early Church for the first three centuries was unanimous in its belief that the day of the Lord would occur at the completion of the sixth day—the six thousand years since Adam. The twenty-three writers I studied, including Methodius, Victoranios, Justin Martyr, and Tertullian, all taught that this was the apostolic teaching. However, the Lord Jesus Christ is sovereign. He changed His mind about judging Ninevah, despite Jonah's forty-day prophecy, when the whole city—from slave to king—repented. He delayed His judgment on that city for one hundred years.

However, Jesus warned us, "Watch therefore, for you know neither the day nor the hour in which the Son of Man is coming" (Matthew 25:13). His words to the disciples regarding the fig tree and "putting forth leaves" clearly tie Armageddon to the generation that is living when the nation of Israel is reborn. Every time the fig tree is used in the Bible symbolically, Israel is the subject of the prophecy. Our generation has witnessed the miraculous rebirth of Israel, the rise of the Revived Roman Empire, the rise of Babylon, and hundreds of other unique prophecies. We have witnessed more fulfilled prophecies in this last decade than in the previous two thousand years. We can have confidence that our generation will see the fulfillment of the rest of the prophecies. However, as I said, God is sovereign. We cannot and must not set dates. In God's perfect timing all these things will be fulfilled. Each of us has an appointment to meet Jesus Christ. We will either meet Him as our returning Savior or we will meet Him as our returning Judge. The appointment is set. It will not be postponed.

The Armageddon Battle Plan

The initial battle plan will be a military contest for world supremacy. The combatants will be the nations of the East rebelling against the Antichrist and the western nations. An army of two hundred million men will cross Asia, killing over one-third of humanity (more than one billion) on its terrible journey to the killing ground of Armageddon (Revelation 9:18). Where will such an enormous army come from?

The Armies of the East

In our 1986 trip to Communist China, Kaye and I discussed with Chinese officials the tragic effects of the one-child policy on the massive 1.1 billion population of that country. Young couples are selectively aborting female fetuses to make sure they give birth only to male babies because, legally, they can only have one child. The result is that each year China has nine male babies born for every girl. This astonishing problem is a population and military time bomb. By the late 1990s China will have more than 125 million young men of military age without any women to marry. If you remember the photos of the Tian'An Men Square demonstrations you saw very few girls. The same situation is developing in North Korea and northern India. Modern tests that detect the sex of the fetus allow couples to selectively abort babies that are of the wrong gender.

Now for the first time we can understand how an incredible army of two hundred million soldiers will be produced in this generation. The kings of the East will have the manpower to produce an unstoppable army to contest the world's leadership for the next thousand years. China and Japan now have a thirty-year Friendship Treaty. The combination of Japan's military-industrial complex with China's staggering resources and manpower will produce the awesome army described in Revelation. Reliable military reports from western intelligence sources say that China has built enormous military roads across southern China and occupied Tibet. These roads serve no commercial purpose and lead from the center of China towards the Middle East. The recent flurry of Chinese military hardware sales, including sophisticated Silkworm missiles, to Iran, Iraq, Saudi Arabia, and Yemen indicates their growing interest in this area of the world. The "kings of the East" know that the Middle East is the key to world control. If anyone feels that China, Japan, and India are content to let the West rule the world for the next thousand years, look carefully at the histories of these countries.

Across the Euphrates River

In order to reach northern Israel this army will have to cross the Euphrates River which has served as a military barrier to invasion for thousands of years. The book of Revelation declares that the Euphrates River will dry up to allow the two hundred million man army of the "kings of the East" to cross into Israel. In January, 1990, the president of Turkey pushed a button that closed the recently built dam now blocking the great river. The river dropped 75 percent in one day. Truly we are entering the age of the Messiah as one prophecy after another is fulfilled before our eyes.

The Confederation of Western Armies

The huge armies of the East will come into Israel to battle the Western armies of the Antichrist for the rule of this planet. The prophet Daniel describes the Antichrist's rise and military defeat: "At the time of the end the king of the South shall attack him; and the king of the North shall come against him like a whirlwind...and he shall enter the countries, overwhelm them, and pass through. He shall also enter the Glorious Land, and many countries shall be overthrown (11:40-41). This passage indicates that the confederacy of nations that join in the final rebellion against the tyranny of the Antichrist will include the "kings from the east," the "king of the South" and the "king of the North." The biblical phrase "king of the South" has always identified Egypt and her African allies. The "king of the North" identifies nations to the north of Israel. These possible candidates include Syria, Turkey, or even the remnants of "Gog and Magog," the Russians who survived the military destruction several years earlier. Daniel tells us that "many countries shall be overthrown" including Egypt, Libya, and Ethiopia by the hand of the Antichrist. However, "these shall escape from his hand: Edom, Moab, and the prominent people of Ammon" (vv. 41-42).

At that crucial moment in the Antichrist's counterattack, "news from the east and the north shall trouble him; therefore he shall go out with great fury to destroy and annihilate many" (v. 44). The mobilization of the two hundred million man army of the kings of the East, together with additional forces from the north, will warn the Antichrist that the final Battle of Armageddon is coming. The response of the man of sin will be decisive. Daniel says that "he shall plant the tents of his palace between the seas and the glorious holy mountain" (v. 45). The satanic forces of the Antichrist will assemble in Israel to meet the coming onslaught. He will establish his headquarters sacrilegiously on the Temple Mount, which will once more be a military stronghold. The Bible prophecies his doom: "Yet he shall come to his end, and no one will help him" (v. 45). When the Lord Jesus Christ is your opponent, no one can help. The Antichrist's doom is certain.

The Entrance of the White Horse

When the battle is at its height, Jesus Christ riding on a white horse will descend from Heaven with His army of angels and Christian saints, also on white horses. "Then I saw heaven opened, and behold, a white horse. And He who sat on him was called Faithful and True, and in righteousness He judges and makes war" (Revelation 19:11). Then John prophesied our participation in this battle to save the planet and Israel: "And the armies in heaven, clothed in fine linen, white and clean, followed Him on white horses" (v. 14). Jesus Christ, the Angel of the Lord, will personally lead His military forces against the Antichrist's satanically inspired armies. "It shall be in that day that I will seek to destroy all the nations that come against Jerusalem" (Zechariah 12:9).

After the armies have assembled for battle, the Lord will come from Bozrah, far to the south of Jerusalem. "The Lord has a sacrifice in Bozrah, and a great slaughter in the land of Edom.... For it is the day of the Lord's vengeance, the year of recompense for the cause of Zion" (Isaiah 34:6,8). Consider the fact that the world's military might will pour into the Middle East. Today there are over 570 million men in the world's standing armies and reserves. Isaiah says that Jesus Christ will personally destroy those who come to defeat His people: "Who is this who comes from Edom, with dyed garments from Bozrah...? For I have trodden them in

My anger, and trampled them in My fury; their blood is sprinkled upon My garments" (Isaiah 63:1,3).

The final battle will occur several days later as the rest of the Antichrist's armies surround Jerusalem to attack and devastate her (Zechariah 12:2-11). The Lord prophesied that Jerusalem will be the focus of those huge armies that survived the terrible Battle of Armageddon in the north. God will destroy these armies "though all nations of the earth are gathered against" Jerusalem (Zechariah 12:3). Zechariah's prophecy describes something that appears to be very similar to the awesome effects of a neutron bomb that will be used against the armies attacking the Holy City: "And this shall be the plague with which the Lord will strike all the people who fought against Jerusalem: Their flesh shall dissolve while they stand on their feet. Their eyes shall dissolve in their sockets, and their tongues shall dissolve in their mouths" (Zechariah 14:12).

The people of Israel, especially the tribe of Judah, will prevail against overwhelming odds through the supernatural help of Christ. The prophet declares that "the one who is feeble among them in that day shall be like David, and the house of David shall be like God, like the Angel of the Lord before them" (v. 8).

In an earlier prophecy Daniel said: "[The Antichrist] shall be one who makes desolate, even until the consummation, which is determined, is poured out on the desolate" (9:27). This strange declaration promises that although the Antichrist will cause great desolation, this era of history will end with the total destruction of him and his forces. John describes the climax of the battle: "And I saw the beast, the kings of the earth, and their armies, gathered together to make war against Him who sat on the horse and against His army. Then the beast was captured, and with him the false prophet...These two were cast alive into the lake of fire burning with brimstone. And the rest were killed with the sword" (vv. 19-21).

God's Purpose in the Battle of Armageddon

There are three reasons why God will destroy the armies of the nations at Armageddon. The first is that they are determined to destroy His Chosen People Israel. The Lord say, "I will also gather all nations, and bring them down to the Valley of Jehoshaphat; and I will enter into judgment with them there on account of My people, My heritage Israel, whom they have scattered among the nations" (3:2). This tragic hatred of the Jews reveals that their profound hatred of God has motivated these people throughout history. God will judge the nations for persecuting Israel and attempting to kill the Jews who have returned from exile.

The second reason why God will judge the nations at Armageddon is because the nations have failed to repent of their sins. As John tells us in Revelation 16:9, the men "blasphemed the name of God who has power over these plagues; and they did not repent and give Him glory." Despite the miracles of the Great Tribulation period, most men will choose to die with a curse upon their lips rather than turn from their sinful rebellion.

The third reason for the destruction is that God will finally judge mankind for our total abuse of this planet and its resources. The doomsday weapons and their destruction as described in the Bible's accounts of the Tribulation period reveal man's contempt for the earth which God gave to us. Revelation 11:18 declares that God will "destroy those who destroy the earth."

The Day of the Lord

The prophet Zechariah says: "Behold, the day of the Lord is coming, and your spoil will be divided in your midst. For I will gather all the nations to battle against Jerusalem; the city shall be taken, the houses rifled, and the women ravished. Half of the city shall go into captivity, but the remnant of the people shall not be cut off from the city. Then the Lord will go forth and fight against those nations, as He fights in the day of battle. And in that day His feet will stand on the Mount of Olives" (14:1- 4). This fascinating prophecy gives us more details about the events following the climactic Battle of Armageddon. The armies north of Israel, involving hundreds of millions of soldiers, will be devastated by the heavenly army of Jesus Christ. However, as Zechariah says, the surviving enemy armies will continue to assault Jerusalem and the tribal areas of Judah for some days after the first Armageddon battle. The curious mention of Judah and the phrase "governors of Judah" and "house of David" in Zechariah 12:6 and 7 suggests that Elijah the prophet and the other witness may restore the genealogies of the tribes by then. As Jerusalem begins to fall to the enemy, one-third of the women in the city will be taken captive. Then the Lord Jesus Christ will descend on the Mount of Olives as Zechariah proclaimed. When His heel strikes the mountain where He spent so many hours two thousand years ago, the ground will split asunder creating a crevice running from the Dead Sea through the mountain to the Mediterranean. "Then you shall flee through My mountain valley, ...and all the saints with you" (Zechariah 14:5). Revelation 16:18-21 describes an enormous earthquake greater than any other in history that will divide Jerusalem into three parts as the other cities of the world fall.

The rebuilt city of Babylon will also be destroyed. The mention of Jerusalem dividing into three parts suggests that perhaps the three great valleys that define the city--Hinnom, Tyropoeon, and Kidron--will open to the depths as a result of this devastating earthquake: "'And it shall come to pass in all the land,' says the Lord, 'That two thirds in it shall be cut off and die, but one third shall be left in it: I will bring the one third through the fire, will refine them as silver is refined, and test them as gold is tested'" (Zechariah 13:8-9). This prophecy shows the utter horror of the Great Tribulation period. Only one third of the Israelites will survive the battle. Yet the promise is clear that every one of the survivors will accept their Messiah and His salvation. The thousands of years of rebellion will end forever. The Lord promises that "they will call on My name, and I will answer them. I will say, 'This is My people'; and each one will say, 'The Lord is my God'" (v. 9).

The book of Revelation also tells us that more than two thirds of the inhabitants of the Gentile nations will die in the various wars and judgments poured out during the awful period.

In the next chapter we will discuss more about the coming of the Messiah.

CHAPTER 16

The Coming of the Messiah

The prophecy of the coming of the Messiah is our bridge to eternity. It connects human history from the Garden of Eden to the Millennium and the Kingdom of the Messiah. As we approach the final years of the twentieth century, those who are aware of this prophecy are gripped by a growing messianic expectation. The Messiah is coming! His return will complete God's plan of redemption as predicted by the Law and the Prophets.

In this chapter we will examine a number of prophecies that give us a preview of the Messiah's coming and the dramatic aftermath. We will also explore material about Jesus that was censored from the Mishnah Torah for almost seven hundred years. Israel has longed for her Messiah through all her generations, and Christians have awaited the second coming of Christ. "He who testifies to these things says, 'Surely I am coming quickly.' Amen. Even so, Come, Lord Jesus!" (Revelation 22:20).

The Person of the Messiah

From the beginning, Jewish rabbis have pondered over the identity of the coming Messiah. Is the Messiah a man or is He God? Many prophecies ascribe miraculous powers to the Messiah. He will transform the whole world, including the hearts of men and women. Christians accept that the Messiah who came and who must return is the Son of God, a member of the Trinity. Jews usually focus on the fact of the Messiah's humanity. However, they also believe the passages in Scripture that say He will live forever, redeem mankind, and transform the world into the Kingdom of God.

How can this be true if He is only a man? Usually the rabbis will admit that He is more than just a man but they are careful to deny that the Messiah could be God. They fear that this conclusion comes too close to the Christian interpretation of Scripture.

Their problem, however, is that many Old Testament passages clearly identify this Messiah with the Angel of the Lord. This Angel of the Lord is not a normal created angel. The Bible clearly indicates that the Angel of the Lord is actually God Himself. In fact, a close examination of these Old Testament passages and the Jewish paraphrases written before the time of Christ reveal that the Jews originally understood these passages as referring to the mysterious Angel of the Covenant as God. The importance of this detail cannot be overestimated. These passages clearly reveal that this Angel of the Covenant is Jehovah, the coming Messiah, Jesus the Christ.

This issue is also important to Christians. Many believers fail to recognize that Jesus appeared numerous times to man in the Old Testament. While some Christians see the God of the Old Testament as a stern, unyielding, and judgmental Jehovah, they tend to feel differently toward Jesus Christ. As Paul says in 1 Timothy, "God was manifested in the flesh, justified in the Spirit, seen by angels, preached among the Gentiles, believed on in the world, received up in glory" (1 Timothy 3:16). Some see Jesus, the Son of God, almost as a "different" God than the God revealed to the prophets and patriarchs.

God revealed Himself as Jehovah-Jesus Christ throughout the Old Testament. Frequent references tell of God's physical appearance to the patriarchs and prophets. God also visibly appeared to Israel as a cloud of glory in the wilderness and, later, in the Tabernacle and Temple. Who appeared to these Old Testament saints --God the Father, or Jesus the Son of God, the coming Messiah? This is important because a proper understanding of Jesus' role in the Old Testament will enable us to appreciate in a new way God's unfolding plan for man's redemption. It will enable Christians to see that God has not changed and will not change: He "is the same yesterday, today, and forever"

(Hebrews 13:8). There are three important points to consider: (1) the Person who appeared to these saints is truly God and not an ordinary angel; (2) He is not God the Father; (3) He is in fact Jesus Christ, the Coming Messiah.

The Angel of the Lord Was Not an Ordinary Angel

While ordinary angels often appeared to saints in the Old Testament, we should not confuse these beings with the appearances of the Lord. As one example, consider the account of the two angels who appeared to Abraham and Sarah to tell them about the son Sarah would have in her old age. When the angels were through delivering the happy news, they "turned away from there and went toward Sodom." But, the verse continues, "Abraham still stood before the Lord" (Genesis 18:23). This word "Lord" in the original is "Jehovah."

Another example is seen when Jacob met "a Man" who "wrestled with him until the breaking of day." Later in the passage, Jacob says he was going to call that place "Peniel," Face of God, because "I have seen God face to face, and my life is preserved" (Genesis 32:24,30).

When the Angel of the Lord appeared to Moses in the burning bush He said, "I am the God of your father—the God of Abraham, the God of Isaac, and the God of Jacob" (Genesis 3:6). No ordinary angel would dare make that claim. Moses was aware of this because he "hid is face, for he was afraid to look upon God." The term "Angel of the Lord" indicates that the Person is not an ordinary angel. The word "angel" means "messenger." It can refer to an angel, a created being in heaven, or it can refer to the office of being a messenger for someone else. However, in those cases where the Old Testament identifies the divine person as the Angel of the Lord the context clearly indicates it is not an ordinary angel. When Stephen, that great evangelist and deacon, preached his final and fatal sermon, he referred to Moses at the burning bush. "An Angel of the Lord appeared to him in a flame of fire in a bush, in the wilderness of Mount Sinai. When Moses saw it, he marveled at the sight; and as he drew near to observe, the voice of the Lord came to him, saying, 'I am the God of your fathers'" (Acts 7:30-32). In these verses the words "Angel of the Lord" and the word "Lord" (Jehovah) are used interchangeably for the same person. The Angel of the Lord who appears in the Old Testament is God.

This Divine Person Was Not God the Father

The Bible clearly reveals that "no one has seen God at any time. The only begotten Son, who is in the bosom of the Father, He has declared Him" (John 1:18). This divine Person who was called the Angel of the Lord was not God the Father. In another passage God says that "no man can see Me and live!" (Exodus 33:20). Yet many Old Testament saints met this divine Being called the Angel of the Lord and lived. If you saw God and lived, it was Jesus the Son of God who appeared. This person acts as a messenger of Jehovah. The Angel of the Lord, the messenger, must be different from the One who sent Him. Since both individuals are divine, we must conclude that the Old Testament declares in these passages that Jehovah and the Angel of the Lord are two divine persons. Yet the Bible also strongly asserts that there is only one God: "Hear, O Israel! The Lord is our God, the Lord is one!" (Deuteronomy 6:4). This is the mystery of the Trinity-Father, Son, and Holy Spirit—but only one God. Other passages reveal the person of the Holy Spirit, but they will be discussed in a future book.

The Divine Person Is Actually Jesus Christ, the Messiah

Jeremiah was given one of the greatest prophecies of the Old Testament: "'Behold, days are coming,' declares the Lord, 'when I will make a new covenant with the house of Israel and with the house of Judah, not like the covenant which I made with their fathers in the day I took them by the hand to bring them out of the land of Egypt'" (Jeremiah 31:31-32). The Angel of the Lord who made the first covenant with Moses was God Himself. Now the prophet Jeremiah declares that the same One will make a new covenant with Israel. The book of Hebrews declares that

Jesus Christ is "the mediator of a better covenant, which has been enacted on better promises" (Hebrews 8:6). The writer then continues by quoting Jeremiah's prophecy and identifies the maker of both the old and new covenants as Jesus Christ (vv. 7-10). If the maker of the new covenant and the old covenant are the same, then Jesus Christ is the Angel of the Lord, the Jehovah who appeared repeatedly in the Old Testament.

Jesus the Messiah continually works, from the Garden of Eden to the coming Battle of Armageddon—from Genesis to Revelation, to redeem mankind. Jesus the Messiah spoke the truth when He declared: "I am the Alpha and the Omega, the first and the last, the beginning and the end. Blessed are those who wash their robes, that they may have the right to the tree of life, and may enter by the gates into the city" (Revelation 22:13-14).

The Promise of the Messiah

"I believe with a perfect belief in the coming of the Messiah. Even though he may delay, I will wait every day for him to come." In this Jewish Code with its Thirteen Principles of faith, Maimonides declared that righteous Jews must believe in the coming Messiah. He stated: "Anyone who does not believe in him or does not wait for his coming, denies not only the declarations of the prophets, but also those of the Torah and Moses, our Teacher." This great teacher declared that it is vital for those who follow God to actively pray for the coming of the Messiah and the fulfillment of the Torah.

Two Sets of Prophecies About the Messiah

Careful students of Scripture—both Old and New Testament, will find two sets of prophecies concerning the coming Messiah: the Suffering Messiah and the Messiah-Redeemer. In His role as the Suffering Messiah He would suffer and die. In the second set, the Messiah-Redeemer will save His people, return the exiles, rule the earth, and live forever. Rabbis and Jews of the first century wondered about the order in which these prophecies would be fulfilled.

Naturally, as they suffered under the brutal occupation of Rome, they longed for the good news of the Messiah-Redeemer who would save them from their enemies.

Therefore, when Jesus told His disciples that He would suffer death, even his closest followers said, "Not so, Lord!" Jesus had to rebuke his disciple Peter for presuming to reject God's will for His Son. Jesus' cousin, John the Baptist, who had declared that Jesus was the "Lamb of God" also wondered about the two sets of apparently opposing prophesies. When John was awaiting his execution at Masada he sent two of his disciples to ask Jesus: "Are you the Coming One, or do we look for another?" (Matthew 11:3). John the Baptist, inspired by God, obviously knew that Jesus was the Messiah. However, he would naturally want to know the truth about Christ. Would Jesus fulfill the Suffering Messiah prophecies by dying at that time, or would he fulfill the prophecies of the Redeemer Messiah by setting up His kingdom?

After Jesus died and rose again, early Christians understood that this first coming fulfilled the prophecies of Isaiah and David: the Suffering Messiah who would die for man's sins (see Isaiah 53, Psalm 22). By the end of His ministry among them, His close followers had already begun to anticipate Jesus' return as the Messiah Redeemer to fulfill the prophecy of Isaiah 9 who would establish the Kingdom of God forever. They finally could ask Him: "Tell us, when will these things be? And what will be the sign of Your coming, and of the end of the age" (Matthew 24:3).

Qualifications of the Messiah

One of the hardest thing for Jews to accept about Jesus is the fact that He died without setting up the Kingdom of God. Yet, one of the leading Jewish scholars, Moses Maimonides, set down a list of qualifications of the coming Messiah that detail the coming of Christ. In the first section he describes the initial set of Suffering Messiah prophecies: "If a king will arise from the house of David who is learned in Torah and observant of the Mitzvot, as prescribed by the written law and the oral law, as David, his ancestor was, and will compel all of Israel to walk in [their light] and reinforce the breaches; and fight the wars of God, we may, with assurance, consider him the Messiah."

An examination of the Gospel record reveals, first, that Jesus fulfilled the prophecies as the Son of David. Maimonides declared in another place, "There is no Messiah-king in Israel except for the descendants of David and Solomon." Jesus also astonished His listeners as one "who is learned in Torah and observant of the mitzvot." Jesus allowed Himself to be sacrificed at Calvary to accomplish His redemptive purpose for mankind. His ultimate sacrificial gift to believers fulfilled the prophecies of Isaiah 53 and Psalm 22.

In further describing the qualifications of the coming Messiah, Maimonides says: "If he succeeds in the above, builds the Temple in its place, and gathers the dispersed of Israel, he is definitely the Messiah....He will then improve the entire world, [motivating] all the nations to serve God together as [Zephaniah 3:9] states: 'I will make the peoples pure of speech that they all will call upon the Name of God and serve Him with one purpose'" (Halachah 11:4). In this second section Maimonides details the hope of the Redeemer Messiah that will be accomplished in the second coming of Christ. When Jesus returns as the promised Messiah, He will build the Fourth Temple as described in Ezekiel 40 and 48 and gather the exiles into the Millennial Kingdom of God.

Was Jesus the Messiah?

For the past two centuries, many Jews have rejected the claim of Christ on the grounds that Jesus was a myth, not a real historical figure. Generations of Jews have been taught that the writings of Matthew, Mark, Luke, and John were unreliable documentation that were written long after the events described. Theories of the higher critical school of the last century categorically denied the early existence of the Gospels. These theories have been overturned by recent scholarly research. It is virtually impossible to seriously claim today that the Gospels were fabricated after all living witnesses had died. Even liberal scholars today admit that the Gospels were widely distributed before A.D. 70, before the burning of the Temple. This early dating of the Gospels is vital evidence of their truthfulness. The existence of widely distributed written records about the teachings, miracles, prophecies, death, and resurrection of Jesus within thirty-five years of the events provides tremendous proof of their reliability. No one in the first century would have taken these accounts seriously if living witnesses could deny their truthfulness. We have more reliable historical evidence of the life, death, and resurrection of Jesus that we do about the life of any other character of ancient history, including Julius Caesar.

Maimonides, in one fascinating section of the Mishnah Torah, refers to the problem of the history of Jesus and His partial fulfillment of the Messianic prophecies: "If he [the Messiah] did not succeed to this degree or he was killed, he surely is not [the redeemer] promised by the Torah. [Rather] he should be considered as all the other proper and complete kings of the Davidic dynasty who died. God only caused him to arise in order to test the many, as [Daniel 11:35] states: 'and some of the wise men will stumble, to try them, to refine, and to clarify until the appointed time because the set time is in the future'" (Halachah 11:4).

Maimonides concluded that Jesus' death proved that He was not the promised Redeemer Messiah. The conclusion was accepted by Jewish scholars for thousands of years. However, Maimonides makes an astonishing admission: if the person legitimately fulfills part of the prophecies but is killed before completing the restoration of the Temple, etc., he must be considered legitimately as "all the other proper and complete kings of the Davidic dynasty who died." In other words, Maimonides concluded that Jesus was not an imposter. A "proper king of the Davidic dynasty" is a potential Messiah-King of Israel.

Maimonides then considered historical evidence he had discovered about Jesus of Nazareth. As the greatest Jewish scholar of medieval times he had studied the extensive rabbinical libraries that contained historical materials from the first century. In his day, many documents of the Sanhedrin records about the trial of Jesus still existed, including Talmudic passages that were later censored.

Censored References to Jesus in the Mishnah Torah

During years of research I uncovered mysterious references to the existence of passages from the Mishnah Torah that had been censored. This material referred directly to the history of Jesus of Nazareth. As I searched and wrote to bookstores containing rare manuscripts, I continually ran into stone walls. I was told that this information was either unavailable or non-existent. It is quite difficult to find Jewish material about the Messiah in bookstores. Fortunately, my long search was finally rewarded when I met a book collector in the Jewish Quarter of the Old City of Jerusalem in the spring of 1989. His partner did not want to sell me a copy. However, after thirty minutes of hard negotiations I was able to obtain the treasured copy. Since then, over fifty individuals I know have tried and failed to obtain this edition of this material.

In an earlier chapter I indicated the reason for censoring these Talmudic and Mishnah Torah passages about Jesus. Part of the material refers to Jesus in a less than flattering light due to the Talmud's rejection of the Gospel claims of Jesus as Messiah. During the persecution of the Jews by the Catholic Church, ignorant bigoted priests would occasionally quote these passages to incite riots against the Jews. Some Church leaders, knowing that this was a terrible misuse of Jewish commentaries, met with Jewish leaders in Europe to find ways to prevent future persecution. The rabbis, wanting to end the persecution, also felt that something should be done about these controversial writings. This unusual convergence of interests led to a joint decision in A.D. 1200 to censor these passages about Jesus. This material was removed from these historical volumes in both monastery and rabbinical libraries and, consequently, not included in future editions of the Mishnah Torah. For seven hundred years this wonderful historical material about Jesus of Nazareth was lost to the world. Most present editions refer to the fact that censored material about Jesus was removed.

Fortunately, several manuscripts that contained this censored material escaped the hands of the religious authorities. Maimonides had left his original manuscripts in Yemen when he died. These Yemenite manuscripts of the Mishnah Torah were brought to Israel when the Jews of Yemen returned to the Promised Land. These missing portions about Jesus were published in 1987 by Rabbi Eliyahu Touger and the Maznaim Publishing Corporation, Jerusalem, Israel. The word "CENSORED" was overprinted on the book jacket, and the textural notes explain the curious history of the censored portions about Jesus. The following are quotes from this excellent commentary:

> Jesus of Nazareth who aspired to be the Messiah and was executed by the court was also [alluded to] in Daniel's prophecies, as [ibid. 11:14] states: 'the vulgar [common] among your people shall exalt themselves in an attempt to fulfill the vision, but they shall stumble. Can there be a greater stumbling block than [Christianity]? All the prophets spoke of the Messiah as the redeemer of Israel and its savior, who would gather their dispersed and strengthen their [observation of] the Mitzvot [the commandments]. [By contrast, Christianity] caused the Jews to be slain by the sword, their remnant to be scattered and humbled, the Torah to be altered, and the majority of the world to err and serve a god other than the Lord.

> Nevertheless, the intent of the Creator of the world is not within the power of man to comprehend, for His ways are not our ways, nor are His thoughts, our thought. [Ultimately,] all the deeds of Jesus of Nazareth and that Ishmaelite who arose after him will only serve to prepare the way for the Messiah's coming and the improvement of the entire world, [motivating the nations] to serve God together, as [Zephaniah 3:9] states: "I will make the peoples pure of speech that they will all call upon the Name of God and serve Him with one purpose" (Halachah 11:4).

What makes this passage so amazing is that Maimonides admits the basic historical account about Jesus:

He was a legitimate teacher, He aspired to be the Messiah, He was executed by the Sanhedrin. Additionally he declares that Jesus was a legitimate king of Israel, descended from King David, and that He was referred to in the prophecies of Daniel. Maimonides obviously struggles with the problem of the failure of Jesus to set up His kingdom. He could not understand the reason for Jesus' death or Christianity's subsequent persecution of his Jewish people. However, he trusted God's mysterious paths and believed that ultimately the deeds of Jesus of Nazareth will prepare men's hearts for the Redeemer Messiah's coming. Maimonides wondered about the meaning of the Cross and the death of Jesus. He asked: "Can there be a greater stumbling block than [Christianity]?" The Apostle Paul used the same words to describe his people's reaction to Jesus: "We preach Christ crucified, to the Jews a stumbling block and to the Greeks foolishness, but to those who are called, both Jews and Greeks, Christ the power of God and the wisdom of God" (1 Corinthians 1:23-24).

The Timing of His Coming

In my book *Armageddon – Appointment With Destiny*, I quoted from over a dozen first-century Christian and Jewish writers showing their belief that the Messiah would come after six thousand years. Daniel the prophet clearly predicted the triumphant return of the Messiah, the Prince, in his great prophecy of the Seventy Weeks. Daniel 9:24-27 tells us that the termination of the seventy weeks of years (490 years) assigned to Israel will occur at the final battle of Armageddon, ending the last seven years of this age: "Seventy weeks are determined for your people and for your holy city, to finish the transgression, to make an end of sins, to make reconciliation for iniquity, to bring in everlasting righteousness, to seal up vision and prophecy, and to anoint the Most Holy" (Daniel 9:24).

Notice that the prophet says that the last event which will end this age will occur only when the High Priest anoints "the Most Holy." This verse is described in Jewish commentaries on Daniel as referring to the coming Messiah. Though most modern commentators do not expound on this feature of the prophecy, I believe it is a definite prediction about the anointing of the Messiah. This will be the final event that ends the Tribulation period and ushers in the Millennial Kingdom. Jesus of Nazareth was never anointed with the oil of anointing during His first advent two thousand years ago. Yet His formal titles of "Christ" and "Messiah" prophetically refer to His future "anointing" with this special ointment.

The Anointing of the Messiah

God, when He was instructing Moses about His laws and ceremonies, instructed him to collect certain oils and spices. Moses was to "make from these a holy anointing oil, an ointment compounded according to the art of the perfumer. It shall be a holy anointing oil....And you shall anoint Aaron and his sons, and sanctify them, that they may minister to Me as priests. And you shall speak to the children of Israel, saying, 'This shall be a holy anointing oil to Me throughout your generations'" (Exodus 30:25,30-31).

The "Holy Anointing Oil"

The Kings of Israel, including Saul, David, and Solomon were anointed with this precious oil. Moses Maimonides said that "when a King was appointed, he was anointed with oil reserved for this purpose....Once a King is anointed, he and his descendants are granted the monarchy until eternity, for the monarchy is passed down by inheritance." First Samuel 16:11-13 describes David's anointing: "Samuel said to Jesse, 'Are all the young men here?' [Jesse replied], 'There remains yet the youngest, and there he is, keeping the sheep.'...Now he was ruddy, with bright eyes, and good-looking. And the Lord said, 'Arise anoint him; for this is the one!' Then Samuel took the horn of oil and anointed him in the midst of his brothers; and the Spirit of the Lord came upon David from that day forward" (1 Samuel 16:11-13). The Bible required that the Messiah must come from the tribe of Judah and the line of King David. The Mishnah Torah says that all of the ancient kings of the Davidic dynasty were anointed near a stream. The stream indicated the perpetual reign promised to David's

eed. That is why the genealogy of Jesus of Nazareth was so
nportant to writers of the Gospels.

According to Talmudic material, one of the ingredients
f the anointing ointment was an oil called *afars'mon*, from
1e sap of a type of balsam tree. Queen Cleopatra of Egypt
nce asked Mark Anthony, the ruler of Rome, to provide her
vith a special grove of these rare balsam trees that grew near
ericho. The only other place where the tree could be grown
vas at a wadi known as Ein Gedi near Qumran. The oil from
1e sap of the tree was so pure that it required no refining. It
vas used in perfumes and medicines that were so expensive
nly the rich could afford them. During the period of the
econd Temple this oil was extremely rare and very
aluable.

When Rome invaded Qumran in A.D. 70, the retreating
ssenes burned the only remaining grove of balsam trees to
eep the precious oil out of the hands of the Romans. For
vo thousand years the rabbis believed that this special
nointing ointment was extinct because of the loss of this
ne special ingredient. How could they anoint the future
Iessiah without the proper anointing ointment?

he Copper Scroll and the Holy Anointing Oil

After twenty centuries of belief that the anointing
intment was lost forever, a group of Christian
rchaeologists following directions given in the Copper
crolls found a flask containing the ointment. The clay flask
ad been buried in a cave by the Essenes and Temple priests
ore than two thousand years ago. This was one of the
recious Temple objects that had been hidden from
ivading Roman forces in hopes that future generations
ould find it and place it in the rebuilt Temple in
reparation for the coming Messiah.

In 1989, under the direction of Dr. Joseph Patrich of the
Iebrew University's Institute of Archaeology, a group of
rchaeologists and volunteers, including my friends Dr.
ary Collett and Dr. Nathan Meyers, found the flask of oil in
ne of the caves some distance from where the Arabs first
iscovered the Dead Sea Scrolls in 1947. The clay flask was

down in a hole over three feet deep, protected by fibers an
wrapped in palm leaves. Despite being hidden in the hottes
spot on Earth for thousands of years, the oil wa
miraculously preserved. A small stone plugged the to
spout and a hardened plug of oil sealed the tiny hole in th
side of the flask. Subsequently, Professor Zeev Aizenshta
and Dorit Aschengrau, at the University's Casali Institute o
Applied Chemistry laboratories, tested the oil. Carbon 1
dating determined that the oil was placed in the containe
during the first century, the time of the Second Temple. The
found the oil's chemical composition was unique. One dro
in water turned the water milky white, exactly as ancien
documents suggested it should.

The Hilchot Beit HaBechirah (4:1) recorded that th
priests hid this precious anointing ointment before th
Temple was destroyed. The Lord has miraculousl
preserved it until it could be discovered in our generatio
It is no accident that this oil of anointing should reappea
after all these centuries. It has been given to the chief rabb
of Israel until it can be put in the rebuilt Third Temple an
used to anoint their long-awaited Messiah. The "anointe
One" is surely coming soon.

The Reconvening of the Great Sanhedrin

The Great Sanhedrin was the supreme court of law fo
Israel until Jerusalem and the Temple were destroyed i
A.D. 70. It was responsible for establishing legislative an
executive powers, including capital punishment until th
Romans restricted this power. The word "Sanhedrin" wa
derived from the Greek word for "assembly," in fact, i
members were called "the Men of the Great Assembly." Ezr
the priest established the Sanhedrin when the Jews returne
to Jerusalem from Babylon, but their ancestry dates back t
the forming of a council of seventy elders which Go
commanded Moses to develop to share the burdens o
governing the nation of Israel (see Numbers 11:16,24-2!
The seventy elders and Moses made up a governi
assembly of seventy-one. This assembly continued from th
Exodus until the Babylonians captured the Israelites in 6(
B.C.

The Sanhedrin met in the Chamber of Hewn Stone in the Inner Court of the Temple. The High Priest also served as the president of the Sanhedrin.

The Sanhedrin in the Sixth Millennium

The Israel Torah Foundation and other orthodox religious groups in Israel are now calling for the formation of the Sanhedrin in the Sixth Millennium to enable Israel to rebuild the Temple and anoint the Messiah. They appealed to the rabbis of the world to come together in Jerusalem and elect the seventy-one most qualified rabbis worldwide into a Sanhedrin.

A few quotes from the brochure entitled The Sanhedrin in the Sixth Millennium show how the foundation of this prophetic movement corresponds with all other Messianic prophecies being fulfilled in Israel today: "The rebirth of the State of Israel has given rise to ardent hopes for the re-establishment of the Great Sanhedrin as the guiding light for the Jewish People."

"The prophecy of redemption is being fulfilled in our days with the ingathering of the Exiles and the liberation of the Land. Yet the great task of rebuilding the Temple is still before us. It is written that the Temple of Jerusalem will be rebuilt by a king of the Davidic line, who will be installed by the High Court of Seventy-One, that is, the Sanhedrin."

"The Sanhedrin is needed today to provide the Jewish Nation with the political and spiritual leadership it must have to achieve the long-awaited redemption of the People and the Land."

Their literature refers to the Genesis account of the creation of the heavens and the earth in six days together with the setting aside of the seventh day as a holy Sabbath. As we approach A.D. 2000, they believe that this period of history is significant as the completion of the sixth millennium since creation. "Our era is the sixth millennium after the Creation. The wisdom of our sages prescribes that each day of creation represents a millennium (1000 years) and therefore our era is the Eve of the Seventh Day, that is, the Sabbath Eve....This is the Eve of the "Perfection of

Days," the Eve of the Coming of the true Messiah—Son of David."

This call for the reformation of the Great Sanhedrin has great prophetic significance. It is essential to establish a legal High Court of rabbis capable of determining the laws and rules for the Third Temple. Jesus, in Matthew 24:20, told the Jews to "pray that your flight may not be...on the Sabbath" when the Jews were restricted to journeying no farther than a thousand paces. This suggests that the Sanhedrin and its authority will be established in Israel in our generation before the Antichrist enters the Temple to declare that he is god.

This call to form a new Sanhedrin is one of the most significant of prophetic developments since Israel became an independent State on May 15, 1948. Step by step the Lord is motivating Israel to fulfill the necessary steps leading to the Third Temple and the Age of the Messiah.

The Urim and Thummim

Exodus talks about the mysterious Urim and Thummim that was to be "put in the breastplate of judgment" which would "be over Aaron's heart when he goes in before the Lord." The Bible and various Jewish writings frequently refer to the Urim and Thummim which was used for divine guidance. According to Yoma 73b, the High Priest would consult this device on special occasions to determine the will of the Lord for the people, usually concerning whether or not they were to go to war. The Hilchot Kelai HaMikdash (10:11) makes an unusual statement regarding the Urim and Thummim. It tells how the High Priest would enter the Holy of Holies with his back to the king. As the High Priest faced the Ark of the Covenant, the king would ask his question in a low voice. "Immediately the Holy Spirit would descend on the priest. He would look at the breastplate and see, in a prophetic vision, how [the answer] would stand out in bold letters from the breastplate." This description indicates that the twelve precious stones that made up the breastplate were marked with letters. The particular stones with the appropriate letter would glow to reveal God's will in answer to the question.

A prophecy in Ezra indicates that the Urim and Thummim will finally be restored to Israel for guidance when Elijah and the Messiah appear: "They should not eat of the most holy things till a priest could consult with the Urim and Thummim" (Ezra 2:63). The search for the Breastplate of the High Priest according to the instructions in the Copper Scroll takes on a unique importance in light of these prophecies.

Three Commands To Israel

Moses, in the book of Deuteronomy, recorded three special commandments that God demanded Israel fulfill once she entered the Promised Land. They would: (1) build a Temple for God; (2) anoint a king; (3) blot out the memory of years of tribulation.

In the first command, God said "You shall seek the place where the Lord your God chooses, out of all your tribes, to put His name for His habitation; and there you shall go" (Deuteronomy 12:5). Israel was told to build a Temple in a special place—Mount Moriah. This site was chosen by God centuries before when He told Abraham to build an altar on which to sacrifice his only son to God. This was a test of Abraham's loyalty. Isaac was rescued from death by the Angel of the Lord. Years later, David was sent to this same place to build another altar. Toward the end of David's reign, God commanded the king to buy a piece of land that belonged to the Jebusite, Araunah. Araunah used the land on Mount Moriah as a threshing floor. In this place David built a second altar to the Lord to end the plague. Then, when Solomon prepared to build the first Temple, he was told to build it "on Mount Moriah, where the Lord had appeared to his father David, at the place that David had prepared on the threshing floor" (2 Chronicles 3:1). The Third Temple will be rebuilt at this same location. They cannot build the Temple anywhere else other than the exact site shown to King David three thousand years ago.

The scholar, Maimonides, in the Mishnah Torah recounts the promises of the coming King: "In the future, the Messianic King will arise and renew the Davidic dynasty, return it to its initial sovereignty. He will then build the

Temple and gather the dispersed of Israel. In his days, all the statutes [laws] will return to their previous state. We will offer sacrifices, observe the Sabbatical and Jubilee years according to all the particulars mentioned by the Torah" (Hilchot Melachim U'Mischamotehem V' Hilchot Melech MaMachiach—The Laws of the Kings and their Wars and the laws of the Messianic King).

In this passage Maimonides confirmed the rabbinic understanding that the Messiah, the Redeemer, will build the Temple as prophesied in Zechariah 6:12: "Behold the Man whose name is the BRANCH! From His place He shall branch out, and He shall build the temple of the Lord." The Jewish sages' understanding of this passage has led many Jews to believe that they should do nothing to further the plans for the Third Temple until the Messiah—the Branch comes to build it. However, other Jews in Israel believe that they should prepare to rebuild the Third Temple. Many Christian prophecy teachers, including myself, believe that the Jews will build the Third Temple in the near future. The coming Messiah will build the Fourth Temple in the Millennial Kingdom (Ezekiel 40-48).

The establishment of the Kingdom of God under the Messiah is the true goal of human history as outlined by the Word of God. Jesus the Messiah will lead the nations to true peace, prosperity, a knowledge of the Lord, and pure service to our God in His Messianic Kingdom. Many have believed that the Church can somehow prepare the world for the Kingdom and create the preconditions that will allow Jesus the Messiah to rule from the Throne of David. However, the Bible clearly declares that only the coming of the Messiah will bring about the Kingdom of God. The prophet Daniel predicted that Christ will come suddenly during the reign of the ten nation confederacy of the Antichrist. The Messiah will triumphantly destroy the nations who will fight against Christ's armies, and then He will set up His eternal Kingdom that will cover the entire earth. The prophecy states that the nations of the Antichrist will be destroyed, pulverized as dust. The details of this prediction totally contradict the concept that the Church can gradually "Christianize" the nations of the world until, after a long period of time, the world becomes so spiritually transformed that it willingly accepts the Messiah's rule. The prophets Joel, Zechariah, Malachi, Matthew, and John repeatedly describe a violent conflict called the Battle of Armageddon that will end with the victory of Jesus Christ and His heavenly army.

In our final chapter we will explore the tremendous prophecies about the coming Kingdom of God. Will the twelve tribes of Israel finally receive their inheritance in the Promised Land? What is the role of the Church in governing the Earth after Christ's return? Why will Israel resume the Temple worship system? We will examine the glorious promises of the transformation of the Earth under the reign of Jesus the Messiah.

CHAPTER 17

The Messiah and the Millennial Kingdom

The Millennium will witness the final fulfillment of the hopes and dreams of humanity. When Jesus Christ, the Prince of Peace rules from the Throne of David we will finally enter into the Age of Redemption. Yet this topic of the Millennium has aroused a great deal of controversy and discussion over the years. In the book *Heaven – The Last Frontier* I discussed at some length the arguments for accepting this Millennium as a literal period of one thousand years that will follow the return of Jesus Christ as Messiah. For over three hundred years the early New Testament Church unanimously accepted the reality of a literal Millennial reign of Christ and the saints on a redeemed Earth. This is a very strong argument for accepting this doctrine. Revelation 20 repeats six times that this period will last one thousand years. Many passages in the Old Testament also discuss the coming Kingdom of God. The Millennium is not the total duration of God's Kingdom on Earth, it is simply the first chapter of His eternal Kingdom. The Earth will continue forever, renewed by fire when the first one thousand years end. In this chapter we will explore God's tremendous promises concerning the exciting period known as the Millennium.

The biblical Millennium, when the Messiah rules the earth, will begin when the Great Tribulation and the Battle of Armageddon end. After that, as John describes in his vision in Revelation, "an angel" will come down from heaven carrying "the key to the bottomless pit." The angel will take "the dragon, that serpent of old, who is the Devil and Satan, and bound him for a thousand years." He will be "cast into the bottomless pit" where he will stay "so that he should deceive the nations no more till the thousand years [millennium] were finished" (Revelation 20:1-3).

During this period, the Messiah Jesus Christ will rule from the Throne of David in His Millennial Kingdom. Mankind will then enjoy all they have hoped for and dreamed of since Adam and Eve were banished from the Garden. The citizens of the Millennial Kingdom will be those survivors of the Great Tribulation and the Battle of Armageddon. Tragically, the Bible tells us that only one-third of all Jews and approximately one-third of all Gentiles will survive.

The first thing Christ will do as He begins His reign is to judge the nations. This is not simply the judgment of the "good and evil" deeds of individuals, but a judgment of how the nations have treated the Jews and Christian believers throughout the centuries, especially during the preceding Great Tribulation.

The Judgment of the Nations

"When the Son of Man comes in His glory, and all the holy angels with Him, then He will sit on the throne of His glory. All the nations will be gathered before Him, and He will separate them one from another, as a shepherd divides his sheep from the goats" (Matthew 25:31-32).

The book of Joel tells us that this judgment of the nations will take place in the Valley of Jehoshaphat: "For behold, in those days and at that time, when I bring back the captives of Judah and Jerusalem, I will also gather all nations, and bring them down to the Valley of Jehoshaphat; and I will enter into judgment with them there on account of My people, My heritage Israel, whom they have scattered among the nations" (Joel 3:1-2).

The Valley of Jehoshaphat, better known by its biblical name "Kidron Valley," lies between the Mount of Olives and the Temple Mount in Jerusalem. It is one of three valleys that define the city of Jerusalem. For a thousand years the blood of millions of sacrificed animals flowed from the Temple altar through stone pipes and narrow tunnels to soak into the soil of the Kidron Valley. Gardeners in ancient

Jerusalem collected this incredibly rich soil and sold it to those who needed the best top soil available. The beautiful Garden of Gethsemane, where our Lord prayed the night He was betrayed by Judas, is situated in the Kidron Valley. From this holy place the great Messiah-King will judge every nation that has existed since Adam and Eve's rebellion in the Garden of Eden.

Representatives from all the nations will gather together to be judged according to how they have received the Jews throughout history, and how they have treated Gentile believers in Christ since the Resurrection and throughout the Great Tribulation. Nations that fed the hungry, gave drink to the thirsty, housed the homeless, clothed the naked, visited the sick, aided the imprisoned will "inherit the kingdom prepared for you from the foundation of the world" (Matthew 25:33-34). These are the sheep nations. Jesus says, that those who cared for the least of His servants will receive a reward just as though they had rendered that care to Him. They will continue to exist as nations, blessed forever—through the Millennium and beyond into eternity on the new Earth.

Of the "goat" nations, however, those who cursed and oppressed His servants, Jesus will say, "'Assuredly, I say to you, inasmuch as you did not do it [fed, housed, clothed, visited and ministered] to one of the least of these, you did not do it to Me.' And these will go away into everlasting punishment" (vv. 45- 46). This judgment will not mean the end of the nation/state system, but it will mean the end of the "goat" nations.

A prophecy in Zechariah says that all the nations that are left "shall go up from year to year to worship the King, the Lord of hosts, and to keep the Feast of Tabernacles" (Zechariah 14:16). In this prophecy we see that nations will continue to exist as separate political entities under the reign of the Messiah, and will send representatives to the Temple for the Feast of Tabernacles forever.

Even after the Millennium, when the New Jerusalem will descend out of heaven to Earth: "The nations of those who are saved shall walk in its light, and the kings of the earth bring their glory and honor into it" (Revelation 21:24). These nations will live on into eternity and, the Bible assures us, their political systems including "kings" will continue and will bring glory to the eternally reigning Messiah.

The Millennial Kingdom of Christ

In this wonderful thousand-year reign of Jesus the Messiah there will be many features that our present Earth, since the fall of Adam and Eve, has lacked. On the physical side, Isaiah tells us that the "desert shall rejoice and blossom as the rose; it shall blossom abundantly and rejoice" (35:1-2). The Dead Sea will live again and be filled with "a very great multitude of fish" (Ezekiel 47:9). The animal kingdom will be transformed: "The wolf and the lamb shall feed together, the lion shall eat straw like an ox" (Isaiah 65:25). Mankind will once again administer the earth for the Lord as Adam and Eve were commanded to do.

But the greatest change will be in the hearts of Earth's citizens. There will no longer be war or bigotry, and the chosen people will receive a new spirit that will cause them to want to obey God. The most significant aspect of the Millennium to believers in Christ is that the Church of Jesus Christ will reign with Him. We will "inherit the kingdom prepared for [us] from the foundation of the world" (Matthew 25:34).

The Dead Sea Will Live Again

The Dead Sea, the lowest point on the Earth's surface, and the surrounding desert have been desolate since the days of Sodom and Gomorrah. They stand as a symbol of the Earth's curse. Yet Ezekiel says that during the Millennium, the Messiah will restore the Dead Sea by healing the water that flows from beneath the Temple through the desert and into the sea.

"He brought me back to the door of the temple; and there was water, flowing from under the threshold of the temple toward the east, for the front of the temple faced east; the water was flowing from under the right side of the temple, south of the altar....Then he said to me: 'This water flows toward the eastern region, goes down into the valley, and enters the sea. When it reaches the sea, its waters are healed'" (Ezekiel 47:1,8).

The earth beneath the Temple will open to allow water from the huge subterranean sea beneath Jerusalem to flow forth. As this living water makes its way through the parched Judean wilderness, the banks will spring into a rich growth of trees and vegetation. "Every living thing that moves, wherever the rivers go, will live. There will be a very great multitude of fish, because these waters go there; for they will be healed, and everything will live wherever the river goes. It shall be that fishermen will stand by it from En Gedi [on the shore of the Dead Sea] to En Eglaim; there will be places for spreading their nets. Their fish will be of the same kinds as the fish of the Great Sea, exceedingly many" (vv. 9-10). This prophetic detail about fishing inspired a pastor friend of mine in Florida to believe that life in the Millennium may be more fun than he previously thought.

The Animal Kingdom Will Be Transformed

God created the animal kingdom to function in harmony with His laws and principles. However, one of the consequences of the sinful rebellion of Adam and Eve was the tragic introduction of violence and death into the animal kingdom as well as in mankind. The "mark of Cain," the sign of violence, has afflicted all biological life so that all life today exists by killing other life. But in the Millennium, "The wolf also shall dwell with the lamb, the leopard shall lie down with the young goat, the calf and the young lion and the fatling together; and a little child shall lead them. The cow and the bear shall graze; their young ones shall lie down together; and the lion shall eat straw like the ox. The nursing child shall play by the cobra's hole, and the weaned child shall put his hand in the viper's den. They shall not hurt nor destroy in all my holy mountain, for the earth shall be full of the knowledge of the Lord as the waters cover the sea" (Isaiah 11:6-9).

This prophecy in Isaiah indicates that the original peaceful form of nature will return in the Kingdom of God. Some have wondered if it is truly possible that God will transform the animal kingdom as the prophet describes. The

One Who created all the universe, including the Earth with its animals and humans, is certainly capable of restructuring biology so that the carnivore is able to derive nourishment from vegetation.

A truly wonderful manifestation of the Messianic rule of the Prince of Peace will extend even to the animal kingdom. All of nature will bask in the divine protection of the Lord Jesus Christ.

Mankind Will Again Administer the Earth for God

Often when people consider eternity, or life on Earth during the Millennium, they wonder what they will do to fill the endless days. They fear they will not have anything interesting to do with their lives. Yet the Bible's prophecies tell us that life after the Messiah sets up His Kingdom will be interesting and exciting. It will proceed much as it does now, only without the drudgery of toil and the curse of sin that forces us to earn a living by the "sweat of your face." Purposeful economic activity will remain a major part of the lives of a redeemed humanity that enters into the Millennial Kingdom after Armageddon as well as those born during the Millennium. "They shall build houses and inhabit them; they shall plant vineyards and eat their fruit....And My elect shall long enjoy the work of their hands " (Isaiah 65:21,22). Without drudgery of meaningless labor, citizens of the Millennial Kingdom will enjoy purposeful activity, accomplishing their joyful part in God's Kingdom. Ezekiel says that they will fish in the Dead Sea; Isaiah talks about gold and incense being delivered to Jerusalem (60:6); "sons of foreigners shall build up your walls" (v. 10); ships shall sail from afar, bringing home the exiles (v. 9). These verses tell us that natural people living during the Millennium will have many interesting and productive activities to fill their time with. The resurrected saints, the raptured Church of Jesus, will assist the Messiah in "ruling and reigning" over the natural Jews and Gentiles living on Earth.

God set up Adam and Eve in the Garden of Eden to tend and take dominion over creation. Those in His Millennial Kingdom will be given the same administrative role.

Israel Will Have a New Covenant

The Messiah will rule Earth "with a rod of iron" during the Millennium (Psalm 2:9; Revelation 2:27; 19:13). On Mount Sinai God gave Israel a Law which they continually broke. But in the Millennial Kingdom He will implant the Law of Christ within the inward spirit of the men and women of Israel: "Not according to the covenant that I made with their fathers in the day that I took them by the hand to bring them out of the land of Egypt, My covenant which they broke, though I was a husband to them." Rather, "I will put My law in their minds, and write it on their hearts; and I will be their God, and they shall be My people" (Jeremiah 31:32-33).

Ezekiel prophesied: "I will give you a new heart and put a new spirit within you; I will take the heart of stone out of your flesh and give you a heart of flesh. I will put My Spirit within you and cause you to walk in My statutes, and you will keep My judgments and do them. Then you shall dwell in the land that I gave to your fathers; you shall by My people, and I will be your God" (Ezekiel 36:26-28).

All People Will Follow the Lord Willingly

One of the most remarkable features of the Kingdom of Christ is that men will no longer need to be taught and admonished to know the Lord. "'No more shall every man teach his neighbor, and every man his brother, saying, "Know the Lord," for they all shall know Me, from the least of them to the greatest of them,' says the Lord. 'For I will forgive their iniquity, and their sin I will remember no more'" (Isaiah 31:34). When Christ comes He will redeem the hearts of all men and women, from the lowest to the highest rungs of society, forgiving their sins forever. That transformed humanity in the Millennium will partake of the same incredible knowledge of the Lord that, until now, has been experienced only by the most devout servants of God.

Isaiah's phrase "from the least of them to the greatest of them" indicates that society will not be a homogenized group without distinctions. Even in the Millennial period with unlimited opportunities, resources, and time, people will still manifest their differences in desire, ambitions, and efforts. These personality differences will produce a hierarchy of society—from the least to the highest—under the perfect justice and administration of Christ. Heaven is a hierarchy with cherubim, seraphim, "living creatures," archangels, angels around the throne, warrior and messenger angels, elders, the Bride of Christ, the 144 thousand, and "great multitude which no one could number." Our God loves variety. The Kingdom of God on Earth will provide people with the opportunity to explore and express their individuality and creativity.

Anti-Semitism and Bigotry Will End

One of the greatest features of the Millennial Kingdom will be the change of heart toward the Jews. Christ will finally eliminate the ancient anti-Semitism that so often erupted in the hearts of nations. Hatred of the Jews is the mark of a heart that has not been touched by God's love. Anti-Semitism is the sign of a civilization unredeemed.

Satan's intense hatred of God has manifested itself throughout history in the persecution of the people of Israel. He hoped to destroy God's people—the vessel chosen to reveal His Word and God's Redeemer, Jesus of Nazareth. Therefore he has done everything in his power to inspire nations and individuals to do violence to the Jews. Even though Jesus conquered Satan when He went to the Cross the devil still "walks about like a roaring lion, seeking whom he may devour" (1 Peter 5:8). In His Millennial reign, however, Jesus will cause Satan to be bound and cast into the bottomless pit for a thousand years. A bound Satan will no longer provoke Gentile nations to hatred and persecution of God's chosen people and His Bride of Christ, the Church.

After centuries of intermittent persecution, it is natural for Jews to fear and have a profound distrust of Gentiles. But when the Messiah, the Prince of Peace, reigns in Jerusalem both Jews and Gentiles will finally appreciate each other and live in peace. "Whereas you have been forsaken and hated, so that no one went through you, I will make you an eternal excellence, a joy of many generations" (Isaiah 60:15).

The Gentile Nations Will Be Reconciled and Blessed

When the Messiah returns, the Gentile nations will finally enter into the blessings which God promised them from the beginning of time. God told Abraham that his seed would ultimately bless all nations on Earth. "I will bless those who bless you, and I will curse him who curses you; and in you all the families of the earth shall be blessed" (Genesis 12:3). The seed of Abraham, Israel, has already blessed all of humanity in the transmission of God's revelation through the written Word, and through Jesus the Messiah, "the Word" (John 1:1). Israel has also contributed enormously in science, medicine, law, and philosophy.

However, the Gentiles will experience the final fulfillment of their blessing when the Millennium begins. Isaiah prophesied: "Arise, shine; for your light has come! And the glory of the Lord is risen upon you. For behold, the darkness shall cover the earth, and deep darkness shall cover the earth, and deep darkness the people; but the Lord will arise over you, and His glory will be seen upon you. The Gentiles shall come to your light, and kings to the brightness of your rising. Lift up your eyes all around, and see; they all gather together, they come to you; your sons shall come from afar, and your daughters shall be nursed at your side. Then you shall see and become radiant, and your heart shall swell with joy; because the abundance of the sea shall be turned to you, the wealth of the Gentiles shall come to you" (Isaiah 60:1-5). In the Millennium the Jews and Gentiles will be reconciled to each other in complete understanding of their distinct roles in God's unfolding plan for the redemption of the planet. The nations will honor the Messiah and His throne in Jerusalem by blessing Israel materially in every way.

Israel was destroyed many times in history because she failed to sanctify God's holy name and become a light to the Gentiles. When their hearts are transformed spiritually by the return of Christ their Redeemer-Messiah, God's Chosen People will reflect His holiness and spirit perfectly.

Jerusalem Will Become the City of Peace

While generations of Jews and Gentiles have prayed for the peace of Jerusalem, the tragic history of the city illustrates man's ability to endure the pain of war rather than avoid it. One promise of the Millennial Kingdom is that the City of David will finally enjoy the peace she has sought through all her generations.

After the devastation of the Great Tribulation and the climactic Battle of Armageddon, the guns will be finally silenced and the violence of war will cease for a thousand years. "Thus says the Lord: 'Behold, I will extend peace to her like a river'" (Isaiah 66:12). The true peace of the Messiah will flow "like a river" from the changed hearts of Jews and Gentiles. Except for one brief rebellion after the Millennium when "he (Satan) must be released for a little while" (Revelation 20:3) from the bottomless pit into which Satan was cast, war will completely cease. When you contemplate the terror, pain, suffering and death from thousands of years of warfare, it is difficult to envision a world at peace with itself and with God. Can you imagine the projects we can plan and accomplish with the huge resources on this planet when we no longer spend trillions of dollars each year on weapons, armies, police, insurance, etc.? Then Jerusalem will truly be the city of peace in a world at peace.

Throughout history the locked gates of a city symbolized the lack of peace in the hearts of men. The gates will finally be opened forever to allow access to the city of Jerusalem. Israel will receive her blessing and will then enjoy the promised peace and prosperity that have eluded her during countless centuries of living in the "valley of dry bones."

Jerusalem Will Have a New Name

Not only will Jerusalem's image be changed to that of a city of peace, she will also receive a new name. Isaiah predicted the changes in the city under the reign of Messiah: "You shall be called by a new name, which the mouth of the Lord will name. You shall also be a crown of glory in the hand of the Lord, and a royal diadem in the hand of your God. You shall no longer be termed Forsaken, nor shall your land any more be termed Desolate; but you shall be called Hephzibah [My Delight in Her], and your land Beulah [Married]; for the Lord delights in you" (Isaiah 62:2-4).

When Jerusalem turns from sin, the Lord will delight in her and she will delight in the presence of the Messiah as He reigns from the throne of David. In addition, the prophet says that Israel has been Desolate since she rejected Christ as Messiah, but she will finally rejoice in her new name Married. God uses the image of joy and contentment in marriage to symbolize the final state of Israel when she turns from her unfaithfulness and enjoys her reunion with the God of Abraham, Isaac, and Jacob.

Israel's Borders Will Be Expanded

When the Messiah returns to set up His Kingdom, Israel will finally possess all the land God promised Abraham over four thousand years ago. Solomon was the only one who came close to taking all the land God gave the Israelites. Ezekiel the prophet outlines the boundaries of the new kingdom of Israel during the Millennium (See Ezekiel 47:15-21).

The Northern Border: from the Mediterranean to Hethlon to Hamath (vv. 15-17).

The Eastern Border: from Hauran and Damascus through Gilead and from the Jordan River to the Dead Sea (v. 18).

The Southern Border: from Tamar to the waters of Kadesh to the Mediterranean Sea (v. 19). (God promised Abraham that his seed would, at some point in Israel's future, include the Arabian Peninsula as far as the Euphrates River, Genesis 15:18-21).

According to Ezekiel 48:1-29, the tribal divisions from north to South in the Promised Land will be as indicated on Diagram 1. Each tribal division will run east from the Mediterranean Sea in parallel zones.

The Tribal Division in the Millennium

Dan
Asher
Naphtali
Manasseh
Ephraim
Reuben
Judah
The Holy Portion for the Prince
Benjamin
Simeon
Issachar
Zebulun
Gad

Closeup of the Holy Portion

For the Prince	Kohanim		For the Prince
	Levites		
	Suburb	City	Suburb	

The Tribes of Israel

John, in the book of Revelation (7:4-8), talks about the sealing of the "one hundred and forty-four thousand of all the tribes of the children of Israel," twelve thousand from each of the twelve tribes of Israel. There are 144 thousand Jewish Witnesses during the tribulation period. Reading carefully, you will see that this list of tribes differs from the original allocation of tribes and lands which the book of Joshua talks about (Joshua 15-22).

Tribal Allocations

Joshua's Twelve Tribes	Revelations Twelve Tribes
Judah	Judah
Manasseh	Manasseh
Benjamin	Benjamin
Simeon	Simeon
Zebulun	Zebulun
Issachar	Issachar
Asher	Asher
Naphtali	Naphtali
Reuben	Reuben
Gad	Gad
Dan	Levi
Ephraim	Joseph

The tribe of "Joseph" was not mentioned in Joshua because Joseph's two sons, Ephraim and Manasseh, received tribal allotments. The tribe of Levi was also not mentioned in Joshua's list because Levi was the priestly tribe that inherited the six cities of refuge and the tithes of the people. To make up the twelve tribes in the list in Revelation, the tribe, "Joseph" replaces his son "Ephraim" and "Levi" replaces "Dan." Why is the tribe of Dan not included in the "Revelation" account? Most scholars believe that the reason for their elimination may stem from their defiance of God's law concerning idolatry. When King Jeroboam set up two golden calves, one in Bethel and the other in Dan, the people of Dan chose to worship the calf rather than go to the Temple at Jerusalem (See 1 Kings 12:26-30).

Ezekiel, however, prophesies that the tribe of Dan will be redeemed and take their place once again with the twelve tribes during the Millennium. Their sin will finally be forgiven when Christ returns to save Israel at the Battle of Armageddon. When Ezekiel lists the division of the land during the Millennium, Dan is again included (see Ezekiel

48). The tribe of Levi will not receive a tribal portion of the kingdom because their portion belongs to God. They will once again receive their material blessings and tithes as priests from each of the twelve tribes, as they did when Joshua allocated the Promised Land. "It shall be, in regard to their [Levites] inheritance, that I am their inheritance. You shall give them no possession in Israel, for I am their possession. They shall eat the grain offering, the sin offering, and the trespass offering; every dedicated thing in Israel shall be their's. The best of all firstfruits of any kind, and every sacrifice of any kind from all your sacrifices, shall be the priest's; also you shall give the priest the first of your ground meal, to cause a blessing to rest on your house" (Ezekiel 44:28-30). The Levites shall live on property near the fourth Temple that will be built by the Messiah. They will not be able to "sell or exchange any of it; they may not alienate this best part of the land, for it is holy to the Lord" (Ezekiel 48:14).

The Millennial Temple

For three millennium the history of Jerusalem has revolved around the site of the Temples of Solomon and Herod, both of which have been destroyed. For twenty centuries, rabbis argued over whether or not the Jews should rebuild the Temple if they ever regained the Holy City. Now, since the Six-Day War in 1967, Israel is in possession of the land and the Temple Mount. Now the argument that rages in the yeshiva schools in Jerusalem is, Will we build the Temple and then the Messiah will come? or, Will the Messiah come as Zechariah prophesied and build the Temple Himself?

The Bible's answer to both questions is clear: Yes! First, the Orthodox Jews in Israel will build the third Temple, and then, after the Messiah returns He will build the fourth Temple, north of Jerusalem as described by Ezekiel.

This generation will witness the building of the third Temple by the Jews in Israel. That Temple is the one the Antichrist will defile during the "abomination of desolation" prophesied by Daniel. It will ultimately be cleansed by Jesus Christ when He enters the Temple through the sealed Eastern Gate. Zechariah prophecies a fourth Temple that will be built during the Millennium.

"Behold, the Man whose name is the BRANCH! From His place He shall branch out, and He shall build the temple of the Lord; yes, He shall build the temple of the Lord. He shall bear the glory, and shall sit and rule on His throne; so He shall be a priest on His throne" (Zechariah 6:12).

Jewish Worship Will Be Restored in the Temple

In the Millennium the Lord will restore the ancient priesthood of Israel to conduct worship services in the Fourth Temple. In Ezekiel 40—48 the Lord describes the linen robes they will wear and details the ministry of sacrifices they will perform each day in the rebuilt Temple.

God, in His command to Moses (Leviticus 23:1-41), laid out the laws of the various annual feasts for Israel. In speaking of the Feast of Tabernacles He said: "You shall keep it as a feast to the Lord for seven days in the year. It shall be a statute forever in your generations. You shall celebrate it in the seventh month" (v. 43). This command, along with the prophecy in Isaiah 66:21-23, prove that the feasts will be commemorated annually. Worship in the Temple will continue on Earth forever, even after God creates His Millennial Kingdom. "'I will also take some of them for priests and Levites,' says the Lord. 'For as the new heavens and the new earth which I will make shall remain before,' says the Lord, 'So shall your descendants and your name remain. And it shall come to pass that from one New Moon to another, and from one Sabbath to another, all flesh shall come to worship before Me,' says the Lord" (Isaiah 66:21-23).

Ezekiel, in another prophecy, describes Jewish priests who will administer worship in the Temple that will be built by the Messiah during the Millennium. These priests and kohanim will be descended from the tribe of Levi and the sons of Aaron who are born in the Millennium. You will find a description of the laws governing these priests in Ezekiel 44, verses 15 through 18.

The Sacrificial System Will Continue

One of the most perplexing ideas to students of Scripture is the idea that God intends that the annual feasts, along with animal sacrifice, will continue into the Millennium. Many Christians who have studied the prophetic portions in Zechariah 14, Isaiah 66, and Ezekiel 40 to 48, which clearly describe these Millennial worship ordinations, are confused by the idea. They ask, "Didn't the sacrifice of Christ eliminate animal sacrifices forever?"

The New Testament describes in many places the fundamental truth that God's sacrifice of His only Son Jesus Christ upon the cross dealt with the sin problem once and for all. The book of Hebrews, quoting David's Psalm 40, says: "'Sacrifice and offering, burnt offerings, and offerings for sin You did not desire, nor had pleasure in them' (which are offered according to the law), then He said, 'Behold, I have come to do Your will, O God.' He takes the first that He may establish the second. By that we will have been sanctified through the offering of the body of Jesus Christ once for all" (Hebrews 10:8-10). In this passage God says that He did not want the Jews to simply follow the ancient law of outward sacrifice as a ritual, because God sanctified those who believe in Jesus' offering His own body on the cross.

Then in verses 3 and 4, Hebrews says, "But in those sacrifices there is a reminder of sins every year. For it is not possible that the blood of bulls and goats could take away sins." We understand from these references that animal sacrifice could never atone for the sins of rebellious men. Only the complete sacrifice of Jesus could ever totally atone for our sins. However, God clearly demanded the sacrifices from Adam to Christ. Those sacrifices were acts of obedience to the direct command of God, as well as acknowledgments of one's own personal sinfulness and need for God's forgiveness. Animal sacrifices covered the sins of the people temporarily until the prophesied Messiah would come and offer Himself once and for all as the necessary atonement for sin. If animal sacrifice can never atone for sin, why would God allow Israel to resume such sacrifice in the Third Temple, prior to Armageddon, and then demand that Israel continue such sacrifice in the Millennium? There are two reasons why I believe this is true.

First, the early Jewish-Christian Church continued to offer sacrifices in the first century. A close examination of the book of the Acts of the Apostles shows that Paul and other Jewish- Christian believers participated in the offering of sacrifices in the Temple whenever they were in Jerusalem. They did this until the Temple was burned in A.D. 70. Gentile believers in Christ were never involved in the sacrifices because God's command in the Old Testament was only to the Jews. Jewish-Christians who went to the Temple to preach, such as Paul, had to obey the sacrificial practices or they would never have been permitted to continue preaching day after day. Historical evidence is conclusive that first-century Jewish believers continued in this practice for thirty-eight years, until A.D. 70. Once the Temple was burnt to the ground, sacrifice was impossible, and the whole issue became unimportant.

The Jerusalem church told Paul that people had heard that "you teach all the Jews who are among the Gentiles to forsake Moses, saying that they ought not to circumcise their children nor to walk according to the custom" (Acts 21:21). Because Paul was so successful in spreading the gospel to the Gentiles, the Jerusalem church was reluctant to do anything that would hamper his work. But they did not want Paul to alienate the "many myriads of Jews there are who have believed" and who were "all zealous for the law" (v. 20). So they suggested that Paul, as a Jew, openly demonstrate his continued obedience to the law of Moses and take the Nazirite vow, along with four other men. They instructed Paul to "take them and be purified with them, and pay their expenses so that they may shave their heads." In doing this, Paul would show them "that those things of which they [the believing Jews] were informed concerning you are nothing, but that you yourself also walk orderly and keep the law" (Acts 21:24).

Paul followed their suggestion and took the Nazirite vow (see Numbers 6), shaved his hair, purified himself and, when the days of purification were completed, offered a sacrifice in the Temple. "Then Paul took the men, and the next day, having been purified with them, entered the temple to announce the expiration of the days of purification, at which time an offering should be made for each one of them" (v. 26). Even though Paul continually affirmed that his belief in Christ's atonement did not make him reject God's commands for the Jews, He still insisted that salvation came only through the Christ's once-and-for-all-time sacrifice on the cross.

Second, New Testament writers used the legal sacrificial system to illustrate very important points concerning Christ's sacrifice on the Cross. When Paul and other church leaders observed the Law of Moses it served to graphically explain that these sacrifices were only a shadow of the final sacrifice of God's Son. The daily sacrifices and Temple rituals were types of Jesus Christ. As I mentioned in an earlier chapter, when the priest took his knife and cut the Passover lamb's throat to kill it instantly, he would say, "It is finished." When he placed the lamb on the vertical spit he would tie its outstretched front legs to the cross-beam spit. He would wrap the lamb's intestines around the animal's head while it was being roasted. This was called "the crown of the Passover." Jewish-Christian teachers would have compared the prophetic significances of these details to the events that transpired during Jesus Christ's crucifixion.

These examples of the way early Jewish believers used God's law to teach God's great love when He sacrificed His only Son on the cross will be repeated during the Millennium. The Two Witnesses and the 144 thousand Jewish witnesses which the book of Revelation speaks about may refer to the ongoing Temple sacrifices as they witness to the Jews of the Tribulation, just as Paul did two thousand years ago. They will be able to show how these sacrifices commemorate the one complete sacrifice of Christ at Golgotha.

Then again, during the Millennial Kingdom of Christ, the illustration of animal sacrifices may again be used to teach the billions of Jews and Gentiles born during that thousand year period that the cost of our salvation was the blood of the innocent Lamb of God. The sacrifices in the Temple will remind those who are born during that blessed time of peace on Earth that the cost of our salvation has always been the shed blood of the Lamb. Perhaps during that idyllic time the children of the Millennium will find it hard to understand the horror of sinful rebellion and the terrible cost of our redemption from sin. Offering an innocent animal in the Millennial Temple may serve as a tremendous teaching tool to those new generations.

The fact that Scripture clearly prophesies that animal sacrifice will resume at the Temple does not in any way suggest that such a sacrifice will effectively provide a covering for the sins of those people. "For it is not possible that the blood of bulls and goats could take away sins" (Hebrews 10:4). Just as animal sacrifice did not take away sin in the past, it will not take away sin in the future. The only thing animal sacrifice ever accomplished was to express that a man acknowledged his personal sin and his obedience to God's command at that time. Without the shedding of the blood of Jesus Christ, the Lamb of God, man would never have been able to be saved from sin. Only by accepting the completed sacrifice of Jesus Christ on the cross can we be saved. All those who have ever been saved or ever will be saved—from Abel to the last person born in the Millennium—are saved through the sacrifice of Jesus Christ. From Adam until eternity, salvation can only be found in Christ's atoning work on the Cross. There is only one plan of salvation—Jesus Christ.

As the Bible so clearly declares: "Jesus said...,'I am the way, the truth, and the life. No one comes to the Father except through Me'" (John 14:6).

The Church Will Reign With Christ

Jesus will not rule the nations of the Millennium alone; the resurrected believers of the Church will reign with Him to provide the leadership necessary to create a just society, not only in government but also in the priesthood. Those who have often toiled for the Lord without recognition or reward in this life, will reign openly before the nations in that glorious day when Jesus manifests His servants. Consider the song the twenty-four elders sang to the Lamb in Revelation 5:9-10: "You have redeemed us to God by Your blood...and have made us kings and priests to our God; and we shall reign on the earth." Also the declaration of the Apostle Paul: "If we endure, we shall also reign with Him" (2 Timothy 2:12). Even after the Millennium those whose names are written in the "Lamb's Book of Life" will "reign forever and ever" on the New Earth (Revelation 22:5). Unlike the earthly priesthood, which is subject to weakness and human frailties, the royal priesthood of the believers in the Millennial Kingdom of Christ will function in perfect holiness and power.

At the end of the thousand-year reign of Christ, God will release Satan from his chains in the "bottomless pit" and allow him to tempt mankind one last time. Amazingly, after a thousand years of peace, prosperity, and righteousness under the Messiah, a multitude of those people born during the Millennium will join Satan in his final rebellion.

These rebellious people will be descendants of those Jews and Gentiles who survived the Great Tribulation. Although they will grow up knowing about the Messiah ruling in Jerusalem, they will secretly hold rebellion in their heart. Since Jesus will "rule with a rod of iron" they will bide their time until the final rebellion at the end of the Millennium. Revelation 20:7-9 declares that "Satan will be released from his prison and will go out to deceive the nations which are in the four corners of the earth, Gog and Magog, to gather them to battle." When they attack "the camp of the saints and the beloved city...Fire came down from God out of heaven and devoured them." This final rebellion will prove that mankind will fail every single test of obedience that God provides.

The Great White Throne Judgment

This judgment will occur at the end of the one thousand year Millennial Kingdom. This last judgement before the Throne of God in Heaven will involve every single sinner from Cain to the last sinner who dies fighting this last battle of history.

"Then I saw a Great White Throne and Him who sat on it, from whose face the earth and the heaven fled away...And I saw the dead, small and great, standing before God, and books were opened...the dead were judged according to their works..." (Revelation 20:11,12).

This solemn judgment will determine the degree of punishment of all sinners. The decision of Heaven or Hell was determined by their previous rejection of the only plan of salvation God provided – the blood of Jesus Christ. All who will stand before God on that day will be sinners. The wicked angels, both those imprisoned for their sins recorded in Genesis 6 and the fallen angels of Satan, will also be judged at this time. In II Peter 2:4 he prophesied: "God did not spare the angels who sinned, but cast them down to Hell and delivered them into chains of darknes, to be reserved for judgment." Paul tells Christians: "Do you not know that the saints will judge the world?" (I Corinthians 6:3). In Matthew 25:41 Jesus declared the destiny of those who chose to reject His salvation: "Depart from Me, you cursed into the everlasting fire prepared for the devil and his angels." Notice that the everlasting fire was originally prepared for the devil and his angels. God earnestly desired that every man and woman will repent of their sins and accept His salvation.

Christians will not appear at the Great White Throne judgment. The sins of Christians have been judged forever on the cross when we accepted Christ as our personal saviour. However, the life and works of Christians after they became believers will be judged in Heaven at the Bema Judgment Seat of Christ as recorded in II Corinthians 5:10. "For we must all appear before the judgment seat of Christ, that every one may receive the things done in the body, according to what he has done, whether good or bad." Rewards and crowns will be given out to the faithful servants of Christ but there will be no punishments.

Final Choices

The Lord has not left us in darkness concerning the time of the Messiah's return. Although we cannot know "the day nor the hour in which the Son of Man is coming" (Matthew 25:13), the Bible suggests that He is coming back to Earth in our generation. Someday soon the heavens will be shattered "with a shout, with the voice of an archangel, and with the trumpet of God" (1 Thessalonians 4:16) announcing to the Church the awesome news that "Messiah is here!" At that moment Jesus Christ will appear in the clouds to receive His Bride, His faithful Church, rising supernaturally in the air to meet their Lord and King. The believers will return to Heaven for the glorious marriage supper of the Lamb. In that wonderful marriage feast the Old Testament saints who arose earlier (see Matthew 27:52-53) will be the friends of the Bridegroom Jesus. All Christians will appear in the coming judgment of Christ to receive their rewards for their faithfulness to Christ on Earth.

In 1 Thessalonians 2:19, Paul talks about our hope in the coming rapture of the saints: "For what is our hope, or joy, or crown of rejoicing? Is it not even you in the presence of our Lord Jesus Christ at His coming?"

Meanwhile, on the planet below, men will experience hell on Earth under the savage rule of Satan's Antichrist. The wrath of God will be poured out on an unrepentant world. The terror and horror of those unrelenting years of war, famine, and death will surpass anything that human language could depict. Though there will be some who will choose Christ in those terrible times, the cost of their choice will be their instant martyrdom. Those who accept the invitation of the Lord today can avoid that terrible time of persecution, that "time of Jacob's trouble" (Jeremiah 30:7). This promise to the Church does not imply that we can expect to escape all persecution and trials as Christians. The Bible repeatedly warns us about the tribulations and persecutions we must experience in our walk with Christ. If the Lord delays the Rapture much longer, the Church in North America will begin to experience the same savage persecution that has afflicted Christians throughout history, including many nations in the Third World today.

It is not just philosophical or religious speculation that each of us will someday meet Jesus the Messiah face to face: "It is appointed for men to die once, but after this the judgment" (Hebrews 9:27). God declares that "all have sinned and fall short of the glory of God" (Romans 3:23) and it is impossible for a holy God to allow an unrepentant sinner into a sinless Heaven. In light of the incredible evidence about Jesus the Messiah, and the many signs that His return is very near, each of us must make our final choice. Every day sinful rebellion leads men inexorably toward hell and an eternity without God. "For the wages of sin is death, but the gift of God is eternal life in Christ Jesus our Lord" (Romans 6:23). However, God loved everyone of us so much that He sent His Son the Messiah to accept the punishment of hell for everyone who would confess his sin and ask forgiveness. In the Gospel of John, the prophet declared: "But as many as received Him, to them He gave the right to become children of God, even to those who believe in His name" (John 1:12).

Men want to make spiritual matters so complicated but God declares that salvation is very simple. Who will become the god of your life? Jesus or you? Either you will allow Jesus to become your Lord, admitting you are a sinner in need of a pardon, or you will insist on remaining the god of your life, even though your decision will lead you to hell. In the end it is your choice. You choose Heaven or Hell for your eternal destiny. You can choose to follow the Messiah and meet Him in the Rapture as your Savior. Or you can reject His claims to be Lord of your life and choose to meet Him as your judge at Armageddon. Paul quoted Isaiah when he said, "Every knee shall bow to Me, and every tongue shall confess to God" (Romans 14:11; Isaiah 45:23).

The keeper of the Philippian prison where Paul and Silas had been incarcerated was put in a position to make this final choice. God used an earthquake to miraculously break the chains that bound the two preachers and open the prison doors. The warden awoke and saw the doors open and, fearing that the prisoners had escaped, drew his sword to kill himself. When Paul called out that all the prisoners were still there, the frightened jailer recognized the power of the Messiah. He called out, "Sirs, what must I do to be saved?" Their reply to the jailer has never changed: "Believe on the Lord Jesus Christ, and you will be saved, you and your household" (Acts 16:30-31). After taking them out of the prison the jailer made his final choice: "He rejoiced, having believed in God with all his household" (v. 34).

Our world continues its fateful journey towards its appointment at Armageddon in the "valley of decision" (Joel 3:14) You must make your choice: Who will you put your faith in?

If you have already chosen to follow Jesus the Messiah, I would like to encourage you to become actively involved in the accomplishment of the Great Commission of our Lord and Savior. In Matthew 28:19-20 Jesus commanded, "Go therefore and make disciples of all the nations, baptizing them in the name of the Father and of the Son and of the Holy Spirit, teaching them to observe all things that I have commanded you; and lo, I am with you always, even to the end of the age." The truth that the return of the Messiah is near should motivate each of us to a renewed love of Christ and a willingness to witness to those around us. I have written these books to encourage Christians and also provide them with prophecy research materials that they can give to their friends and neighbors. The amazing events of the Persian Gulf War and the turmoil in Russia are causing many to ask what is ahead for the Earth. We receive letters each day from readers whose loved ones have come to know Jesus as their Messiah through reading this material. This growing concern about Bible prophecies regarding these last days, is opening the door to the greatest opportunity to witness in our lifetime. I trust my books and tapes will prove worthwhile to your personal study and witnessing.

During the last twenty-eight years I have enjoyed the tremendous experience of studying the prophetic truths about the Millennium, Heaven, and the coming Messiah. However, the purpose of prophetic study is not simply to inform you, but also to transform you through the renewing of your minds by Jesus the Messiah. The study of the truth about the Messiah has changed my life forever. I will continue to study until I meet Jesus face to face in Heaven. The Apostle John, speaking about the Messiah's return, declared that "everyone who has this hope in Him purifies himself, just as He is pure" (1 John 3:3).

John records an astonishing promise that will be fulfilled in this generation: "Beloved, now we are children of God; and it has not yet been revealed what we shall be, but we know that when He is revealed, we shall be like Him, for we shall see Him as He is" (1 John 3:2).

The prophet John saw the Messiah's glorious return: "The kingdoms of this world have become the kingdoms of our Lord and of His Christ, and He shall reign forever and ever!" (Revelation 11:15). On that wondrous day we shall join with all the saints of God and sing:

> "We give You thanks, O Lord God Almighty,
> The One who is and who was and who is to come,
> Because You have taken Your great power and reigned."

CHAPTER 18

The Messiah and the Dead Sea Scrolls

The Dead Sea Scrolls were discovered in several caves to the west of the ancient salt sea in 1947. This discovery of the most ancient Bible manuscripts ever found transformed the world of biblical scholarship. Prior to this, the oldest Old Testament biblical texts available to scholars were manuscript copies dated about A.D. 1100. In other words, the oldest text of a biblical book, such as Isaiah, was an A.D. 1100 copy of a copy of a copy of a copy. When the Dead Sea Scrolls were initially released, scholars were delighted to find every single book of the Old Testament except the book of Esther. The importance of this discovery cannot be overestimated. In one moment, scholars were able to step back over one thousand years closer to the original writing of the manuscripts. They were astonished to discover that the biblical manuscripts from A.D. 1100 that guided the translators of the King James Version in A.D. 1611, were identical "word for word" with the ancient Dead Sea biblical scrolls written some two hundred years before Christ. How could the Bible's text have remained so accurate over two thousand years of copying?

The Masoretic Scribes

This new discovery confirmed the incredible accuracy of the Masoretic scribes and Christian monks who laboriously copied these biblical texts over the centuries. The name Masora describes the Jewish scribe's work of carefully "counting" the verses, chapters, and letters of the Hebrew biblical text. The Jews' love of the Word of God caused them to copy each letter with astonishing accuracy. The Masoretic scribes counted every single letter in every verse of the books of the Bible and wrote this information in the margins to ensure total accuracy. For example, they recorded that the book of Genesis (Bereishis) contained precisely 1,534 verses in the Hebrew text. They stated the middle verse of Genesis was: "By the sword shalt thou live" (Genesis 27:40). After the copying was completed, several master scribes would check each book meticulously. If one mistake was discovered, they cut up and burned the incorrect copy. The Jews called these scribes Masora, "the hedge or fence of the law," because they protected the sacred text from corruption. Some scholars believed this succession of Masora scribes began about the time of Ezra the Scribe about 520 B.C. and continued until the year A.D. 1030. For a certain period they carried on their sacred task from schools in Tiberias on the Sea of Galilee. Their awesome devotion to the sacred Word of God preserved the biblical text "letter for letter" over twenty centuries. Later, Christian scribes copied the New Testament Scriptures with the same accuracy and love of God. If only Christians today loved the Bible as much as those ancient scholars.

Eleven complete scrolls and thousands of fragments of others were discovered in the Qumran Dead Sea Caves from 1947 to 1956. A large number of the initial manuscripts were discovered by the Bedouin tribesmen of Ta'amireh. Archaeologists located a large number of significant manuscripts in the 1950s. The last major addition to the scroll treasures came in the year 1967 when the very important Temple Scroll, that had been found by Bedouins some years before, was finally purchased for the Israeli government by the Israeli archaeologist Yigael Yadin. In this treasure trove of Dead Sea manuscripts they found multiple copies of Genesis, Isaiah, and a number of other significant biblical texts that attested to the incredible accuracy of our current Bible texts. Several important texts reveal that the Essene community expected a coming Messiah and a final apocalyptic War Between the Sons of Light and the Sons of Darkness. These expectations certainly parallel the hopes and beliefs of the early Christian community in Israel.

Dr. Sukenik, Yadin's father, purchased the Dead Sea Scrolls in their original wrappings and jars from a dealer in Bethlehem and made the first English translation of them. In 1947 the first scrolls were found in a cave in the Judean desert wrapped in linen and stored in earthenware jars with lids. While Dr. Sukenik recognized their great antiquity, he had difficulty convincing the scholarly world. He sent a piece of the linen wrappings from the scrolls to be tested by a laboratory in Europe. Unfortunately, the radioactive testing methods used in 1947 tended to damage the test material. In order to avoid this problem, the linen covering rather than the actual scroll material was tested. The carbon-14 test of the linen yielded a date between the second century B.C. and the beginning of the first century A.D. This result confirmed that the scrolls were produced by the Essenes and buried for safekeeping in A.D. 68. In the last few months of 1991 Swiss laboratories have finally tested the original scroll material and have confirmed this first-century dating.

The Mysterious Essene Community and the Dead Sea Scrolls

At the time of Christ there were three significant Jewish religious communities, the Pharisees, the Sadducees, and the Essenes. The ascetic Essenes lived primarily in three communities: Qumran at the Dead Sea, the Essene quarter of Jerusalem (Mt. Zion), and Damascus. They appear to have existed from approximately 200 B.C. until the destruction of their communities in Jerusalem and Qumran by the Roman armies in A.D 68. Very concerned with purity, they separated themselves from the temple worship in Jerusalem. In their love for the Word of God they faithfully copied out each of the scrolls of the Old Testament in their scriptorium in the village of Qumran. New evidence indicates that these men of God were aware of the new religious leader in Israel known as Jesus of Nazareth and the group of writings about Him known as the New Testament. Many have suggested that John the Baptist and the Zealots mentioned in the Gospels of the New Testament must have known the Essenes. Many scholars have suggested that John the Baptist and Jesus of Nazareth were influenced by the Essenes. However, the new evidence from the just-released scrolls would suggest that the Essenes were influenced by both Jesus and the Gospel accounts.

Flavius Josephus wrote about the Essenes in his classic history of the period, *Wars of the Jews* (II. 8,2–13) and his *Antiquities of the Jews* (XIII. 5,9; XV. 10,4.5; and XVIII. 1,2–6), providing most of the details known about them until the discovery of the scrolls in 1947. Josephus and the Jewish writer Philo tell us that there were over four thousand members in the sect, all living in

Israel. They must have accumulated considerable wealth, as members turned over their possessions to the group when they joined. Evidence suggests that the group rejected slavery and warfare but believed in resurrection and angels. Yet they were closely connected to the group known as Zealots who violently resisted the Roman army at Masada. Most writers believe the name Essenes means "pious ones" or perhaps "silent ones." They usually wore white robes and were very careful to observe the Sabbath festival. In A.D. 112 the Roman governor Pliny described an Essene community on the western shore of the Dead Sea. This village of Qumran was finally discovered almost two thousand years later. The Christian historian Eusebius, writing around A.D. 300, said that the Essenes were connected in their beliefs to Christianity.

From the moment of their discovery, many Christian scholars speculated that the scrolls contained evidence of the new faith of Christianity. For over forty years, their hopes and dreams were frustrated by the decision of the original scroll scholars to withhold publication of a significant number of these precious scrolls. When some scholars speculated openly that there must be evidence of Christ in the unpublished scrolls, the group of original scroll scholars vehemently denied their claims. Now, after a delay of over forty years, the last group of unpublished scrolls is beginning to be released to the world. To the great joy and surprise of many scholars, there are a number of definite references and allusions to the New Testament and, more importantly, to Jesus of Nazareth.

The initial group of scholars was made up primarily of Catholic biblical-text specialists chosen by the Jordanian antiquities authorities because the Dead Sea caves were under the jurisdiction of Jordan at that time. Ironically, the Jordanians insisted that no Jews be allowed to work on these Jewish scrolls. Access to the scrolls has been controlled by the original team members and the Ecole Biblique et Archéologique Française, a well-respected Catholic institution sponsored by the Pontifical Biblical Commission of the Vatican. The scrolls themselves were primarily stored in the Rockefeller Museum in Arab East Jerusalem, just outside the old city walls. Although the Rockefeller Museum fell into the hands of the Israeli government during the Six Day War in 1967, the Israelis curiously agreed to allow the original team to maintain absolute control over these priceless Jewish treasures. This monopoly has kept them out of the hands of all Jewish scholars. In practical terms, this meant that access to the scrolls was restricted to the original scroll team and their graduate students. Many equally qualified scholars at hundreds of academic institutions have spent forty frustrating years awaiting access to these incredibly valuable manuscripts.

While some team members published a minor part of the texts, the team responsible for the greatest cache of scrolls discovered in Cave 4 has been the slowest to release its material. Over three hundred texts from the other caves have been published since 1949. However, the team with Cave 4 scrolls has only published one hundred out of the five hundred scrolls. By the late fall of 1991 over 80 percent of the Dead Sea Scrolls from the Cave-4 team remain in the hands of an extremely small group of academics. Some have suggested a conspiracy to keep the scrolls out of the hands of other scholars. However, the truth is more likely that the original team simply enjoyed the total authority and power their undisputed possession provided to them. They were assured of great academic positions, publishing contracts, and the best graduate students available. If a student wanted access to these scrolls, his only option was to work for one of the original scroll team members or successors. The team acted as if the scrolls were their personal possession, rather than a treasure owned by all mankind.

In the last several years, the *Biblical Archaeological Review* has launched a public campaign demanding the release of these scrolls to the wider academic community that desires to understand the origins of Judaism and Christianity. Years ago a special concordance of the fifty-two thousand words used in these scrolls was established in secret for use by the original team. This concordance was obviously of no use to anyone without the scrolls. However, in 1991, Dr. Ben-Zion Wacholder and Martin Abegg of Hebrew Union College in Cincinnati used a sophisticated Macintosh computer and software program to reconstruct the original texts from this concordance. This innovative computer approach allowed them to reassemble the texts and make them available to other scholars. Naturally the original team decried this effort and claimed that their work had been stolen.

Years ago, in an attempt to preserve the scrolls from possible destruction in war, the Israeli authorities authorized the microfilm duplication of the original scrolls. These three thousand negatives were to be held for safekeeping in several different libraries around the world. After the release of the reconstructed computer texts by Hebrew Union College, William Moffett, director of the Huntington Library, one of the four depositories, began to release the remaining unpublished scrolls to qualified scholars worldwide. In the next several years we should see the publication of a great number of texts that will enhance our understanding of the first century of this era and the birth of Christianity.

A Dead Sea Scroll Reference to the Crucified Messiah

In the final months of 1991 the world was astonished to hear that one of the unpublished scrolls included incredible information about a "Messiah" figure who had suffered for the iniquities of men. The scroll was translated by Dr. Robert Eisenman, professor of Middle-Eastern religions at California State University. He declared, "The text is of the most far-reaching significance because it shows that whatever group was responsible for these writings was operating in the same general scriptural and Messianic framework of early Christianity." Although the original scroll team continually claimed that there were no references to early Christianity in the unpublished scrolls, this new evidence totally contradicts their position. This single scroll is earthshaking in its importance for historians and theologians. As Dr. Norman Golb, professor of Jewish history at the University of Chicago, said, "It shows that contrary to what some of the editors said, there are lots of surprises in the scrolls."

This remarkable five-line scroll, held unpublished by the scroll team for forty years, contains incredible information about the death of a Messiah figure. It refers to "the Prophet Isaiah" and the passage (Chapter 53) that identifies the Messiah as one who suffers for the sins of his people. This Jewish Essene scroll is an amazing parallel to the New Testament Christian understanding that the Messiah would first suffer death before ruling in glory forever. Many scholars felt that the only Jewish expectation during the first century revolved around a Messiah that would rule gloriously forever. The exciting discovery of this scroll reveals that there were some among the Essenes who understood the dual role of the Messiah exactly as the Christians did. The phrases in the scroll identify this Messiah as the "Shoot of Jesse" (King David's father), the "Branch of David," and declare that he is the one who was "pierced" and "wounded." The word "pierced" reminds us of the messianic prophecy in Psalms 22:16: "they pierced my hands and feet." The Prophet Jeremiah (23:5) says, "I will raise unto David a righteous branch."

The scroll also describes a "leader of the community" that was "put to death." This clear reference to the historical Jesus of Nazareth is creating shock waves for liberal scholarship that assumed the Gospel account of Jesus was mere myth. The evidence of history is that Jesus is the only messianic claimant that was crucified. Also, as confirmed by the Gospel genealogies, Jesus of Nazareth is the sole figure who proved by the genealogical records kept in the Temple that He was the "Son of Jesse." Additionally, the scroll identifies the Messiah as "the sceptre," which may be a reference to the Genesis 49:10 prophecy, "The sceptre shall not depart from Judah, nor a lawgiver from between his feet, until Shiloh come; and unto him shall the gathering of the people be."

These scrolls buried in A.D. 68 attest to the historical truthfulness of the New Testament record of the life of Jesus and His crucifixion. They suggest that this Jewish Essene writer knew that Jesus of Nazareth was the "suffering Messiah" who died for the sins of His people. As Dr. Lawrence Schiffman, professor of Judaic studies at New York University, stated, "It's a very, very important text. This proves how important it is for us to have access to everything."

The "Son of God" Scroll

Another fascinating scroll, discovered in Cave 4 and known as 4Q246, refers to the hope of a future Messiah figure. This is another of the scrolls that have been kept unpublished for over forty years. Astonishingly, it talks about the Messiah as "the Son of God" and the "Son of the Most High." These words are amazingly similar to the language of the Gospel of Luke, 1:32 and :35. The entire text is still being translated in Jerusalem, but the following section was provided to me on my recent trip to Israel.

The Text of Scroll 4Q246

"He shall be called the Son of God, and they shall designate (call) him Son of the Most High. Like the appearance of comets, so shall be their kingdom. For brief years they shall reign over the earth and shall trample on all; one people shall trample on another and one province on another until the people of God shall rise and all shall rest from the sword."

The Text of Luke 1:32 and :35

"He shall be great, and shall be called the Son of the Highest: and the Lord God shall give unto him the throne of his father David."

"And the angel answered and said unto her, the Holy Ghost shall come upon thee, and the power of the Highest shall overshadow thee: therefore also that holy thing which shall be born of thee shall be called the Son of God."

Anyone comparing these first-century texts must be struck by the startling similarity of concept and wording used to describe this messianic leader. One of the great differences between the Christian and Jewish conceptions of the promised Messiah revolves around his relationship to God. While the Jews have taken the position that the Messiah will be a man, such as Moses, with a divine mission, the Christians believe that the Messiah would be uniquely "the Son of God." The Jewish view usually holds that the concept of a "Son of God" violated the primary truth of monotheism found in Deuteronomy 6:4: "Hear, O Israel: The Lord our God is one Lord." The Christians believe that Jesus' claim to be the Son of God is not a violation of Deuteronomy 6:4. Rather, Christians believe that the Father, the Son, and the Holy Spirit are revealed in the Bible to be One God, revealed in three personalities, not three separate gods. Therefore Christians understand the statements about Jesus as the Son of God as being in complete conformity with the truth of monotheism—there is only one God. It is fascinating in this regard to consider these statements in this first-century Jewish text: "He shall be called the Son of God, and they shall designate (call) him Son of the Most High."

These statements suggest the possibility that either the Essenes accepted the messianic claims of Jesus or they at least anticipated this concept. Either one of the possibilities opens up new areas for exploration. Another possibility that must be considered is this: Is it possible that this scroll 4Q246 is quoting from the Gospel of Luke that was widely circulated at the time according to early Christian witnesses? Luke the physician claimed to be writing the Gospel of Luke as an eyewitness. In Luke 1:1–3 he says: "Forasmuch as many have taken in hand to set forth in order a declaration of those things which are most surely believed among us, Even as they delivered them unto us, which from the beginning were eyewitnesses, and ministers of the word; It seemed good to me also, having had perfect understanding of all things from the very first, to write unto thee in order, most excellent Theophilus."

The presence of the identical wording of Luke 1:32 and 35 in a Jewish Dead Sea Scroll buried in a cave in A.D. 68 stands as a tremendous witness to the early existence of the Gospel records. If the Gospels were written and distributed within thirty-five years of the events of the life of Jesus, then they stand as the best eyewitness historical records we could ever hope to possess. It would be almost impossible to distribute the Gospel accounts to thousands of people in Israel within thirty-five years of the events unless they were true accounts. If the Gospels had been untrue, many witnesses would have stood up and contested the accuracy of their accounts. The records of the first century do not reveal that anyone contested the basic details of the life, death, and resurrection of Jesus. In fact, as shown in the earlier chapters, the ancient historical records in the writings of Roman and pagan historians, the Talmud's account of the crucifixion, and Flavius Josephus's account of Christ all confirm the truth of the Gospel record.

Possible New Testament Quotations in the Dead Sea Scrolls

In 1971 a Spanish biblical scholar named José O'Callaghan studied some of the fragments of scrolls discovered in Cave 7 at Qumran. He was looking for correspondences between these fragments of Greek scrolls and the Septuagint, the Greek translation of the Hebrew Old Testament that was widely used by Jesus and the Apostles. These fragments contain only small portions of each verse and, after almost two thousand years, are greatly damaged. In some cases only small fragments containing three or four lines of a verse remain from an original scroll. It required considerable detective work to put these fragments together.

One day Dr. O'Callaghan carefully examined several small scroll fragments located in a photo page in *The Discoveries of the Judean Desert of Jordan*. To his great surprise he noticed that several did not fit any Old Testament text. These fragments were listed as "fragments not identified." To his amazement Dr. O'Callaghan found that these Greek-language fragments bore an uncanny resemblance to several verses in the New Testament. He discovered the Greek words "beget" and a word that could be "Gennesaret," a word for the Sea of Galilee. The fragment containing "Gennesaret" appears to be a quotation of the passage referring to the feeding of the five thousand found in Mark 6:52–53 that states: "For they considered not the miracle of the loaves: for their heart was hardened. And when they had passed over, they came into the land of Gennesaret, and drew to the shore."

If these texts are actually portions of these Christian writings, they would be the earliest New Testament texts ever discovered. *The New York Times* responded, "If O'Callaghan's theory is accepted, it would prove that at least one of the Gospels, that of St. Mark, was written only a few years after the death of Jesus." The *Los Angeles Times* headlined "Nine New Testament Fragments Dated A.D. 50 to A.D. 100 Have Been Discovered in a Dead Sea Cave." It stated that "if validated, [they] constitute the most sensational biblical trove uncovered in recent times." O'Callaghan's material has been published in several scholarly journals including *Biblica*.

Cave-7 Fragments Possibly Connected with the New Testament

Dr. O'Callaghan ultimately identified eight different scroll fragments from Cave 7 that appear to be quotes from New Testament passages. The fragments appeared to O'Callaghan to be portions of: Mark 4:28, 6:48, 6:52–53, and 12:17, Acts 27:38, Romans 5:11–12, I Timothy 3:16, and James 1:23–24.

For the earth bringeth forth fruit of herself; first the blade, then the ear, after that the full corn in the ear. (Mark 4:28)

And he saw them toiling in rowing; for the wind was contrary unto them: and about the fourth watch of the night he cometh unto them, walking upon the sea, and would have passed by them. (Mark 6:48)

For they considered not the miracle of the loaves: for their heart was hardened. And when they had passed over, they came into the land of Gennesaret, and drew to the shore. (Mark 6:52–53)

And Jesus answering said unto them, Render to Caesar the things that are Caesar's, and to God the things that are God's. And they marvelled at him. (Mark 12:17)

And when they had eaten enough, they lightened the ship, and cast out the wheat into the sea. (Acts 27:38)

And not only so, but we also joy in God through our Lord Jesus Christ, by whom we have now received the atonement. Wherefore, as by one man sin entered into the world, and death by sin; and so death passed upon all men, for that all have sinned. (Romans 5:11–12)

And without controversy great is the mystery of godliness: God was manifest in the flesh, justified in the Spirit, seen of angels, preached unto the Gentiles, believed on in the world, received up into glory. (I Timothy 3:16)

For if any be a hearer of the word, and not a doer, he is like unto a man beholding his natural face in a glass: For he beholdeth himself, and goeth his way, and straightaway forgetteth what manner of man he was. (James 1:23–24)

Naturally, as with other matters connected with the controversial Dead Sea Scrolls, many scholars disagreed with the conclusions of Dr. O'Callaghan, and the debate still continues twenty years later. More work needs to be done. However, the recent publication of Scroll 4Q246 and its identical reference to "the Son of God" as found in Luke 1:32 and 35 would lend support to the possibility that these fragments are related to the above New

Testament passages. We have great hopes, related to Dr. Gary Collett's new Qumran cave dig described in an earlier chapter. One of those hopes is that we may discover additional New Testament references and other Christian records in the newly detected scroll jars.

The Melchizedek Scroll and the Coming Messiah

Another exciting scroll that also relates to the New Testament was discovered in Cave 11. It is called the Melchizedek Scroll because its subject matter is the role of the mysterious figure known as Melchizedek, King of Salem.

In the Old Testament Genesis account, Melchizedek is called "the priest of the most high God" and it is he to whom Abraham "gave . . . tithes of all" (Genesis 14:18–20). In Psalms 110:1–5 David talks about the Messiah, "my Lord," as a Melchizedek figure who will both rule "out of Zion" and act as Israel's priest. King David also suggests that this Melchizedek is, in fact, the Messiah: "The Lord hath sworn, and will not repent, Thou art a priest for ever after the order of Melchizedek. The Lord at thy right hand shall strike through kings in the day of his wrath" (Psalms 110:1–5).

Melchizedek in the Book of Hebrews

The inspired New Testament writer of the book of Hebrews developed this theme of Melchizedek as the real Messiah. He also identifies Him with messianic titles including, King of Righteousness and King of Peace. He reveals that Melchizedek was more than a mere man: "Without father, without mother, without descent, having neither beginning of days, nor end of life; but made like unto the Son of God; abideth a priest continually" (Hebrews 7:3). The Holy Spirit declares that Jesus, "made perfect . . . became the author of eternal salvation unto all them that obey him; Called of God an high priest after the order of Melchisedec" (Hebrews 5:9–10). Jesus is our eternal Messiah "because he continueth ever, hath an unchangeable priesthood. Wherefore he is able also to save them to the uttermost that come unto God by him, seeing he ever liveth to make intercession for them. For such an high priest became us, who is holy, harmless, undefiled, separate from sinners, and made higher than the heavens" (Hebrews 7:24–26). This declaration in Hebrews that Melchizedek is both Messiah and also God was considered a radical departure from the Jewish views of the first century.

In this connection it is fascinating to explore this newly revealed Melchizedek Scroll that was written by Jewish Essenes and buried prior to A.D. 68. This scroll reveals a startling convergence of the messianic ideas of this Dead Sea Scroll and those of the New Testament book of Hebrews. The following lines are from a recent translation of this Dead Sea Scroll.

> And concerning that which He said, In (this) year of Jubilee each of you shall return to his property. . . . And it will be proclaimed at the end of days concerning the captives as He said: To proclaim liberty to the captives. . . . Its interpretation is that He will assign them to the Sons of Heaven and to the inheritance of Melchizedek; for He will cast their (lot) amid the portions of Melchizedek who will return them there and will proclaim to them liberty, forgiving them (the wrongdoings) of all their iniquities. . . .
>
> And the Day of Atonement is the end of the tenth Jubilee, when all the Sons of (Light) and the men of the lot of Melchizedek will be atoned for. . . . For this is the moment of the Year of Grace for Melchizedek. And he will, by his strength, judge the holy ones of God, executing judgment as it is written concerning him in the songs of David, who said Elohim has taken his place in the divine council; in the midst of the gods he holds judgment. . . . And Melchizedek will avenge the vengeance of the judgment of God. . . . This is the day of Peace/Salvation concerning which (God) spoke through Isaiah the prophet, who said, (How) beautiful upon the mountains are the feet of the messenger who proclaims peace, who brings good news, who proclaims salvation, who says to Zion: Your Elohim (reigns). Its interpretation; the mountains are the prophets . . . and the messenger is the Anointed one of the spirit, concerning whom Daniel said, (Until an anointed one, a prince) . . . its interpretation, to make them understand all the ages of time. . . . In truth . . . will turn away from Satan . . . by the judgment(s) of God, as it is written concern-

ing him, (who says to Zion); your Elohim reigns. . . .
And your Elohim is Melchizedek, who will save them
from the hand of Satan.

This unusual first-century B.C. prophetic midrash from Cave
11 is composed of thirteen fragments. It was first published in
1965 by A. S. van der Woude as *"Melchizedek als himmlishe
Erlosergestalt"* in *Oudtestamentishche Studien* printed in Leiden
(pp. 354–73). Additional material appeared in an article from M.
der Jonge and A. S. van der Woude called *11Q Melchizedek and
the New Testament* in the text *New Testament Studies* published
in 1966 (pp. 310–26). Dr. J. T. Milik, one of the top Dead Sea
Scroll scholars, also discusses this text in the *Journal of Jewish
Studies.*

The Features of the Melchizedek Scroll

There are a number of extraordinary features found in this
scroll including many references to this mysterious Messiah-
Melchizedek figure. Several phrases describe the period when the
Messiah will appear. The phrases from this scroll about the timing of Melchizedek-Messiah's appearance include:

the End of Days
the End of the Tenth
  Jubilee Cycle
the Year of Jubilee
the Day of Trumpets in
  7th Month
the Day When Elohim
  Reigns

the Day of Atonement
the Year of Grace
the Day of Vengeance
the Day of Peace and
  Salvation

These phrases also curiously parallel both Old and New Testament references to the Messiah.

Melchizedek's Identification As the Messiah

Another startling feature of the Melchizedek Scroll involves
its amazing identification of Melchizedek with the promised Messiah. Some of the key phrases of identification include:

the Messiah
the Anointed One who proclaims Salvation

the Prince
the Judge
the Avenger
Elohim
the High Priest of the Year of Jubilee
the Messenger of God
Michael the Great Prince

Even a casual consideration of these names will remind one
of the titles applied to Jesus the Messiah in the Bible. Beyond
question, the most incredible thing about this particular scroll is
the writer's identification of Melchizedek with both the Messiah
—"the anointed one"—and Elohim. Elohim is the plural form of
the name of God and has the connotation of absolute divine
power. Although the Old Testament Hebrew text uses a number
of different words for God, the word Elohim appears most frequently. This declaration in the scroll that the Messiah is Elohim
(God) is an amazing parallel to the New Testament doctrine that
Jesus of Nazareth is both Messiah and God. Until the discovery of
these Dead Sea Scrolls, most scholars believed that there was no
acceptance of this New Testament doctrine outside the Christian
community. These scrolls will fundamentally alter the historical
understanding of the claims of Jesus the Messiah. It is obvious
that there are a number of significant parallels between the book
of Hebrews and this Dead Sea Scroll regarding the role of Melchizedek as the coming Messiah, the Son of God.

In other passages, this scroll connects the coming of the Messiah with the Year of Jubilee, which concludes with the final "redemption of the land" and the captives. This clearly parallels the
biblical view of Jesus as our great high priest who will proclaim
the Great Jubilee and "the restitution of all things." In Acts 3:21,
Paul tells us that Jesus the Messiah is the one "whom the heaven
must receive until the times of restitution of all things, which
God hath spoken by the mouth of all his holy prophets since the
world began."

Notice that this Melchizedek figure forgives the people's iniquities just as Jesus, the Son of God, forgives our sins. Obviously,
only God is able to forgive sins. Melchizedek also participates in
the "judgment of the Sons of Heaven and the Holy Ones" just as
the Bible tells us "we must all appear before the judgment seat of
Christ" (II Corinthians 5:10). There is a startling similarity of lan-

guage in the writer's description of "the Sons of Light" that reminds us of Paul's terminology in I Thessalonians 5:5, "Ye are all the children of light."

This scroll also describes Melchizedek as providing "rewards" and carrying out "the vengeance of God." These terms obviously convey the thought that Melchizedek is much more than a mere man or servant of God. He is obviously the Messiah, the Son of God just as the New Testament explains the role of Jesus of Nazareth. The scroll concludes with the information that Melchizedek will "take His place in the Divine Council" and will "judge Satan and destroy him." This reminds us of the words of Revelation 20:10, "And the devil that deceived them was cast into the lake of fire and brimstone."

These unexpected similarities with the New Testament book of Hebrews are extraordinary. Several possible conclusions come to mind. It is possible that the Essene writers of these documents were influenced by the life of Jesus and had some of the New Testament texts in their possession. Another possibility is that these Essene Jews had independently developed a theology surrounding the coming Messiah that followed the New Testament concepts by mere coincidence. There is a third possibility: that the writer of this Melchizedek Scroll was a Jewish Essene follower of Jesus of Nazareth. The recent discovery of the "Son of God" Scroll (4Q246) and the new "Suffering Messiah" Scroll that clearly refers to Jesus, the one who was crucified, add credibility to the notion that this Essene writer was a Jewish Christian.

Many of these mysteries will be solved when the final four hundred unpublished scrolls are published in the next few years. The new dig at Qumran may also uncover additional new scrolls that will help us understand more clearly the messianic beliefs of the men and women who lived when Jesus walked the earth.

SELECTED BIBLIOGRAPHY

Auerbach, Leo. *The Babylonian Talmud*. New York: Philosophical Library, 1944.

Ataur-Rahim, Muhammad. *Jesus — A Prophet of Islam*. Delhi: Taj Company, 1987.

Baylee, Rev. Joseph. *The Times Of The Gentiles*. London: James Nisbet & Co., 1871.

Ben-Dov, Meir. *In The Shadow Of The Temple*. London: Harper & Row, 1982.

Ben-Dov, Meir. *The Western Wall*. Jerusalem: M.O.D. Publishing House, 1987.

Besant, Walter and Palmer, E.H. *Jerusalem — The City of Herod and Saladin*. London: Chatto & Windus, 1908.

Bettenson, Henry. *Documents Of The Christian Church*. London: Oxford University Press, 1967.

Bloomfield, Arthur, E. *A Survey Of Bible Prophecy*. Minneapolis: Bethany Fellowship, Inc., 1971.

Boston, Thomas. *Human Nature In Its Fourfold State*. Philadelphia: Ambrose Walker, 1814.

Boyne, Col. Walter. *Gulf War*. Lincolnwood: Publications International, 1991.

Buck, Rev. Charles. *A Theological Dictionary*. Philadelphia: William W. Woodward, 1825.

Bullinger, E.W. *The Apocalypse or The Day Of The Lord*. London: Eyre & Spottiswoode, 1909.

Butterfield, Herbert. *Christianity And History*. New York: Charles Scribners Sons, 1949.

Comay, Joan. *The Temple of Jerusalem*. New York: Holt, Rinehart and Winston, 1975.

Dean, I. R. *The Coming Kingdom - The Goal Of Prophecy*. Philadelphia: Philadelphia School Of The Bible, 1928.

Desmond, Alice Curtis. *Titus Of Rome*. New York: Dodd, Mead and Company, 1976.

Dewart, Edward, Hartley. *Jesus The Messiah*. Toronto: William Briggs, 1891.

Dupuy, Col. Trevor N. *How To Defeat Saddam Hussein*. New York: Warner Books, 1991.

Edersheim, Rev. Alfred. *The Life And Times Of Jesus The Messiah*. New York: Longmans, Green, & Co. 1896.

Eisemann, Rabbi Moshe. *The Book of Ezekiel*. New York: Mesorah Publications, Ltd., 1988.

Feinberg, Charles. *PreMillennialism Or Amillennialism?* Grand Rapids: Zondervan Publishing House, 1936.

Gilbert, Martin. *The Arab-Israeli Conflict – Its History In Maps*. Jerusalem: Sreimatzky, Ltd. 1984.

Goldstein, Rabbi Morris. *Jesus In The Jewish Tradition*. New York: The Macmillan Company, 1950.

Greenstone, Julius H. *The Messianic Idea In Jewish History*. Philadelphia: The Jewish Publication Society of America, 1948.

Harris, M.H. *Hebraic Literature – Translations from The Talmud, Midrashim and Kabbala*. New York: Tudor Publishing Co., 1944.

Hertz, Dr. J.H. *The Pentateuch and Haftorahs*. London: Soncino Press, 1961.

Higginson, Edward. *Ecce Messias – The Hebrew Messianic Hope*. London: Williams and Norgate, 1871.

Hovery, Alvah. *Biblical Eschatology*. Philadelphia: American Baptist Publication Society, 1888.

Huffman, Jasper. *The Messianic Hope in Both Testaments*. Winona Lake: The Standard Press, 1945.

Jarvis, Rev. Samuel Farmar. *The Church of the Redeemed*. London: Wm. Jones Cleaver, 1850.

Josephus, Flavius. *Complete Works of Josephus*. Grand Rapids: Kregel Publications, 1974.

Keith, Rev. Alexander. *The Signs Of The Times*. Edinburgh: William White & Co., 1832.

Kellogg, Samuel, H. *The Jews Or Prediction And Fulfilment.* New York: Anson D. F. Randolph & Company, 1883.

Kett, Henry. *History - The Interpreter Of Prophecy.* London: Trinity College, 1800.

Kollek, Teddy and Pearlman, Moshe. *Jerusalem.* London: Weidenfeld and Nicolson, 1968.

Lewis, C.S. *A Case For Christianity.* Grand Rapids: Baker Book House, 1977.

Litch, Josiah. *Messiah's Throne And Millennial Glory.* Philadelphia: Joshua V. Himes, 1855.

Lockyer, Herbert. *All The Messianic Prophecies Of The Bible.* Grand Rapids: Zondervan Publishing House, 1960.

Maimonides, Moses. *The Laws of God's Chosen House.* Jerusalem: Maznaim, 1986.

Maimonides, Moses. *The Laws of Kings and Their Wars.* Jerusalem: Maznaim, 1987.

Maimonides, Moses. *Treatise On Resurrection.* New York: KTAV Publishing House, Inc. 1982.

McKinnon, Dan. *Bullseye Iraq.* New York: Berkley Books, 1988.

Milner, Rev. Isaac. *The History Of The Church Of Christ.* Cambridge: John Burges, 1800.

Newton, Bishop Thomas. *Dissertations On The Prophecies.* London: R & R Gilbert, 1817.

Pember, G.H. *The Antichrist, Babylon and the Coming of the Kingdom.* Miami Springs: Schoettle Publishing Co., Inc., 1988.

Pentecost, Dwight, J. *Things To Come.* Grand Rapids: Zondervan Publishing House, 1958.

Peters, George. *The Theocratic Kingdom.* Grand Rapids: Kregel Publications, 1957.

Pusey, Rev. E.B. *The Minor Prophets.* New York: Funk & Wagnalls, 1885.

Pusey, Rev. E.B. *Daniel.* New York: Funk & Wagnalls, 1887.

Read, Hollis. *The Hand of God in History*. Hartford: Robins and Co., 1860.

Reznick, Rabbi Leibel. *The Holy Temple Revisited*. London: Jason Aronson Inc. 1990.

Rossetti, Christina. *The Face Of The Deep*. London: Society For Promoting Christian Knowledge, 1895.

Sale, George. *The Koran with Explanatory Notes*. Philadelphia: J.W. Moore, 1850.

Sasson, Jean P. *The Rape of Kuwait*. New York: Knightsbridge Publishing Company, 1991.

St. John, Robert. *Tongue of the Prophets. Life Story of Eliezer Ben Yehuda*. North Hollywood: Wilshire Book Company, 1952.

Scherman, Rabbi Nosson. *Ezekiel: A New Translation With A Commentary Anthologized From Talmudic, Midrashic And Rabbinic Sources*. Brooklyn: Mesorah Publications, Ltd. 1969.

Seiss, J. A. *The Apocalypse*. Grand Rapids: Zondervan Publishing House, 1960.

Smith, Chuck. *The Tribulation & The Church*. Costa Mesa: The Word For Today, 1980.

Stanley, Arthur, Penrhyn. *Lectures on the History of the Jewish Church*. London: John Murray, 1865.

Taylor, Rev. G. F. *The Second Coming Of Jesus*. Franklin Springs: The Publishing House, 1950.

Thompson, Rev. J. L. *That Glorious Future*. London: Morgan and Scott, 1887.

Trotter, W. *Plain Papers On Prophetic And Other Subjects*. London: G. Morrish, 1869.

West, Gilbert. *Observations On The History And Evidences Of Jesus Christ*. London: R. Dodsley, 1747.

Withers, James. *The Messiah King*. London: S.W. Partridge & Co., 1888.

Yadin, Yegael. *The Temple Scroll*. Jerusalem: Steimatzky Ltd., 1985.

Zlotowitz, Rabbi Meir. Genesis - *A New Translation With A Commentary Anthologized From Talmudic, Midrashic And Rabbinic Sources.* New York: Mesorah Publications, Ltd. 1980.

**Speaking Engagements
or
Teaching Seminars**

Mr. Grant Jeffrey is available for seminars or other speaking engagements throughout the year for churches, conferences and colleges.

Subjects included are Prophecy, Apologetics, Evangelism Training and General Bible Teaching.

Please Contact:

**Grant Jeffrey Ministries
P.O. Box 129, Station "U"
Toronto, Ontario, M8Z 5M4
Canada**

ABOUT THE AUTHOR

GRANT R. JEFFREY has more than twenty-five years of research and teaching experience in the area of Bible prophecy and history. His weekly T.V. program "Appointment with Destiny" airs on the Trinity Broadcast Network and is seen by millions. He is also the author of three bestselling books: *Armageddon: Appointment with Destiny, Heaven: The Last Frontier* and *Messiah: War in the Middle East and The Road to Armageddon.*

Hal Lindsey has taken his millions of faithful readers
on a fabulous journey...

We Deliver!
And So Do These Bestsellers.